FAIR EXCHANGE

Theory and Practice of
Digital Belongings

FAIR EXCHANGE

Theory and Practice of Digital Belongings

Carlos Molina-Jimenez
Dann Toliver
Hazem Danny Nakib
Jon Crowcroft

University of Cambridge, UK

World Scientific

NEW JERSEY · LONDON · SINGAPORE · BEIJING · SHANGHAI · HONG KONG · TAIPEI · CHENNAI · TOKYO

Published by

World Scientific Publishing Europe Ltd.

57 Shelton Street, Covent Garden, London WC2H 9HE

Head office: 5 Toh Tuck Link, Singapore 596224

USA office: 27 Warren Street, Suite 401-402, Hackensack, NJ 07601

Library of Congress Cataloging-in-Publication Data
Names: Molina-Jimenez, C. (Carlos), author. | Toliver, Dann, author. |
    Nakib, Hazem Danny, author. | Crowcroft, Jon, author.
Title: Fair exchange : theory and practice of digital belongings / Carlos Molina-Jimenez,
    Dann Toliver, Hazem Danny Nakib, Jon Crowcroft, University of Cambridge, UK.
Description: New Jersey : World Scientific, [2024] | Includes bibliographical references and index.
Identifiers: LCCN 2023049000 | ISBN 9781800615168 (hardcover) |
    ISBN 9781800615175 (ebook) | ISBN 9781800615182 (ebook other)
Subjects: LCSH: Electronic commerce. | Electronic funds transfers.
Classification: LCC HF5548.32 .M655 2024 | DDC 658.8/72--dc23/eng/20240205
LC record available at https://lccn.loc.gov/2023049000

British Library Cataloguing-in-Publication Data
A catalogue record for this book is available from the British Library.

Cover image: *California Landscape* (https://www.rawpixel.com/image/11932558/california-landscape-william-wendt) by William Wendt, 1920. Public domain image from
Los Angeles County Museum of Art.

For any available supplementary material, please visit
https://www.worldscientific.com/worldscibooks/10.1142/Q0448#t=suppl

Desk Editors: Logeshwaran Arumugam/Ana Ovey/Shi Ying Koe

Typeset by Stallion Press
Email: enquiries@stallionpress.com

Printed in Singapore

To my parents, who taught me to see. All my love.
Dann

To my family.
Hazem

Para mi maestro Ramiro Velázquez Bustamantes y para Mayita.
Carlos

Acknowledgements

This book emerged from the Centre for ReDecentralisation (CRDC), an organization the authors founded to develop and promote the technologies required for living first-class digital lives. We are grateful to the Department of Computer Science and Technology at the University of Cambridge, for acting as a home for the CRDC and cultivating this book, and UK Research and Innovation (UKRI) Digital Security by Design, for funding work associated with this book. We are also grateful to TODAQ for its continuous support of this work.

Thank you to the friends and colleagues who have consistently inspired and challenged us on this journey, and in particular to our early reviewers, whose input proved invaluable. Special thanks to Professor N. Asokan for his feedback, corrections, and refinements on our ideas and Kevin Toliver, who provided detailed and voluminous input and editing on Part 1. We are also thankful to Andrew Hyde at the University of Cambridge Data and Policy Journal for ongoing support across numerous initiatives.

We extend our greatest thanks to the wonderful publishing team at World Scientific, who made this journey smooth and pleasant, who let us stay focused on the important things, and who were exceptionally accommodating of our schedules. Particular thanks to our publishers Laurent Chaminade and Keith Mansfield, production editors Ana Ovey and Adam Binnie, Logesh A for managing the copy editing, and Yolande Koh for editing advice.

Each and every one of you has helped in bringing this work to the world.

Contents

List of Figures

List of Tables

Roadmap

We live in a world of exchanges.

We exchange money for goods and services in many forms, and we also exchange items directly: trading cards, digital assets, a coat check ticket. These exchanges often go smoothly, leaving you and the other party with their expectations met — but sometimes they don't.

Those unfair outcomes are costly. They cost us directly, but more importantly, they cause the majority of our exchanges to be mediated by the largest and most trusted entities, who extract a significant toll for their assistance.

Fair exchange is an area worth studying, researching, and implementing. It has significant relevance in the digital world, and much potential in practical real-world industry applications. Particularly in light of the emergence of the digital economy, the creation of meaningful digital things, and a greater focus on individual autonomy in managing our own affairs directly.

This book aims to highlight the area of fair exchange within research and industry, and to accelerate the pursuit of real-world applications and solutions. This is especially relevant today because, thanks to advances in areas like trusted computing and distributed systems, we have an opportunity to reconsider these problems from a variety of different and largely unexplored angles.

In particular, fair exchange provides an opportunity to redecentralize our digital lives. Efficient digital fair exchange protocols mirror the kinds of exchanges people have had for thousands of years: local transactions, involving locally trusted parties, without requiring the involvement of global institutions or systems. This is a necessary building block for digital lives that we can live locally, instead of just inside corporate data centres.

In the same way you hand a banknote to your local grocer and they hand you a kiwi, you should be able to exchange digital goods with confidence. Fair exchange protocols make that happen.

We start by presenting a framework for understanding fair exchange protocols in Part 1. This framework provides a way to characterize existing protocols by the environments in which their operations are performed, and maps that to limitations on protocol properties and the types of items that can be exchanged.

First, we describe fair exchange protocols and the various properties they can have, such as strength and timeliness. Then we classify the kinds of items that can be exchanged. In particular, copyable items that can be arbitrarily copied are contrasted with unique items, which cannot.

The operations necessary for fair exchange are then defined: the handshake, deposit, verify, synchronize, and release/restore operations. Each of these operations must be run in some kind of environment. Environments have many properties, but the ones that matter for fair exchange are storage, compute, and messaging — and, in particular, how independent these are from the participants. We describe each of these properties in detail and introduce a diagram language used throughout the book for illustrating fair exchange protocols.

Pulling all of this together reveals the fundamental limits of fair exchange. The properties of a fair exchange protocol, and the items it can exchange, are dictated by the environments in which operations occur. These results are succinctly encapsulated by Table 6.1 in Chapter 6.

We finish Part 1 by describing *attestables*, an interface for constrained exfiltration-resistant computing. These are used within Part 2, where we not only apply our framework to existing protocols to understand them better, but also use it to generate new protocols.

These attestable-based protocols can achieve the properties and range of items enjoyed by escrow protocols at much lower costs and risks. One attestable-based protocol that we develop, FEWD (an acronym for "fair exchange without disputes"), is presented in several variations, each tuned to a different use case by distributing the operations of fair exchange to different environments.

The exchange of items, even digital items, does not happen in a vacuum. There are a variety of real-world concerns that may impact an exchange, which we examine from several different perspectives in Part 3. These include technical risks to fairness, but also less quantifiable risks, like that of a participant receiving a defective item.

Legal intervention is considered from a system design perspective. The legal system is used to help obtain a fair outcome in weaker protocols, and to reduce the risk of failed expectations in strong protocols. However, it can also compromise fairness: a fair exchange could be achieved, only to be lost due to unfair legal intervention afterwards. All risk mitigation systems bring risks of their own, and ubiquitous systems deserve special consideration in this regard.

Implementors of fair exchange systems need to be aware of a wide variety of operational concerns, which we cover across a broad spectrum. We also consider various concrete use cases and provide a commercial analysis of the benefits and trade-offs that fair exchange protocols bring to such diverse sectors as healthcare and central security depositories.

Finally, we present a number of fields beyond fair exchange where the techniques and ideas in this book may find application. Our framework and environmental considerations, and attestables in particular, are tools that protocol designers may employ in finding efficient solutions to difficult problems, especially where the cost and risk thresholds of their target use case are narrow and there is little room in the trust stack.

Our vision is for a future where the basic operations of our digital lives — our transactions, purchases, and interactions — do not require trusting large intermediaries to always do the right thing. Fair exchange protocols can reduce that trust burden, which in turn allows it to be spread out among a diverse group of participants to better promote efficiency, fairness, autonomy, and user-centric control.

We look forward to introducing you to the rich field of fair exchange, and hope this book provides you with tools and insights you can use in your work.

Part 1
A Framework for Fair Exchange

Chapter 1

Fair Exchange Protocols

Fair exchange protocols (FEPs) have been a topic of research interest since at least the early 1980s, and a tremendous amount has been written about them. They are inherently cross-domain, touching on distributed systems, cryptography, state management, networking, and ultimately the very essence of digital representations and computation itself.

Any attempt to summarize the field in a single chapter must inevitably come up short, with much good work left out. Here, we primarily highlight aspects that are leveraged throughout the book, including protocol properties like strength and timeliness, varieties of FEPs, and the types of items a given FEP can exchange.

1.1   Definition of Fair Exchange

An *exchange* is an event where participants each give and receive items.

We generally use Alice and Bob as the labels for these participants,[1] and call their respective items D_A and D_B.[2] For instance, if Alice wants to give Bob her item D_A in exchange for his item D_B, and Bob agrees to these terms, they have begun an exchange.

---

[1]We examine exchanges with more than two participants in Chapter 19.

[2]Alice's item D_A may actually consist of several items packaged together. We speak of it as a single item without loss of generality, given that an individual item itself may be arbitrarily complex.

A *fair exchange* is one in which each participant's expectations for the exchange were met: either they received the items promised by the terms of the exchange, or their own items were restored to them. If at the end of the exchange Alice has D_B and Bob has D_A, then the exchange was successful and fair. If Alice has D_A (and Bob doesn't), and Bob has D_B (but Alice doesn't), then the exchange was cancelled and fair. If Alice has D_A and D_B (and Bob has neither), then the exchange was unfair. If neither party has D_A at the end of the exchange, then that exchange was also unfair.

A *fair exchange protocol* (FEP) is a procedure the participants can follow to try to ensure they receive a fair outcome. No protocol can unconditionally guarantee a fair outcome. An item could be struck with lightning, or spontaneously combust, or a malicious AI could compromise the computer systems and steal both items. The world is big and weird and often quite surprising.

A strong protocol can make a powerful promise, though: it can promise that as long as its trust assumptions aren't violated, the outcome of an exchange made using that protocol will be fair. Those trust assumptions often include a trusted third party (TTP), which both participants explicitly trust. Weaker protocols are used as well, often accompanied by a recovery mechanism to resolve disputes.

Protocols have a number of features beyond the strength of the promise they can make, including important considerations like timeliness and invasiveness, which are examined in this chapter. We also examine some standard trust assumptions, and in later chapters we consider additional factors, like the kinds of items that various protocols can exchange.

1.2   History of Fair Exchange

The need for fair exchange extends back to ancient times, and a wide variety of pragmatic solutions have surfaced throughout history. Many of these were what we now label *escrow-based fair exchange*, where a trusted party was charged with gathering and distributing the desired items in order to ensure fairness.

Modern research into FEPs for exchanging digital items can be traced back to the early 1980s (Even and Yacobi, 1980). Oblivious transfer was introduced in a discussion involving the fair exchange of secrets (Rabin, 1981),[3] and has gone on to become a powerful cryptographic technique in its own right, particularly within various models for secure multiparty computation (Even *et al.*, 1985).

The research pace accelerated in the 1990s with Asokan *et al.* (1997), Ben-Or *et al.* (1990), Micali (1997), Zhou and Gollmann (1997), and the introduction of *optimistic* FEPs (Asokan, 1998), which require the TTP only during disputes. A dissection of fair exchange protocols was conducted (Pagnia *et al.*, 1999) which identified sub-problems in fair exchange they called Negotiate, Prepare for exchange, Exchange, Recovery and Resolve.[4] In the late 1990s and early 2000s, the practical relevance of the topic became apparent with the advancement of e-commerce (Onieva *et al.*, 2004; Pagnia *et al.*, 2003; Ray and Ray, 2002).

Cryptographers and distributed systems researchers were both involved in the fair exchange research, with many interesting results coming from each camp. The complexity of fair exchange was analyzed in Pagnia and Gärtner (1999), which demonstrated that the problem of fair exchange in an asynchronous[5] setting is at least as difficult as the problem of reaching consensus in asynchronous distributed systems, and argues that fair exchange cannot be solved without the involvement of a TTP.

The implication is that any place that can guarantee strong fair exchange can also support consensus.[6] And consensus is not easy: the FLP result (Fischer *et al.*, 1985) famously proved that consensus cannot be solved deterministically in an asynchronous distributed system if even one process might suffer a fail-stop failure.

---

[3]That context comes with a set of assumptions about the participants' behaviours that leave ample room for unfair outcomes. It also bears requirements for the deposit and synchronize operations that necessitate being performed in a specialized environment — effectively rendering it an escrow-based protocol.

[4]These classifications are focused on providing modularity with respect to a hierarchy of fairness definitions, in contrast with our operational model which shows the limits of protocols based on the environments in which their operations are performed.

[5]That is, a system with no upper bounds on processing time and message transfer delays.

[6]But cf. Orzan and Dashti (2008), where the authors argue that under certain failure assumptions consensus and fair exchange are incomparable.

An early example of the use of secure processors to support fair exchange is discussed in Tygar (1996), which uses trusted hardware to implement an electronic wallet. Using trusted hardware as the basis of a distributed TTP for probabilistic synchronization is shown in Avoine and Vaudenay (2004), which also builds upon work in Vogt *et al.* (2001a, 2001b) on using smart cards as a trusted execution environment for deposit, verification, and release in fair exchange. The use of trusted components and public bulletin boards (PBBs) as complimentary building blocks is demonstrated in LucidiTEE (Sinha *et al.*, 2019).

FEPs that do not involve any TTPs also have a long history, starting with Blum (1983), which introduced the idea of *gradual release* of the items under exchange. Gradual release protocols are used in several contexts, including contract signing, certified emails, and key exchange, but also have a number of drawbacks (Garay *et al.*, 1999), including a lack of marginal fairness (Chapter 11).

Protocols for fairness in the first decades of the 21st century have often focused either on bringing new kinds of TTPs into existing protocols[7] or on domains that are more amenable to purely cryptographic solutions, such as secure multiparty computing (Chapter 19). There are a variety of features that are needed for real-world fair exchanges, such as the programmatic validation of exchanged items, and aspects that are important for the redecentralization of our digital lives, such as reducing the costs and risks associated with TTPs, which have been receiving varying degrees of focus in the literature.

1.3   Trust Assumptions

All computational protocols base their guarantees on a set of trust assumptions, also called a *trust stack*. Typically, these cover places where there is ample evidence the assumption is trustworthy, but generating a proof is difficult or impossible.

In the case of FEPs, these typically include the standard cryptographic assumptions: the hash functions chosen have collision resistance and preimage resistance; it is computationally infeasible

---

[7]A number of FEPs have been developed which explicitly require trust in various blockchains, for instance.

to generate a valid signature in the digital signature scheme chosen without access to the secret key; and so on. Most of the important properties of cryptographic primitives have not been proven, so they must be added to the set of trusted assumptions.

It also includes assumptions about the implementations of those cryptographic primitives, and the tools and systems built on those primitives, and the implementation of the FEP itself. The laws of physics, and our current understanding of computational machinery, are also implicitly present in that set of assumptions. It is a considerable stack.

Beyond the protocol-level assumptions, each individual exchange also introduces items to the trust stack. Participants generally assume that their devices are under their control and will not fault at a critical moment, for instance. We use the phrase "trust assumptions of the protocol" to cover all the trust assumptions that are required by a particular FEP, both in the abstract and also within a particular exchange.

Note that items on the trust stack are not monolithic: it is not that Alice trusts her device. It is that she trusts her device to act a specific way, for a specific period of time, up to a specific amount. Moving more of the functions of the exchange to Alice's device results in lower cost and risk to her, as long as her device can support the trust weight of the functions she places on it. This is an important technique for redecentralization.

If TTPs are involved in the exchange, they must be explicitly added to the trust stack for the functions they perform. This includes trusted hardware, for instance, which can go wrong in a wide variety of ways. We examine the possibility of relaxing these kinds of assumptions in Part 3.

The trust assumptions of a FEP are one of the primary sources of the risk of an unfair outcome. Indeed, in strong protocols, they may be the only source of risk, as we will see in the following section.

1.4 Strength

A FEP is *strong*, or has *strong fairness*, if fairness cannot be broken without breaking the trust assumptions of the protocol. An escrow-based protocol is strong, because the escrow party is explicitly trusted within the exchange to perform their tasks faithfully. As long as those trust assumptions are not violated — as long as the escrow agent continues to act in a trustworthy manner — then an unfair outcome cannot result.

A FEP is *weak* if fairness can be broken within the trust assumptions of the protocol. For instance, an optimistic front-end is weak, because when Alice sends Bob D_A, he may choose to not send D_B back to her. Bob, who is explicitly not trusted by Alice, may do this without violating any of Alice's trust assumptions.

There are different flavours of weak FEPs. Sometimes evidence is produced that allows the wronged party to be made right by another system. This might be the legal system in a particular jurisdiction, as explored in Chapter 16, or it might be another FEP, like an escrow-based FEP in the case of an optimistic protocol.

In *optimistic* FEPs, the weak front-end is tightly coupled to the strong back-end. This can bring a large amount of efficiency: Alice can send D_A to Bob knowing that if he does not provide D_B in a timely fashion, then she can go to the TTP to achieve fairness. It also provides a strong guarantee of fairness if the front-end fails, though with the costs and risks of running the exchange as a full escrow-based FEP.

Alternatively, the risk of an unfair outcome presented by a weak FEP could simply be accepted by the participants. This is generally the case with protocols like gradual release, although as we show in Chapter 11, it is often possible for one participant to force an unfair outcome for the other participant, depending on the specifics of their exchange.

1.5   Timeliness

A FEP has *strong timeliness* if either party can drive the exchange to completion at any time (Piva *et al.*, 2009). Note that whether the exchange ends in success or cancellation may not be in the control of the party attempting to complete the exchange.

If Alice forces an escrow-based exchange to complete, she will either have Bob's item released to her or her own item returned to her, but it is the escrow agent that decides which of those two results is correct, based on the behaviour of Alice and Bob up to that point.

Alice may wish to cancel the exchange, but if she has already agreed to it and Bob has already received her item, then the escrow agent must release Bob's item to her to preserve fairness.

A FEP has *weak timeliness* if it is guaranteed to finish within a bounded time. This generally means employing a timer of some kind. Some protocols with strong timeliness have a timer to guarantee each exchange finishes within a bounded time, but they must also provide the participants a way to complete the exchange on demand.

If Alice deposits her item in an exchange without weak timeliness, then Bob can wait an arbitrarily long time before he either accepts the trade and releases his item to her or cancels and restores Alice's item to her. For most use cases, this denial of service (DoS) risk is unacceptable, making weak timeliness a minimum requirement for almost all exchanges.

Strong timeliness eliminates the dependency on a timer. This can lead to protocol simplifications by eliminating the need to have a TTP incorporate a cancellation timer. It also eliminates a source of friction for the participants, as choosing the correct deadline for a fair exchange introduces another complication into the handshake operation.

1.6 Other Protocol Properties

A wide variety of properties have been defined in the study of FEPs. Beyond strength and timeliness, the other properties we have found particularly useful in evaluating and creating FEPs are defined as follows.

Note the properties of a FEP are always with respect to a set of trust assumptions and a class of items. That context is important when examining FEPs, many of which have desirable properties only over a small class of items, or only under a large set of trust assumptions.

A FEP is *symmetric* if the actions available to each party are independent of their role in the exchange. Otherwise, the protocol is *asymmetric*, and such protocols generally impose asymmetric cost and risk on the participants.

A FEP is *invasive* if it requires changes to the items (Ateniese, 2004). For example, the TTP might leave a signature on an item recovered from a dispute, which must then be checked by the application to ensure fairness; or the TTP might create an affidavit that tells the application that the contract should be considered as successfully signed. A FEP that is not invasive is called *non-invasive*.

An optimistic FEP is called *invisible*, or transparent, if there is no observable difference between an item that was exchanged optimistically and the same item exchanged through the TTP backend (Asokan, 1998; Micali, 1997). An optimistic FEP that is non-invasive would generally also be invisible, but the opposite is not true, as invisible protocols often change the item structure to suit their needs. In lieu of a commonly accepted term for a FEP without this property, we label these protocols *opaque*.

A FEP provides *non-repudiation* if at the end of the exchange there is evidence conclusively linking the participants to the sending of their items. FEPs that do not guarantee such evidence provide room for *repudiation*.

A FEP that provides *confidentiality* guarantees that only the intended parties have knowledge of the items sent during the exchange. An escrow-based protocol would not generally have confidentiality, since the escrow organization checks the items to ensure they match their descriptions. A *leaky* protocol does not guarantee confidentiality.

A FEP is *clockless* if it does not rely on globally synchronized clocks, or *clockful* if it does. In a clockful protocol, the participants rely on physical clocks to coordinate their actions — for instance, sending messages or cancelling the exchange when a timeout expires.

A FEP is *collusion-free* if it bears no risk that its TTP can abscond with the items or collude with a participant to take both items. If the risk of collusion exists, we say that the protocol is **collusion-risky**. Note that a collusion-free protocol might still produce an unfair outcome if the TTP colludes with one participant by preventing the other from claiming their item, but it cannot take both items for itself.

A FEP is *abuse-free* if no participant can ever prove to an independent observer that they can unilaterally decide whether the protocol completes in success or cancellation. Note that in FEPs with strong timeliness, either party can drive the protocol to completion at any time, so neither party can unilaterally decide how or when it completes, because the other party may make their decision first. Protocols without this property are **abusable**.

A FEP is said to have a *monolithic TTP* if a single TTP is required to be the environment in which all protocol operations occur. Protocols that allow the environment for each operation to be specified independently have *polylithic*, or split, TTPs.

A FEP has a *stateful TTP* when the TTP is aware of the exchange and responsible for keeping some of its state, and modifying its own behaviour based on that state. For instance, escrow-based protocols involve a workflow that prohibits the synchronize operation from occurring until an exchange reaches a particular state. Conversely, we say that the TTP is *stateless* if it does not change its own behaviour regardless of its use in the exchange.

A FEP has a *replicable TTP* if it can be replicated to mitigate the risk of malicious or accidental behaviour unbecoming to a TTP. If replication is detrimental, we say that the TTP is *non-replicable*.

Different use cases demand different properties from FEPs. Strong fairness and strong timeliness are a good start, but sometimes those are unnecessary, while in other cases they are insufficient. Picking a protocol with the right properties for the use case is an important consideration when choosing a FEP.

We turn our attention now to another question of central importance for any fair exchange protocol: what items can it exchange?

Chapter 2

Categories of Items

All items divide neatly into two main groups: *copyable* items, and unique items.

Copyable items are just data. If D_A is copyable, then Alice can retain a copy of it when she deposits it with Bob.

Unique items can't be copied. They have a uniqueness constraint: if D_A is unique, then either Alice can have it, or Bob, but not both. This constraint is generally enforced by a trusted third party (TTP), which Alice and Bob interact with through network messages.

Both of these categories of items must be further refined to be able to identify precisely which items a fair exchange protocol (FEP) can exchange. Many FEPs have been implemented over the decades, and most can guarantee strong fairness only for a subcategory of items. For other items they offer only weak fairness, or no fairness at all: many protocols are strictly limited in the types of items they can exchange.

This motivates presenting a categorization of items based on their relevant properties with respect to FEPs, to provide clear names and descriptions for different classes of items, and aid in our examination of FEPs generally.

2.1   Copyable Items

An item is copyable if Alice can retain a copy of it when she gives it to Bob. More formally, an item is copyable if it observes four key properties:

(1) It is **transferable**: The sender can transfer a copy of the item to the receiver by means of messages sent within the execution of the FEP. This allows for sending the item over the conventional Internet channels, for instance.

(2) It is **verifiable**: The receiver can expose the item to examination within the execution of the FEP to categorically determine that the item meets or fails to meet a set of properties that makes the item acceptable.

(3) It is **idempotent**: The sender can provide the item several times within the execution of the FEP without negative consequences for the sender or the receiver.

(4) It is **entirely data**: The sender can make arbitrarily many perfect copies of the item, which are indistinguishable from the original.[1]

A digital map, for example, is copyable because it meets those four properties. First, it is transferable because Alice can send it from her mobile phone to Bob's mobile phone.

It is verifiable because upon receiving a copy of the map, Bob's device can run a program (for example, a verification of its digital fingerprint) to verify that it matches the map that Bob is expecting, as defined in the setup document.

A map is idempotent because neither Alice nor Bob are negatively impacted if Alice's device sends more than one copy of the map to Bob's device. Finally, a map is just data, and Alice can make as many perfect copies of it as she likes.

The fact that copyable items are just data, and a perfect copy can be kept by the sender, means that the item does not need to be returned to Alice if the exchange is cancelled. She never relinquishes

---

[1]In fact, the sender is generally expected to retain a perfect copy at the conclusion of the exchange, a quality which is exploited in some FEPs to provide fairness guarantees in otherwise impossible situations.

the item, so from her perspective the exchange process can just stop. So long as Bob cannot receive her item through this exchange, then she is still guaranteed a fair outcome.

This property of copyable items allows FEPs to be designed that will work in situations where Alice has no guarantee that Bob will return her item on cancellation. These protocols can have properties such as efficiency or simplicity that might not be achievable if they are required to guarantee that Alice's item will be restored whenever the exchange is cancelled.

The class of copyable items aligns with the fundamental limits of fair exchange, as we will see in Chapter 6 after the remaining foundations of the fair exchange framework are established.

The restrictions on copyable items are as relaxed as possible, to maximize the coverage over items. Some other proposed categories are quite similar, such as the class of forwardable items in Asokan (1998) (items that are electronically receivable, electronically verifiable, and idempotent), though note in particular that copyable items have no restrictions on the nature of their transfer or verification — it does not have to be electronic.

This means that a spoken-word secret is just as much a copyable item as the version typed into a computer. In fact, we can imagine a classic escrow exchange happening with spoken-word copyable items quite easily. Alice and Bob agree to exchange secrets. They both trust Charlie as a confidant for this process. They each tell Charlie their own secret, and what properties they expect the other's secret to have. If Charlie determines that their demands are met, he tells each the other's secret; otherwise, neither learns the other's secret.

Using modern cryptographic techniques when exchanging items like spoken-word secrets or physical items becomes quite a bit more complicated. We briefly consider ways of bringing these worlds together in Section 2.3. For the remainder of the book, we focus on digital items except where otherwise noted, but the principles of our fair exchange framework are generally applicable to all types of items.

Copyable items fall into two primary categories: they might be generic *secrets*, or they may be *instruments* which have a special relationship to a third party. Some secrets can also be verified under encryption, which may allow them to be converted into instruments.

2.1.1 *Secrets*

A secret is a copyable item whose transfer is irrevocably finalized as soon as it is known. Before the exchange, Alice's secret is known by her but not by Bob. After a successful exchange, the secret is known by both Alice and Bob.

Secrets are also known as *secret strings*, but no assumptions are made about the nature of the "strings": they may be ASCII characters, voices singing, bumps on a page, or colours in a painting. In all cases, though, they are copyable.

Secrets include data that are personal, like email and health records; authentication information like usernames and passwords, or a secret phrase for entering a speakeasy; documents requiring limited circulation, like mergers and acquisition paperwork; and proprietary business data like market reports, supply chain information, and maps of shipping routes or pirate booty. The generic example of a secret used in this book is a map.

Note that the sharing of secrets may alter the economic value of the item, depending on its properties. For example, items that represent secret strings may decrease in their commercial value as the number of entities to whom the secret is known increases. Conversely, some items like videos of celebrities and software increase in their commercial value as the number of copies viewed or downloaded increases.

2.1.2 *Instruments*

An instrument is an item that can be manipulated by a TTP in a very specific way. This entity has the ability to either generate a new item with identical properties, or revoke the existing item by releasing its anti-item. The generic example of an instrument exchange is digitally signing a contract.

An instrument is *generatable* if a version of it can be generated by a TTP. For instance, if Alice proves that Bob took D_A but did not deliver D_B to her, then the TTP can generate a replacement D_B for her. Some authors distinguish between strong and weak generability, and regard monetary compensation as a special form of generability (Pagnia *et al.*, 2003).

Any secret can be converted into a generatable item by explicitly depositing it with a TTP. For instance, Alice might deposit D_A with a TTP and receive a deposit receipt in exchange. She can use this deposit receipt to prove to Bob that an item matching the characteristics of D_A is safely deposited with an entity that Bob trusts, and that this TTP is willing to act as the back-end of an optimistic FEP. This allows Alice and Bob to enter into an optimistic exchange for D_A (provided Bob has made similar arrangements). Note that she can continue exchanging D_A with others using this same deposit receipt, so this is a fairly efficient option.

Even more efficient approaches for creating generatable items exist. Alice might be able to encrypt D_A under a well-known key of a TTP. If Bob can use verifiable encryption to verify $\{D_A\}_{K_{\mathrm{TTP}}}$, and trusts the TTP to operate according to the protocol, then he can treat D_A as a generatable instrument.

Another classic example is contract creation. If Alice and Bob both agree that the signature of a specific TTP is acceptable on a specific contract in place of their own signatures, then their signatures over that contract become generatable instruments. In this case, D_B is generatable by definition: instead of a deposit or fancy cryptography, it is simply the definition of an acceptable signature that is changed.

Note that in the latter two examples no prior interaction with the TTP is required. Depending on the average error rate, optimistic protocols for those types of generatable items may yield a high level of amortized efficiency.

An item is *revocable* if a TTP can revoke it. Revocability can be modelled in different ways — for instance, some authors distinguish between strong and weak revocability (Pagnia *et al.*, 2003).

In our framework, revoking a copyable item involves the release of an *anti-item* that nullifies the original item. A revocable item D_A has an anti-item D_A^{-1} that revokes D_A when it is released.

A classic example of revocable items is a payment being made from Alice to Bob. Many payment systems operate using a "pay later" model, where Alice's payment to Bob is really a secret string D_A that he can later redeem for payment from some trusted entity. If that entity also happens to offer a way for Alice to cancel that payment, as well as the facilities necessary to integrate this into an

FEP, then we may consider that cancellation as the release of D_A^{-1}. This prevents Bob from being able to collect his payment from the trusted entity.[2]

2.1.3   *Verifiable under encryption*

Some secrets can be fully verified without exposing anything about the underlying item, other than that it matches the expectations of the recipient. We say that these items are *verifiable under encryption*, or *vercrypt* for short.

Particular care must be taken when exchanging secrets, because as soon as Alice has seen D_B, she has captured its entire value. This aspect of secrets makes verification difficult, because Alice must be prevented from seeing D_B. In general, Alice must employ a TTP of some kind to manually or programmatically verify that the item matches her expectations, but if D_B is verifiable under encryption, then she can verify it locally instead.

A vercrypt item must be *programmatically verifiable*, meaning that it can be entirely verified by computational means, without manual intervention from a human being. We generally limit our examination of items to programmatically verifiable items, except where mentioned otherwise — as in Section 2.3, where we consider digitally inaccessible items; and Chapter 15, where we examine various ways that a participant may fail to have their expectations met in the process of an exchange, and the kinds of risks and risk mitigation techniques that may accompany those failure modes.

A significant advantage of vercrypt items is that they can be turned directly into instruments, allowing them to be exchanged in protocols that cannot provide a fair exchange guarantee over secrets. Various means of making this transmutation have been proposed, for instance, in Cachin and Camenisch (2000), which details an optimistic FEP where Alice can deliver a secret D_A to Bob that has been encrypted under K, the key of a TTP. This allows Bob to go to that

---

[2]Though note that care must be taken to ensure that D_A^{-1} is only released when Alice has failed to receive D_B. Readers who remember paying with cheques, or who have had to deal with credit card chargebacks, may be painfully aware of the lack of fairness in many of these exchanges.

TTP and receive restitution if Alice fails to deliver the unencrypted version to him after Bob has sent his item to her. As long as Bob can use verifiable encryption to verify that $\{D_A\}_K$ would satisfy his expectations if it were decrypted, then he can send D_B to Alice with confidence that the exchange will be completed fairly.

This works for any item whose relevant properties can be verified under encryption, granting us a powerful tool for expanding the class of items that can be exchanged by protocols, such as optimistic ones, which provide strong fairness guarantees for instruments but not secrets.

For example, many types of cryptographic signatures are amenable to being verified under encryption, so that Alice can determine that Bob's signature over a particular document is encrypted under a TTP's key without being able to extract the signature. This converts the secret string of Bob's signature into a generatable instrument that can then be exchanged using a broader group of FEPs.

Verifiable encryption is an active research area, and much progress is being made in expanding the range of properties that can be verified as well as the practical performance of these verifications. As with many applications of modern cryptography, some theoretical techniques for verifiable encryption are prohibitively costly with respect to computational complexity, while others are achievable today on commodity hardware.

2.2 Unique Items

An item is unique if it is not copyable. This simple statement belies a bit of complexity: when we speak of items in this book, we primarily mean things that are digitally transferable and programmatically verifiable, and unless stated otherwise, unique items can be assumed to have those qualities.

That means unique items and copyable items are both transferable and verifiable. As we saw previously, copyable items are idempotent, and are also just data. Unique items are neither.[3]

---

[3]It may be the case that there are not any items that are idempotent but not just data, and vice versa, but it is still worth emphasizing these two aspects separately.

Unique items are not just data. Alice's video game account is not just the data within it. It is not just the username and password she uses to access it. It is an asset — that is, it is an object that changes state over time while maintaining invariants. Alice could send all the data of her user account to Bob, as well as her username and password, but Bob still doesn't have her user account. For instance, she could change the password of the account before Bob has a chance to access it. Or she may be able to convince the video game company to remove Bob's access to the account and restore it to her, perhaps by proving her identity in some fashion. A unique item is not just its data.

Unique items are also not idempotent. If Bob transfers a unit of digital currency to Alice as part of a fair exchange process, he cannot send that same unit to her again, because he has already sent it. This is true of physical items as well: if Bob gives Alice a ten pound note as part of the exchange, he cannot give it to her again later in the exchange, because he does not have it anymore. Giving her another ten pound note will definitely have a negative impact on him.

We can summarize both of those points by saying that unique items cannot be copied.[4] This is expressed as a uniqueness constraint for all unique items that they must have a canonical history. This is generally enforced by a TTP, often the issuer of the unique item, who is the source of truth of its current state.

This third party is an important aspect of unique items. The maintenance of the uniqueness guarantee must be enforced by a mutually trusted party — or, at the very least, a party that the recipient trusts. A unique item that can be duplicated arbitrarily is impossible to value. Given the basic FEP assumption that the participants do not trust each other — if they did trust each other, they would just give each other their items without employing a protocol — a TTP is required to ensure the uniqueness of each unique item.

Unique items can be classified into two subcategories, which are exchangeable by different FEPs. Some unique items, called *assets*, can be moved between accounts, so that Alice can send a message

---

[4]This is a somewhat crude summary, though: what we refer to here as unique items are more generally items that have certain invariants enforced on them, and those invariants may be rather more varied than mere uniqueness. The risks associated with more general invariants causing a loss of fair expectations are examined in Part 3.

changing the management of the asset from her account to Bob's. Other unique items, generically called *accounts*, can only be accessed with a password or some other secret.

2.2.1 Accounts

An *account* is a type of unique item, managed by a third party, where access to the item is provided by a secret, like a password or session token. The generic account used as an example in this book is a video game account. In some examples, this game account is taken to be managed by a centralized service that provides the required interfaces. The third party makes modifications to the account when a request includes the appropriate secret.

One of the modifications that is generally made available is changing the secret. This is necessary for many of the protocols we examine in this book. An account-based unique item that lacks the ability to change its administrative secret is effectively worthless: the first time that secret is exposed, the item is ruined forever. This is why password reset operations are so important, and so ubiquitous, despite representing a large amount of complexity and a correspondingly large amount of security-sensitive surface area.

By definition, one modification the TTP does not make available is moving an account into a different account. The only way to take control of an account is by knowing its secret. However, unlike a copyable item, knowing a secret is not enough to guarantee control of an account, because the secret associated with an account can change.

This is different from an asset, the other type of unique item.[5] Assets can be moved, and control of an asset is usually expressed as access to its account, rather than knowledge of a secret string. Ultimately, we will see that some FEPs provide fairness guarantees over both accounts and assets, while others can provide them only over assets.

There are interesting subtleties within the classification process that arise from the precise ways in which access control mechanisms are employed in FEPs. For instance, an account where the only way

---

[5]Note that the terms *account* and *asset* are really only crude approximations for these classes of items — don't read too much into them.

to update a password is by sending the new password to the server is an account-based unique item. Conversely, if that server provides a way to send a hash (and, for instance, its accompanying salt) to the server, such that the next access to the account must provide a matching password, then this item may qualify as an asset-based unique item instead, and be amenable to exchange in a wider range of FEPs.

The question in the end comes down to this: can a scheme be devised whereby Alice can cause the control of D_A to be transferred away from her, so she can no longer access it, and that Bob can be confident this is true regardless of what Alice does? If this is possible, then the item counts as an asset. If it is not, then the item counts as an account.

Picking up the previous example, if Alice can send a new salted hash to the server, and Bob is able to check that the server has updated the password hash for this item to the new hash, then a protocol could be devised whereby Alice retrieves that hash from a public posting of a mutually TTP, and Bob can verify that the new password hash for the item matches the hash in that public posting of their agreed-upon TTP. Under these circumstances, this item may be counted as an asset, and FEPs that can handle assets but not accounts may be employed.

To the best of our knowledge, no such password update scheme has ever been implemented. Possibly this simply reflects a lack of understanding of the benefits of such a scheme, or the current lack of accessible fair exchange systems for such items, but it is also likely that no such scheme will ever be widely deployed. There are better ways of converting an account into an asset, as we will see in the next section.

2.2.2   *Assets*

An *asset* is the other major category of unique items. The generic asset used as an example in this book is digital money. In some examples, this digital money is presumed to be managed by a publicly addressable digital money ledger, where we may speak of particular "blocks" of updates.

Modifications to an asset are not made based on some secret that is inherent to the asset itself, but rather are authorized by the authority of a proxy, such as an account.

One kind of modification that all assets have is the ability to be reassigned to a different proxy. If something is associated with an account, but can never be associated with a different account, then it is merely a property of that account and not an item itself.

A video game like World of Warcraft (WoW) provides a simple example that demonstrates these two different types of unique items. Alice's WoW account contains several characters. These characters cannot be transferred to a different account: they are simply properties of her account, and are available to whomever controls her account. To relinquish control of her account to Bob, she either needs to tell him her password, and thereby initiate a race to change it, or set it to a different password — and then tell him the new one, setting off another race. If a third party is involved, they need to actively change the password to prevent Alice from cheating in the exchange; they cannot be a passive participant.

Conversely, many of the items her characters possess are transferable. She can easily transfer them to a different account — suppose she sends them to Charlie, a party that both Alice and Bob trust. Alice may even be able to directly prove to Bob that Charlie owns D_A, via marketplace exchange logs, for instance.

The most common way of converting an account-based unique item into an asset is by associating it with a public key instead of a password. This small difference has a big impact on the dynamics of changing control. Instead of sending her password over the wire each time she modifies the item, Alice sends proof that she knows something that no one else does: the secret key matching that item's public key. This means that Alice can apply a modification to the item that changes its public key to a different public key, and potentially can prove to Bob that she has done this, without Charlie being involved.

2.2.3 *Mobile objects*

Of course, a third party is still directly involved in those modifications: the third party that maintains the uniqueness of the unique item. This may be the third party who first created the item (i.e., Blizzard), or the second third party who is running the exchange (i.e., Charlie), or it might even be a TTP, depending on how the item maintainer has configured their service and what access they make available.

Many parties that maintain items make it quite difficult to interface with those items, and do not provide the necessary APIs to modify their items in a programmatic way that is conducive to fair exchange. Others create barriers through expense and latency, as in popular blockchains, which may charge hundreds of dollars or take days to complete a transaction. Those that do offer their own built-in "fair exchange" platforms are often acting as fully trusted escrow agents, with all the concomitant costs and risks, and in particular have access not only to the aggregate market data but also to the full particulars of each individual item.

This is not the case with physical items. If Alice holds a bearer certificate, she can transfer it to Bob directly, without the issuer having any say in the transaction or even any knowledge of it. She can also prove to Bob that the item he is now holding has the full integrity of the issuer.[6]

A data structure called a TODA file (Coward *et al.*, 2022) allows Alice to do the same thing with a digital item. She can transfer it to Bob directly, without the issuer having any say in the transaction or even knowledge of it. And she can prove this to Bob with the same integrity as if he was hearing it directly from the issuer.

This reduces the cost and risk to Alice as the owner of the item, because it eliminates the dependency on the issuer to manage every modification to the item. It also reduces the unnecessary overhead on the issuer to provide those facilities. This allows issuers to focus on issuing assets rather than maintaining their state and facilitating their modifications. Unlike other assets, TODA files can move between custodians, allowing their owner to choose where their state is managed and making them uniquely amenable to any kind of asset-accepting fair exchange process.

2.3   Digitally Inaccessible Items

The word *item* within this work refers primarily to digital items — by which we mean items that can be stored digitally, transferred digitally, and verified digitally. There are a great many non-digital

---

[6]Up to the issuer's anti-counterfeiting techniques, like special ink, holographic implants, quantum dots, or psychic paper.

items, or *inaccessible items*, in the world, however, and we would like to have ways of exchanging those fairly as well. Inaccessible items can still be stored, transferred, and verified, like their digital kin, but the mechanisms for doing so may vary considerably.

Inaccessible items naturally decompose into the same two primary categories as digital items: there are copyable items, like spoken-word secrets, and there are unique items, like a car or a jug of milk. Some inaccessible items, like a photograph, can be as either unique or copyable, depending on whether the value is in that particular physical photograph (perhaps it is signed by the artist) or the information it carries. Others may be represented digitally but have important properties that are subjective in nature and can only be judged by human inspection, making them unable to be verified digitally.

We have already seen an example of an escrow-based protocol for exchanging spoken-word secrets, back in Section 2.1. In fact, escrow-based protocols can be used for any item at all, digital or inaccessible, because all they require is the ability for Alice and Bob to transfer their items to Charlie (a third party they both trust), who stores them temporarily, verifies them, and then transfers them either to their new owners or back to their original owners. Because all items can be stored, transferred, and verified, this simple escrow-based protocol model works for anything.

However, escrow-based protocols come with a significant number of disadvantages, as we will see in Chapter 9. In particular, there is the cost of engaging Charlie, the risk that Charlie steals the items, and the risk that Charlie copies the items. If the items are valuable, those risks are quite significant, which means Charlie must be very trustworthy, making Charlie even more expensive to engage.

Is it possible to exchange inaccessible items without using a fully escrow-based protocol, with all its attendant costs and risks? As we build up our fair exchange framework further, we return to this question, which is ultimately answered in Chapter 6. For now, we turn our attention to the basic operations that every FEP must accomplish.

Chapter 3

The Operations of Fair Exchange

Every fair exchange protocol (FEP) involves five basic operations, carried out to provide its fair exchange guarantee. Understanding these operations, or steps, and how they relate to each other, is the purpose of this chapter. Understanding how these operations relate to their environments, the types of items that can be exchanged, and the resulting FEP properties is the purpose of the first part of this book.

One of the advantages of this operation-focused model is that it allows us to move beyond classical escrow-based FEPs by moving specific operations out of a central trusted third party (TTP). This opens up many new designs for FEPs. In Part 2, we explore these options, both by analyzing existing FEPs with this operational framework and also by introducing new FEPs and combination protocols that mix two or more FEPs together. These can create efficiencies for specific use cases that are unavailable in traditional one-size-fits-all FEPs.

The abstract model in Figure 3.1 shows the order of operations for Alice and Bob, the participants in an exchange that is governed by a FEP.

They first construct a handshake document collaboratively as part of the handshake operation. Then they each deposit their items in the deposit operation, and in the verify operation, their deposited items are verified against the specifications in the handshake document. Finally, the outputs of the verify operation converge into the synchronize operation, which then determines the execution of the release/restore operation.

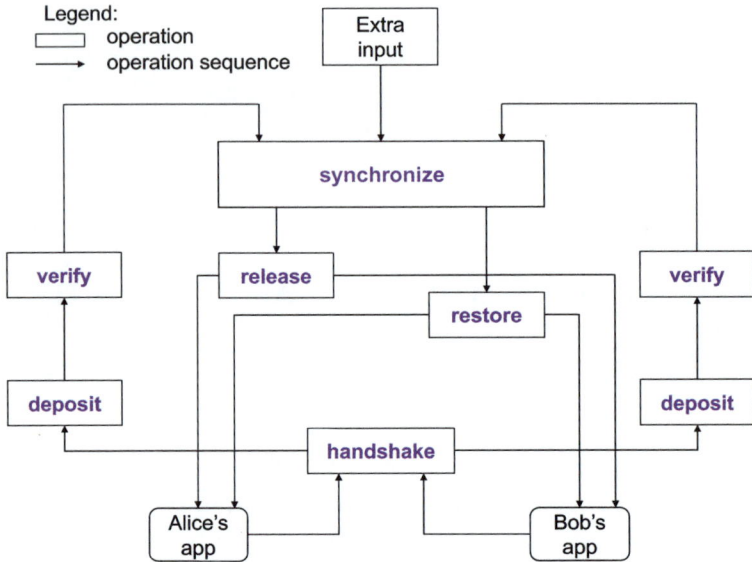

Fig. 3.1.   The five basic operations of FEPs.

3.1   Handshake

The handshake operation solves two distinct problems.

First, it aligns the participants' expectations, forming an agreement on what they are exchanging and the terms of the exchange. Alice and Bob need to express the relevant properties of their desired items, the mechanical properties of the FEP they are using to exchange those items, and any mutually trusted third parties they may need to invoke as part of this exchange.

When both parties agree to those terms, they produce a handshake document H_{AB}[1] for that exchange. Whether this handshake document has any legal standing is an interesting and somewhat orthogonal question we explore in Chapter 16.

Second, the handshake document must provide a unique identifier for the exchange. It is vital that this particular exchange not be confused with some other exchange, even one with the same participants

---

[1] An example of a handshake document used in FEWD is shown in Section 13.1.1.

and items. Without a way to uniquely identify a particular exchange, unfair outcomes may result.

Aligning expectations, the first problem solved by the handshake operation, may mean different things depending on the context. The precision required in the handshake document, and how important this document becomes, can vary depending on the items being exchanged, the nature of the FEP, and how much trust is demanded from and placed in the various trusted parties and mechanisms involved.

Suppose, for instance, that Alice and Bob have decided they will trade some of Alice's apples for some of Bob's oranges. They both trust Charlie, who runs a trading house, to moderate the exchange and prevent any shenanigans; so they arrange to meet at Charlie's and exchange their goods. They each check in their goods as they enter, and Alice connects her apples to Bob's oranges, and vice versa. Charlie strictly enforces the fair exchange guarantee: Alice is free to leave with her apples whenever she desires, but she can only leave with Bob's oranges if they both agree to complete the exchange successfully (in which case she must leave her apples behind).

In this example, the handshake is the check-in process of Alice and Bob entering their goods into Charlie's ledger, and then binding their items together into an exchange — which is necessary to prevent interruption from other exchanges happening in the same trading house. This is sufficient, because Alice will have a chance to directly verify Bob's oranges before accepting the exchange.

Conversely, if Charlie were running a distribution centre, and Alice and Bob sent their fruit to him to exchange on their behalf, they would need to include very explicit instructions about their expectations for properties such as the quality, size, colour, and quantity of the other party's goods. Those details would all be incorporated in that handshake document.

If Alice and Bob are exchanging copyable items, the handshake agreement becomes even more important. Alice needs to explain to Charlie exactly what she requires from Bob's secret document D_B. Charlie may carry out the examination by hand, as we considered in Chapter 2, but we are generally interested in the case where Charlie does this programmatically. This process carries various kinds of risks, depending on the type of item and the properties being considered, which are examined in Chapter 15.

Fairness can also be lost if two different exchange attempts become mixed together. This motivates the second output of a handshake operation: a unique identifier for this exchange. Creating these unique identifiers requires accounting for a number of subtleties, including conflation between different exchanges and replay attacks (Shmatikov and Mitchell, 2002).

Suppose Alice and Bob engage in a number of exchanges over time. In one of these, she says she will give Bob D_A' in exchange for D_B. Bob rejects this, as he considers D_A' to be worth less than D_B.

Later, Alice establishes another exchange attempt with Bob — this time offering D_A in exchange for D_B. Bob accepts. If it is possible that these two exchange attempts could conflate, then Bob could get D_A' while Alice receives D_B, which is an unfair outcome for Bob.

Suppose an escrow service tracks items and handshakes independently. It records that D_B was deposited, but that records do not associate D_B with any particular handshake document. If handshake documents are unsigned or created asymmetrically, then Alice can take advantage of Bob by crafting a second handshake and exchanging for D_B. Even when mutually signed handshakes are required, Alice could deceive Bob by initially agreeing to an exchange of D_A for D_B, which she does not execute. If later D_A goes down in value, or D_B raises in value, she proposes a new exchange of some equivalent item for D_B. Bob re-deposits D_B with the TTP, but she brings the old handshake document instead of the new one, and receives D_B for her D_A, which is unfair to Bob.

A prior cancelled exchange could also be substituted by one party for a current successful exchange. If these two exchanges, which may feature the same users exchanging the same items, have identical identification, then Alice may be able to confuse Bob, or confuse the TTP, resulting in D_B being released to Alice while D_A is also restored to her — an unfair result.

Having a unique and precisely stated handshake document enables the creation of a unique identifier for each exchange process, which also serves to uniquely identify deposits of items, and all other exchange operations. A given handshake document H_{AB} only works for Alice and Bob, and only for the particular D_A and D_B outlined within it, and additionally only works one time.

That last clause is important to emphasize. The exchange that the handshake specifies can only happen once. Any attempt at using it in the future results in exactly the same outcome. Not no outcome, because then Bob runs the risk of losing his document if he is disconnected at the wrong time. Not a different outcome, because then Alice has a chance of unfairly gaining D_B if she runs the protocol a second time.

The "exact same outcome" seems like it would be different for a copyable item than for a unique item. In both cases, though, the successful outcome is to release the item. Charlie will happily release the door behind which Alice put her apples as many times as Bob wants. If Alice's apples are still there, he can take them, and if they aren't, he can't: either way, Charlie performs the same operation.

The handshake's uniqueness guarantee is maintained within the synchronize operation. It is possible to have a stateless synchronizer that still produces the same result regardless of how many times it is run, but in an optimistic protocol, this will generally limit the strong back-end to being release-based (for generatable items) or restore-based (for revocable items), but not both. The choice between release and restore is different from the choice between release and no operation, which requires less overhead.

A stateful synchronizer is able to do more. For instance, within an escrow service, we may think of this as a totally ordered stream of events that are output by the synchronizer and keyed by H_{AB}. Once produced, this stream of events is constant for H_{AB}, and persists between calls to the escrow service. In this case, where the handshake is a unique key and the synchronizer has a long-term memory of the events it has ordered, an optimistic protocol can provide additional functionality.

For instance, suppose Alice begins a revocation attempt for D_A with the TTP in an optimistic exchange, because she didn't receive D_B from Bob. Bob provides D_B directly to the TTP, because he has been unable to send it to Alice for some reason. The TTP has a choice: it could revoke D_A, or it could release D_B to Alice and D_A to Bob. Either of those outcomes is fair, and a TTP that tracks all of that state closely can make either choice, as long as it ensures that once D_A and D_B are released, they cannot be revoked — otherwise Alice could come back later and have D_A revoked while Bob is offline.

In many ways, the strong fair exchange guarantee comes down to ensuring that exactly one of release or restore is activated for a particular exchange. Regardless of which party is invoking that exchange, or how many times the exchange is invoked, the outcome must be the same. This guarantee is provided by the combination of the handshake, synchronize, and release/restore operations. Meanwhile, the deposit operation ensures that the only way the participants may access the items is through release/restore, and the verify operation ensures that each participant's expectations for their received item are met.

3.2   Deposit

The deposit operation protects the interests of both participants. Once the handshake step has completed successfully, Alice and Bob must both deposit their items. When Alice deposits D_A, she wants to ensure that Bob cannot access it, and Bob wants to ensure that Alice cannot modify or destroy it.

For a **copyable item** D_A, once Alice has deposited it, the following requirements must be guaranteed:

- Alice cannot modify or destroy D_A (no takebacks), and
- Bob cannot access D_A (no peeking),
- unless the exchange completes successfully (releasable).

Each of these requirements is critical to the fairness of the FEP.

If Alice were able to modify or destroy her deposited item D_A, then there may be no way for Bob to receive D_A on a successful completion of the exchange process. This is unfair to Bob, so the *no takebacks* requirement is necessary for fairness.

If Bob were able to read D_A prior to the exchange completing successfully, then he could cancel the exchange but keep D_A. This is unfair to Alice, so the *no peeking* requirement is also necessary for fairness.

If the deposited item D_A was not released during a successful completion of the exchange process, then that would be an unfair outcome for Bob, so the *releasable* requirement is also necessary for fairness.

For a **unique item**, the deposit operation is more complicated. In addition to the requirements above for copyable items, there are two more requirements that must be guaranteed once Alice has deposited unique item D_A:

- Alice cannot access unique D_A (no access),
- unless the exchange completes unsuccessfully (restorable).

If Alice were able to access D_A after it was deposited, she could change its access after a successful completion such that Bob would not be able to access it. This yields an unfair outcome for Bob, so the *no access* requirement is necessary for fairness.

If Alice cannot access the item after the unsuccessful completion of the exchange process, then Bob can have D_B but Alice will not be able to access D_A. This is an unfair outcome, so the *restorable* requirement is necessary for fairness.

The requirements presented above for depositing copyable items and unique items are specialized for a classic two-person exchange, but can be generalized to a multiparty exchange. This kind of generalization is discussed further in Chapter 19.

Traditionally, the deposit operation in an escrow-based FEP requires Alice and Bob to each provide their items to a TTP, who acts as an escrow agent. This trusted party fulfills all five requirements above, allowing these agents to take deposit of both copyable items and unique items.

One downside of involving an escrow agent in the deposit step is that while Bob is guaranteed to not be able to read D_A — due to the *no peeking* requirement, and up to the trustworthiness of that escrow agent[2] — the escrow agent can read D_A. This may represent only a minor risk and inconvenience, or it may make it impossible to use an escrow-based FEP, depending on the sensitivity and value of D_A.

Another way of depositing copyable items is through encryption, as we saw with items that are verifiable under encryption in Chapter 2. This can manage the first three guarantees: preventing takebacks by transferring the encrypted file to Bob, preventing peeking through the encryption layer, and allowing Bob to view the item on a successful completion by furnishing him the encryption key. However, encryption alone cannot manage the guarantees required for all unique items, as we will see in Chapter 6.

---

[2]The escrow agent's trustworthiness incorporates not just their desires, but also their abilities. If Bob is able to read D_A, despite the escrow agent's best intentions, that still counts as a trust violation for that FEP.

3.3   Verify

As we saw earlier, the handshake operation establishes a description of the items the two parties are exchanging, which forms the basis of the verify operation.

Ensuring that the correct items are correctly deposited is a pivotal part of the exchange process, which links together the handshake, deposit, synchronize, and restore/release operations. It is essential to verify that the properties of the items and mechanisms of deposit conform to their specifications in the handshake document, which itself must conform to the protocol's specifications. The handshake document also provides the exchange identifier, which both deposits must reference.

The verify step must verify:

- The item matches its description in the handshake.
- The deposit mechanism matches its description in the handshake.
- The handshake is properly formed.
- The deposit is linked to the handshake for this particular exchange.

Typically, only that first check, of an item matching its description, is sensitive information leakage, and the remaining checks can be performed in a dependent environment without negatively impacting the exchange. As a result, we often speak of the validate step as only checking the item against its description, but technically the other aspects must also be validated by this step, or an unfair outcome may occur.

For **copyable items**, like secrets, it is generally the case that Alice is unable to perform validation tests on D_B beyond those listed in the handshake document, and that only a simple binary answer is produced as an outcome of the item validation: either the item has been verified to match the description in the handshake document, or it hasn't.

The succinctness of this result is important to ensure minimal information leakage in a failed verification. If Alice receives information about exactly how D_B fails to match the criteria in the handshake document, she may learn a great deal about the secret contained in D_B, depending on the nature of that criteria. This risk, and steps for mitigating it, are covered in Chapter 15.

It is also important to note the context for verification of copyable items. This might be done by a trusted agent, like an escrow agent, or it may be possible to do it through verifiable encryption, where Alice can verify properties of D_B without having direct access to the underlying information. In either case, in a protocol with strong fairness guarantees Alice must never learn anything about D_B that Bob was unwilling to claim in the handshake document.[3]

For **unique items**, the participants are able to do additional checking beyond the scope of the narrowly defined tests in the handshake document. In fact, in many protocols Alice is able to examine a unique D_B directly and make a decision about whether to proceed based on whatever tests she chooses to employ during that process. In other cases, a trusted agent will proceed on her behalf and make either a computational or a subjective assessment of D_B, depending on the nature of the agent.

For **digitally inaccessible items**, the verify operation is almost identical to digital items. In either case, some agent is provided access to D_B via the deposit mechanism, and is able to perform a series of tests as instructed by the handshake document. This might be Alice directly, in the case of a unique item or a copyable item that is deposited in a manner amenable to verifiable encryption, or it might be an agent that both she and Bob mutually trust, such as an escrow agent, a specialized auditor, or a computational system.

That agent reports the result of their verification as an input to the synchronize operation. This happens directly in the case of a TTP agent: their verification report (true or false), is fed directly into the next step. It can also happen indirectly when a participant is performing the verify operation: Alice may cancel the exchange by simply no longer responding if D_A is copyable. (If D_A is unique, then Alice needs to engage in the remaining steps in order to collect D_A from the deposit mechanism.)

Note the deep relationship between the verify step and the deposit step: the actions available to the verifying agent for examining the item are exactly those exposed by the deposit mechanism. Different deposit mechanisms will allow different aspects of an item to be verified, or may even prevent some desired checks from being able to occur.

---

[3]Weak guarantees may be sufficient when a strong guarantee can be provided by a suitable back-end: optimistic protocols are the classic example of this.

The primary goal of the verify operation is to ensure that the expectations of both parties are met. Many different deposit mechanisms and verification techniques have been proposed over the years to help mitigate the numerous sources of risk that can enter into meeting this goal. These are analysed in Chapter 15 in some detail.

The verify operation must be completed before the synchronize operation occurs. If verification fails, the exchange must be cancelled and the items released back to their original owners to ensure fairness.

3.4   Synchronize

The synchronize operation coordinates the participants to ensure that either they all release, or they all restore. It returns a binary value, corresponding to the success or cancellation of the exchange.[4]

The difference between a strong FEP and a weak FEP is in this sync step. A strong FEP guarantees, up to the security and trust assumptions of the protocol, that the participants will all have a fair outcome — in other words, they will all perform the same action: either release, or restore. However, this always requires a TTP with unimpeded communication channels to both participants. This can be very lightweight, as we have seen; but even so, not every use case can support this cost.

In a weak FEP, the synchronize step sometimes produces an unfair outcome. To guarantee fairness it needs to be backstopped by a strong FEP. An extreme case of this is an optimistic FEP, where the synchronize operation is relatively trivial: after verifying that D_B is deposited correctly, Alice releases D_A directly to Bob, hoping he will send D_B back. If he doesn't, Alice uses the strong FEP that serves as the back-end of the optimistic front-end. Other weak FEPs can use the same strategy of employing a strong FEP as their back-end, if the items being exchanged are valuable.

---

[4]This result of the synchronize step also corresponds from a legal perspective to the participants having signed or denied the handshake contract (Chapter 16).

3.4.1 *Relationship to two generals*

This is very similar to the classic Two Generals Problem, first detailed in 1975 by Akkoyunlu *et al.* (1975), and elaborated in 1978 by Gray (1978).

The story is that two generals, who are camped some distance apart, need to coordinate their attack. Unfortunately, the messengers they send keep getting lost. How does the initiating general know that the responding general has received the message and will attack at the appointed time? The responding general must send a message back — but how do they know the messenger they sent didn't get lost? The initiating general must send a message back. This is clearly an infinite regress.

The standard impossibility results for the Two Generals Problem apply directly to the issue of synchronization in fair exchange,[5] which is not deterministically solvable without guarantees on the communication channels. However, there are many probabilistic solutions: the generals could each send one hundred messages, for instance, in the hope that at least one of them will get through.

Unfortunately, this solution fails in the fair exchange setting, because two participants are mutually adversarial. Rather than two generals working together to overcome a lossy communication channel, Alice and Bob are assumed to be actively trying to cheat each other.

This change of context from a common adversary to a mutually adversarial setting means that simple probabilistic solutions no longer work. Alice can send hundreds of messages to Bob, but he will only reply if doing so is to his advantage.

Other common solutions include having the responding general start by sending regular heartbeat messages to the initiator, indicating they have not yet received a message. The initiating general sends messengers as before, stopping only when sufficient time has passed without receiving heartbeat messages.

This solution also fails when used as the basis of the synchronize step in fair exchange. Bob can simply continue sending the heartbeat

---

[5]As indeed is alluded to by the story in Gray (1978), where the two generals are actually two computers, one in Tokyo and the other in Fuessen, which must perform a fair exchange or face destruction.

messages indefinitely, preventing Alice from ever releasing his document.

The commit coordinator, as described in Gray (1978), proves more effectual for our purposes. This solves the problem by introducing a TTP into the protocol, and requires them to be intimately involved in the process. This provides a sound basis for synchronization, and is precisely what is done by escrow-based protocols and other TTP synchronization methods.

We will see an alternative example of this later, when our public bulletin board (PBB) model is presented in Chapter 4. This model provides a method for reducing the intimacy and trust required from the committed coordinator by relying on a small set of lightweight functions provided by the public bulletin board. In particular, the PBB is employed only for messages related to the synchronize operation, and does need to follow any special rules or even be aware it is being used for this purpose.

The relationship of synchronization to the Two Generals Problem provides a negative answer to the question of whether Alice and Bob can synchronize themselves without a mutually trusted third party involved.

It is somewhat enlightening to take a small step towards formalizing this idea. We begin by restricting the participants, to reduce the surface area under examination.

(1) **Restriction 1**: The participants have no external environment or other parties they can communicate with.
(2) **Restriction 2**: The participants communicate with each other exclusively through messages made up of bits they write, with no other channels or attributes.
(3) **Restriction 3**: A participant is guaranteed access to their counterparty's item once they have received N messages.
(4) **Restriction 4**: A participant can never access their counterparty's item unless they have received N messages.

We grant the participants a boon, in the form of messages that are always delivered, in order, exactly once. This is an unrealistically strong ability, and is enough to solve the Two Generals Problem on its own, but is of no help in the fair exchange synchronization problem because of the mutually adversarial nature of the participants.

Under these conditions, Alice must receive N messages from Bob before she can access D_B, and Bob must receive N messages from Alice before he can access D_A, by Restriction 4.

By Restriction 2, the participants do not have synchronized clocks, or any other kind of mutually synchronized facilities, and by Restriction 1, they do not have access to any external form of synchronization, so they must rely on simply firing messages off to each other.

By Restriction 3, once Alice receives N messages from Bob, she can open D_B. This enforces a sharp transition in their communication: as soon as one participant has received N messages, they can immediately release their desired item and stop sending messages.

The only way to prevent that outcome is for Alice's Nth message to already be sent to Bob by the time she receives his Nth message. But there is no way for Bob to know whether this is the case, by Restrictions 1 and 2. If he sends message N to Alice before he receives message N from her, he does so with no guarantee that he will ever receive her Nth message.

This proof sketch is revealing not just as a way of highlighting the increased difficulty of the fair exchange synchronization problem compared to the Two Generals Problem, but because of what relaxing the restrictions reveals.

Relaxing Restriction 4 provides the participants with a chance they will be able to open their items before receiving N messages. If this chance increases gradually as more and more messages are sent, with a corresponding decrease in the cost paid to exercise that chance, then we have gradual release, a synchronization mechanism and family of FEPs considered in Chapter 11.

Relaxing Restriction 3 yields opportunities for probabilistic games on the opposite side, where after receiving N messages (where N is often 1) there is a chance of being able to open the item, but a chance of being denied as well, with no possibility of reattempt. This is the basis of oblivious transfer, another synchronization method and family of FEPs.

Note that both of these techniques can only provide weak guarantees. Any synchronization relying on probabilistic measures can only ever produce weak FEPs, because either party may get lucky and be able to open their item, while the other side is unlucky and cannot. We examine this thoroughly for gradual release protocols, and highlight exchange parameters that yield a cost- and risk-adjusted measure of fairness called *marginal fairness*.

Relaxing Restriction 2 can provide Alice and Bob with mutually trusted local components, like synchronized clocks, or even attestables, an abstraction we introduce in Chapter 7 that covers both traditional trusted hardware and other formulations of computational trust. These are insufficient for synchronization on their own, as we will see in Chapter 6, but provide a powerful primitive for other fair exchange operations. It is possible that some kind of shared synchronized primitive between Alice and Bob may be discovered that allows them to complete the synchronize step locally, but it would have to have direct messaging capabilities that could bypass any control the participants choose to exert over those messages. Attestables explicitly do not have this: all the messages that Alice's attestable sends or receives are deliberately delivered by Alice.

Relaxing Restriction 1 opens opportunities for the participants to employ a TTP, for instance, a commit coordinator or PBB. This is what all strong FEPs rely on for their synchronize operation, and for good reason, as we will see in Chapter 6.

3.5   Release/Restore

The final step in any fair exchange is to either complete successfully and release D_B to Alice and D_A to Bob, or to cancel and *restore* the items back to their original owners: D_A to Alice and D_B to Bob. We always use the term *release* to mean the item is delivered to its recipient, and *restore* to mean, roughly, that the situation is reset to how it was before the cancelled exchange started. The full operation is referred to as release/restore, or sometimes just R/r for short.

This final operation is focused on the mechanical aspects of reversing the deposit mechanism and extracting the items, as well as delivery to the intended recipient. While we typically think of the synchronize operation as ensuring that exactly one of these two good outcomes (success or cancel) occurs, we can alternatively think of it as ensuring that if release occurs for Alice, it also occurs for Bob, and vice versa, and likewise for restore. This reframing makes it clear that authentication is a vital part of this operation: it is Alice and Bob who must receive the items, not any other party.

For copyable items, release simply means exposing the secret to the recipient. This exposure can never be undone: Alice cannot be forced to forget a secret she has learned, and even if she did forget it, she cannot prove she has.

Correspondingly, the restore operation is not defined for copyable items, and protocols that only concern themselves with copyable items can be simpler as a result. There is no difference between restoring copyable D_A to Alice and doing nothing, since the assumption with copyable items is that the sender retains a copy of the item.

As we saw in Chapter 2 about instruments, there are copyable items that are revocable. In an optimistic protocol, as seen in Chapter 10, Alice may need a TTP to revoke D_A if she has sent it to Bob but she did not receive D_B in return. She does this by granting the TTP the power to create an anti-item D_A^{-1} that will revoke D_A. The TTP releases this anti-item when its release the conditions outlined in the protocol are met within that exchange.

For unique items, release means a full transfer of control. If an account D_B is released to Alice, then she is the only one who knows its new password. Note again the difference between this and a copyable item: Alice is the only one who knows the new control secret; Bob must not be able to keep a copy of it. If an asset D_B is released to Alice, then only her account has control of D_B.

Restoration of unique items is simply the reverse of release. If account D_B is restored to Bob, then only he knows its new password. If asset D_B is restored to Bob, then only his account has control of D_B. It would seem on the surface that the inherent uniqueness of these items would automatically guarantee that Alice and Bob could not both control it, but this is not the case. Race conditions can occur — for instance, if both of them know the new password and they must race to be the first to change the password for D_B; whereas if neither of them know the new password at the end of the exchange, then D_B may be lost forever.

Note that extracting an item from the deposit mechanism is often only half the battle. If Alice has D_B encrypted on her own device, and the key is exchanged as in a gradual release protocol, then release may be as simple as decrypting D_B, but this is the exception. Many FEPs deposit items using other mechanisms, and these must concern themselves with the network delivery of D_B to Alice as part of the R/r mechanism, or, for instance, the network delivery of the appropriate messages to Alice's attestable to allow it to release D_B to her.

They must also concern themselves with Alice's ability to authenticate herself to receive D_B. If Alice is unable to authenticate with a TTP, that creates an unfair outcome for her. If someone else is able to authenticate and take D_B, that creates an unfair outcome for Alice as well.[6]

This authentication can happen in many different ways. It depends on the type of party being authenticated with, such as a TTP or an attestable; the nature of Bob's deposit, such as an explicit deposit of D_B, or an implicit deposit by agreeing to allow the TTP to sign a document on behalf of Bob; and the way Bob and Alice synchronize with each other, for instance, by sending sync tokens consisting of signatures over the handshake document.

Having seen the operations of fair exchange, we next examine the environments in which they are performed.

---

[6] And possibly also for Bob, if D_B is copyable, because now someone has gained access to his secret without paying for it.

Chapter 4

Environments for Operations

We use the term *environment* to describe a place where storage, compute, and messaging are possible, and where different fair exchange operations can occur.

A *dependent* environment is one where a participant controls everything: they can read and write to storage, evaluate and change programs, and send and receive messages at will.

When we talk about an environment being *independent*, we mean that none of the participants in the fair exchange process can interfere with the guarantees of that environment, even if they behave incorrectly according to the protocol.

Independent storage (IS) is an environment where a participant controls the computation and messaging, but there is encrypted storage that they cannot read. For instance, if Bob sends D_B to Alice encrypted under a symmetric key that he knows but she does not, then we say that $[D_B]K_B$ is deposited in an environment with encrypted storage.

An environment with *independent compute* (IC) is one where a participant controls the messages that are sent and received by that environment, but they cannot change the program it is running. Attestables (Chapter 7) define an interface for IC, and provide examples of this environment ranging from trusted hardware-based to cloud provisioned.

An *independent messaging* (IM) environment is entirely controlled by a trusted third party (TTP). The participants can all send and receive messages to this environment freely, and cannot block other participants from doing so. In this chapter, we examine the properties of these environments thoroughly and explain what they contribute to fair exchange protocols (FEPs).

4.1   Dependent Environments

In a *dependent* (or D) environment, a participant controls everything. This might be Alice's laptop, or Bob's mobile device, or perhaps a cloud server one of them is running.

Consider Alice's laptop. She has full control over the storage, compute, and messaging of that environment. She can create or delete any file in its storage. She can also read any file, append to it, or mutate its contents.

She also has full control over its computation. She can evaluate a program, pause its execution, read the process's memory, and change the data and code within it. In particular, she can change a piece of software that is running, either before its evaluation has started or after it has been transformed into a computational process.

Messages that come into this environment are under Alice's complete control as well. She can choose to accept messages from various endpoints, or to deny access to those, using a firewall or proxy. She can do the same thing for messages her applications want to send by using a reverse firewall. She can exercise complete control over message receipt and delivery, and even deliver individual messages on a case-by-case basis if needed.

Another example of a dependent environment is a router that Bob controls. This may not provide a direct way to access storage and computational resources, but Bob can always connect more devices to his router. Every message those devices send to the outside world has to pass through his router, and again he can decide whether to deliver them on a case-by-case basis. This is also true of the messages they receive from the outside world. It is even true of the messages they send and receive to each other.

Note that no other participant in the system, including trusted actors, can change the guarantees within a dependent environment. They cannot stop the owner from destroying storage or compute resources inside the environment. They cannot read messages the owner does not want them to read. They cannot send messages the owner does not want them to send. If they could, then it would be a different kind of environment.

4.2   Independent Storage

Even in Alice's laptop, though, it is not the case that she has complete access to everything that occurs. Other environments can be present inside of a dependent environment. For example, a file may be encrypted with a key to which she does not have access.

Suppose Bob sends D_B to Alice encrypted under a symmetric key that he knows but she does not. We would then say that $[D_B]K_B$ is deposited in an IS environment. Alice controls the computation and messaging, but cannot read D_B.

We would also say that she cannot (usually) write to D_B. Certainly, she can destroy $[D_B]K_B$ by deleting the file, but she can also destroy it by overwriting it. Any attempt to write to D_B by naively changing bytes in $[D_B]K_B$ will result in the destruction of D_B.

Conversely, Alice could promise Bob that she will not look at D_B until the exchange completes, and that she will delete D_B if the exchange terminates in cancellation. This is not an IS, because Alice could break her promise and examine D_B directly.

Note that once Bob deposits $[D_B]K_B$ with Alice, he cannot read it either, because it is inside Alice's dependent messaging environment, which Bob cannot access. If he were to lose his copy of D_B, then Alice would need to deliberately send $[D_B]K_B$ back to Bob for him to be able to access it. An item deposited in an IS is not accessible by any participant.

While an IS usually cannot be written to, there are exceptions where a well-defined boundary can be created that sufficiently constrains the writing process as to maintain the isolation boundary. Homomorphic encryption is an example of this. It allows interacting with an IS, but only through a boundary that prevents arbitrary read/write behaviour.

Note that IS does not exist as a top-level environment. It has no compute abilities, so it must be embedded inside a computational environment.

4.3   Independent Compute

An IC environment is a computational environment where no participant can modify the program that is running or read its memory.

This is a specific form of *exfiltration-resistant computing*, a broader term for a computing system that provides safeguards around access to the computational processes. IC environments can be embedded inside a dependent environment — in fact, they must be embedded inside a messaging environment, as they have no messaging ability.

Suppose Bob promises to change his secret key and encrypt it so that he can't access it. If he performs this task in a dependent environment, he could always change his mind and modify the program or peek into its memory to find the new secret key.

With independent computation, though, whether embedded in his dependent environment or at arms length, Alice can trust the process boundary to prevent Bob from keeping a copy of the new key. Attestables define an interface for IC, and Chapter 7 provides additional examples of this environment.

Bob can still destroy the process: by switching off the device, sending a terminate message to its host, issuing a kill command from a terminal, or whatever the appropriate method is for that particular environment. And of course, he can block messages to and from the process, which is observationally equivalent to terminating it.

Other than Bob's ability to destroy it, though, these independent computations cannot be disturbed by any participant. Nothing can change the rules that process is following. Additionally, nothing can look inside the process.

This actually requires a stronger isolation mechanism than IS, where encryption under a symmetric key is enough to provide the necessary guarantees. In the case of independent computation, the data are being actively used in the process, so the isolation mechanism should also rule out leaks through side channels, and must therefore be quite robust.

4.4   Independent Messaging

Every participant can freely send messages to an environment with IM, and receive messages from it, without any other participants being able to intercept those messages or interfere with their delivery.

This kind of environment must be entirely controlled by a TTP. In the context of a FEP, that party makes a guarantee that it will send and receive the required messages for each participant without interference from other participants.

These services may be very lightweight, offering only read and append-only write access to IS,[1] or it may offer a fully independent computing environment for running arbitrary programs.[2]

Suppose Alice and Bob wish to perform the synchronize operation between themselves. Bob promises that after he receives Alice's sync token he will send a message to her with his own, but without IM there is no way to guarantee he will send it.

Conversely, if they make use of an IM service that offers read and append-only write access to IS, then Alice and Bob can quite easily synchronize by both posting their sync tokens to the service.

Note that the guarantee provided by an environment with IM is quite strong, but also very specific. It does not guarantee that Bob will be able to deliver a message to the service immediately: he may be offline, or have lost his device, etc. It does guarantee that there is nothing Alice can do to keep Bob from reaching the service, beyond some bounded window of time. Whatever she tries — DDoS, simjacking, cutting his cable — he will eventually be able to reestablish connection with the service and send and receive messages.

Whether this is an appropriate assumption to make depends on the resources deployed by the service, as well as the resources available to Alice and Bob. How long the participants should have to resume contact, in protocols that make use of timeouts, is also a question that depends on the resources of the participants and trusted parties in the exchange. In general, it should be the case that a service trusted by Alice and Bob to provide an IM environment has many more resources than either participant.

4.4.1 *Public bulletin board*

We introduce two specialized abstractions for IM environments, which we employ liberally throughout this work, in the same way that the attestable abstraction is used for IC environments.

The first is an append-only data store called a public bulletin board (PBB). PBBs have been used to provide fairness for secure

---

[1]Note that independence is always from the perspective of the participants, not the trusted parties. Whether the trusted party can read the plaintext in this storage or not is a different issue.

[2]It is also possible that an IM service could offer just mutational write access to IS, or other kinds of relatively weak service offerings.

multiparty computation (Choudhuri *et al.*, 2017), as an alternative to using a more robust TTP that offers a larger set of features but also requires more space in the trust stack.

A PBB makes a small set of guarantees around its service:

(1) It is **accessible**: all exchange participants can read the PBB's posts.
(2) It is **immutable**: posts to the PBB cannot be changed.
(3) It is **ordered**: all participants always see posts in the same order.
(4) It is **verifiable**: the lists of posts it delivers are cryptographically signed.

The accessibility guarantee of a PBB ensures that it remains an IM environment. The verifiable requirement is most easily handled by message signing. The immutability and ordering requirements can be resolved at the data structure level, for instance, by having the PBB wrap posts in blocks that use hash pointers to form a linked list. They could also be resolved by the PBB simply swearing that those posts appeared in that order. In either case, participants will need to trust the PBB, as it could fork a hash-based linked list, or even maintain two different lists for the different participants.[3]

We examine these guarantees, and various implementations that achieve them, further in Chapter 17.

Note that a PBB offers nothing beyond those simple guarantees: no computation of arbitrary programs, and no additional interfaces or functionality. It is possible to use a more full featured service as a PBB, but from the perspective of FEPs, the PBB features are sufficient for its tasks, and limited enough for it to be run efficiently and with a minimum of risks, whether operational or data exposure. It merely stores and replays messages it has received. It lists those messages in a total order, and signs its own messages.

4.4.2   *Trusted third party*

The second abstraction for IM environments represents a service provided by a TTP. This includes escrow services that run specialized programs for facilitating each fair exchange operation.

---

[3]The PBB could leverage some external integrity for this, to reduce its trust barrier, and in many cases it might make sense for it to do so.

It can also include more generic services that allow arbitrary programs to be run in an environment that offers both IM and IC for user-provided (or at least user-selected) programs. A TTP can be used piecemeal within a FEP for providing an environment for individual operations, or may combine several operations into a single service offering.

A TTP combines the guarantees of an attestable with those of a PBB, and requires a level of trust in the service provider that accounts for both of those sets of guarantees.

Chapter 5

A Diagram Language for Fair Exchange

The four basic environments introduced in the previous chapter are abstractions we use to describe the properties of the environment in which different fair exchange operations are being performed. In this chapter, we introduce a diagram language that we use in subsequent chapters to explain fair exchange protocols (FEPs). In particular, we use the diagrams to explain the risks faced by the executions of the operations involved in FEPs.

5.1 Environment Diagrams

5.1.1 *Dependent environments*

A dependent environment (Figure 5.1) is an abstraction over any system that can send and receive messages. Alice's laptop is a dependent environment. Her router is a dependent environment. If her laptop is connected to the Internet through her router, this is a form of composition. This nesting of environments suggests that a diagrammatic approach would be useful.

A simple box suffices for this simple environment. We use rectangles of different configurations to indicate environment boxes. These can represent a particular piece of hardware or an entire network of computing environments. When it is important to be specific, we show the individual process that messages are being delivered to.

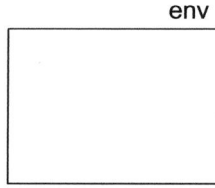

Fig. 5.1.   Dependent environment.

Fig. 5.2.   Independent storage.

Fig. 5.3.   Computational process.

This can be modelled at any level of complexity, but our concern is not architectural precision, it is showing the elements that are relevant to the FEP under discussion.

5.1.2   *Independent storage*

Independent storage (IS) is an abstraction over encryption. An application can provide IS: Bob can encrypt D_B under K_B to produce $[D_B]K_B$. He can send that to Alice, and now she has D_B contained within an IS environment. Where is that environment? Somewhere Alice controls, like her laptop.

Here again we have nested environments, with this IS environment sitting inside her dependent environment. We denote IS with a circle (Figure 5.2). When it is necessary to show specific processes in an environment, those are indicated by rounded rectangles (Figure 5.3).

5.1.3 Independent compute

Independent compute (IC) environments fit between the other two independent environments. They must be embedded in a messaging environment, like IS, but they provide an arms-length place for computation to proceed, like IM environments can.

We define an abstraction for IC environments called *attestables*. An attestable is a service that offers the guarantees that are essential to IC — namely, that the rules of the process cannot be changed once it is started, and that the data inside it cannot be observed — and adds to those a third guarantee, which is that the attestable service can attest to those first two guarantees.

Attestables come in many forms, ranging from cloud-based services to third-party devices to embedded secure enclaves. The trade-offs of these different forms with respect to FEPs, as well as accompanying implementation details, are discussed in detail in Chapter 7.

We denote an attestable — in other words, an environment that can attest that it offers independent computation — using a thin rectangle box with a second thin box inside (Figure 5.4), representing the isolation mechanism that keeps external processes from peering inside the independent computation environment.

5.1.4 Independent messaging

A service that offers IM is an abstraction over some entity that is trusted by all the participants to provide the IM guarantees, in addition to whatever other services it offers that are used within the protocol.

We denote a service that offers IM using a box with a thick border (Figure 5.5), to indicate that its messaging layer is protected from interference by participants. This is the most basic form of an IM environment, and in our diagram language it is synonymous with a public bulletin board (PBB), which provides IM without computation.

On the other end of the spectrum are trusted third parties (TTPs), IM environments that provide services requiring independent computation.

att

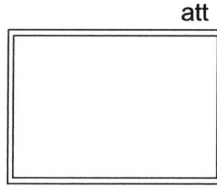

Fig. 5.4.   An attestable.

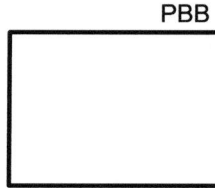

PBB

Fig. 5.5.   A PBB offers IM without computation.

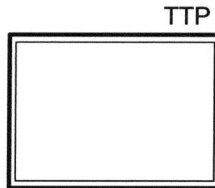

TTP

Fig. 5.6.   A TTP offers IM with computation.

We indicate this type of environment by composing the thick outer box for IM with the thin inner shell of independent computation (Figure 5.6). This is an obvious composition, because a TTP provides the guarantees and has the risks of both a PBB and an attestable.

If this party provides all five fair exchange operations through a single unified interface, we call it an *escrow service*. This uses the same graphical denotation that other TTPs do. The trade-offs of escrow-based fair exchange are considered in detail in Chapter 9.

The diagrams above serve as the basic abstractions for modelling of the environments wherein the fair exchange operations are performed.

As we shall see in the next chapter, these are the right abstractions for being able to understand the fundamental limitations of any FEP, simply by drawing its picture.

5.2 Composition and Errors

Here we look at the ways the diagrams can be composed, and highlight some particular illegal diagram configurations.

5.2.1 *Basic composition*

We compose dependent environments in the obvious way, as seen in Figure 5.7, by sticking the boxes inside each other.

In this example, we can think of the outer environment, *env*, as representing something like a participant's home network router, for instance.

Attestables can also be composed with dependent environments in a natural way. In Figure 5.8, we see an attestable inside a participant's dependent environment.

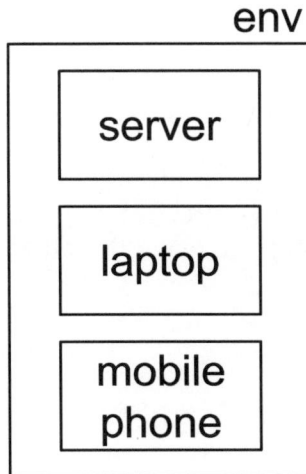

env

```
┌─────────────────────┐
│  ┌───────────────┐  │
│  │    server     │  │
│  └───────────────┘  │
│  ┌───────────────┐  │
│  │    laptop     │  │
│  └───────────────┘  │
│  ┌───────────────┐  │
│  │    mobile     │  │
│  │    phone      │  │
│  └───────────────┘  │
└─────────────────────┘
```

Fig. 5.7.   Three devices deployed within an environment.

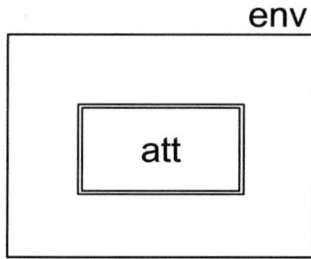

Fig. 5.8.   Attestable deployed within an environment.

This attestable might be a standalone device on Alice's network, or a USB key plugged into her laptop. It could also be a secure enclave on her laptop or a trusted component on her mobile phone, with those particular local environments abstracted out in this diagram.

5.2.2   *Arrows*

There are several different arrow types used in the diagrams in this book, as seen in Figure 5.9.

Arrows that describe something in the diagram are always dashed, so they stand out from the arrows that describe the process or protocol.

Arrows indicating a communication channel have arrows on both ends. We assume these channels are secured with end-to-end encryption when traversing networks, unless noted otherwise.

Single-headed arrows represent either a message being sent or a state transition, depending on the type of diagram. In either case, these form a step in a process being described.

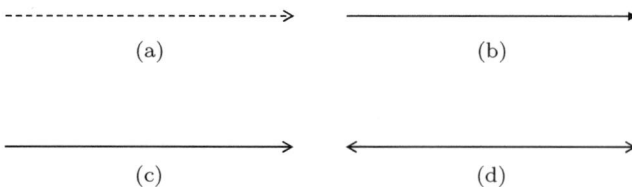

Fig. 5.9.   Arrow notation. (a) Description, (b) State transition, (c) Message, and (d) Channel or secure channel.

A Diagram Language for Fair Exchange 57

5.2.3 Composite diagrams

Diagrams can be composed through inclusion of a process inside of a dependent environment, as we have seen. In Figure 5.10, the process app_A is placed within the dependent environment env_A. In this arrangement, env_A provides app_A with its computational needs. Note that env_A has full access to app_A, and can both read its memory and alter its data and instructions.

A second way to compose diagrams is to connect them with arrows. The arrow labelled D_A shows a message being passed from app_A to app_B. The message itself is a cleartext version of D_A, though note that as it traverses the open network — represented by the gap between env_A and env_B — we assume it is encrypted within the communication channel.

Also note that the message arrow passes through the boundaries of env_A and env_B. These environments control all messages sent to the processes inside them or delivered from those processes, and can read, modify, delete, or arbitrarily delay the deliveries of any message, and can reorder sequences of messages.

An attestable att_A is represented in Figure 5.11, composed inside a dependent environment env_A. Here att_A is sending a message to its sibling in env_A, a process called app_A. Note that env_A has full access to this message as well, as it does to all messages passed between processes within it. It does not have access to any internal messages sent in att_A, nor to any processes or data inside att_A. Generally, we display attestables like att_A as singular units, but processes can be composed inside an attestable if necessary.

The message in this example is $\{D_A\}_K$, which is Alice's document D_A encrypted under a key K, which in this case is a key belonging to att_A. This means that app_B and env_B cannot read D_A (and neither

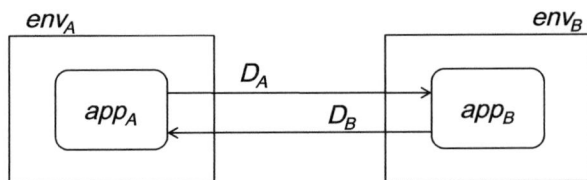

Fig. 5.10.   Environments with apps.

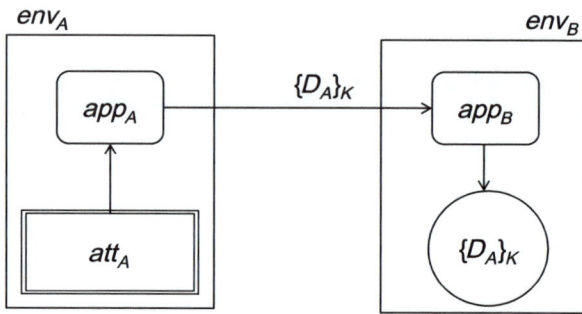

Fig. 5.11.   Environments with apps, an attestable, and IS.

can app_A or env_A, though they already have access to D_A), but it can write it into the IS, which is shown as the circle containing $\{D_A\}_K$ inside env_A.

5.2.4   *Diagrammatic errors*

Some configurations are illegal within these environment diagrams, the equivalent of syntax errors in a programming language.

Putting an IM environment inside another environment is an obvious error (Figure 5.12). Sending messages independently means they are not passed through some other environment.

Note the caveat about the protocol diagram: the environment belonging to some TTP is not expected to create and maintain a point-to-point connection to the participants of the exchange. It is perfectly acceptable to send those messages through other trusted carriers, who thereby become part of the ambient trust stack for this particular exchange. We model this by effectively rolling up the

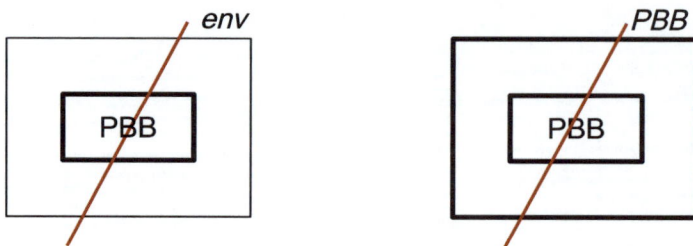

Fig. 5.12.   Never nest IM environments.

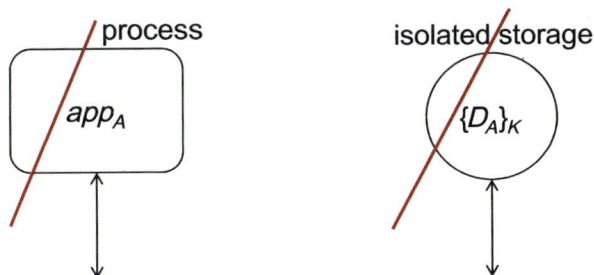

Fig. 5.13.   Always nest processes and IS.

networks the TTP is using to communicate to the participants within the TTP itself, so that the TTP box effectively contains both the proper TTP entity as well as all of the services it pays for, directly and indirectly, resulting in its ability to receive packets from and send packets to each participant.

IS environments and processes must exist inside an environment that provides compute — in other words, they need to be nested in a rectangular box.

Putting processes or IS environments as top-level entities in a protocol diagram is a syntax error (Figure 5.13). Communication arrows cannot go directly to those rounded shapes, they must pass through a rectangular box first.

The rectangular boxes, both thick and thin, are what provide computing resources for our environments, and neither a process nor an IS environment can do anything without compute. (In particular, IS environments are just data.)

5.3   A Distributed System Example

As an example of the environmental diagram language, we take the model of FEWD, as seen in Figures 5.14 and 5.15. We return to these figures later, in Chapter 13, where this new FEP is introduced and these diagrams are properly explained in that context.

For now we focus on them as representative examples of our diagram language, and in particular the contrast between the two figures, which highlights the kind of abstraction enabled by this diagram language. We make use of this abstraction for the

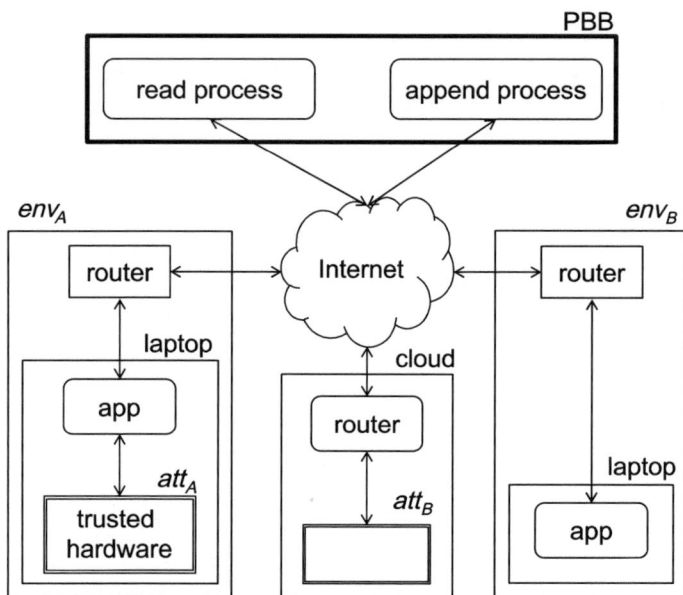

Fig. 5.14.   Deployment of FEWD on the Internet.

remainder of the book, without resorting back to the more detailed diagram style of Figure 5.14.

5.3.1   *Diagrammatic abstraction*

Starting from the top of Figure 5.14, we see that the PBB maintains two processes, one for appending content and another for responding to read requests for the current list of content. Even this more detailed view is quite abstract, of course, and possibly wrong: the PBB may implement this as a single process, or these may actually be many different processes, spread across many different machines residing in a data warehouse, a federated network, a distributed system processing, a smart contract, or even an *ad hoc* consensus system.

From the perspective of environment diagrams, these differences are irrelevant. We note processes in diagrams to clarify functionality and provide names to different aspects of the system, but make no distinction between a coroutine, an OS-level thread, a Unix-style process, an application composed of many local processes, or a distributed system.

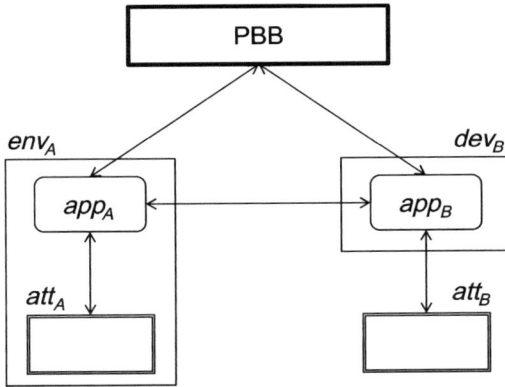

Fig. 5.15.   FEWD abstracted as a distributed system.

In Figure 5.15, we see the view of the PBB has been simplified, and we simply assume it has the standard PBB interfaces as described in Chapter 4. This is our standard way of representing a PBB in environment diagrams.

Alice's environment, which we generally label as env_A, contains a box representing her router in Figure 5.14. In many ways, this router represents the edge of her control over messages: until they are delivered to her router Alice cannot see them, and once they leave her router towards the open Internet, she cannot retract them.

One way to draw this is to have all arrows into env_A enter through her router, and then flow out from there. Another is to have env_A absorb the router into it, so that the environment boundary contains the router as part of its structure, and arrows passing through the edges of the env_A box are messages that pass through Alice's router, where she can exercise control over them.

In fact, there is an even stronger guarantee present, which is that arrows between boxes in env_A also pass through Alice's hardware network router, and she can exercise control not only over messages flowing through the boundary but also those that flow through the space denoted by the top level of env_A.

In particular, if there were two laptops in env_A, the arrows between them would go through the router. As there is only one laptop, and as isolating it as an independent device does not add anything to our understanding of this particular configuration of FEWD, we can do the same abstraction over Alice's laptop and absorb it into env_A. Now there are two layers at which Alice can exercise control within env_A — though of course she could add many more, if desired.

We see this abstraction applied in Figure 5.15, along with the de-emphasis of the particular instantiation of att_A. As discussed in Chapter 7, it doesn't matter what att_A is, it only matters that Alice and Bob trust it in their respective appropriate ways. Whether it is a trusted hardware on her laptop, a USB key she plugs into her laptop, or a separate piece of hardware connected to her router, the resulting abstraction is the same.

On Bob's side of Figure 5.14, we see he has a somewhat more complicated setup, where the application that is driving his side of this fair exchange process is on his laptop and behind his router, but the attestable he is using is a cloud-based one, which he communicates with over the Internet.

We perform the same absorption of Bob's router and laptop in Figure 5.15 that we did for Alice, though with the change that the resulting environment is labelled dev_B to emphasize that it collapses to a single device.

To communicate with his attestable, Bob must send messages over the open Internet, which are then further dispatched by the routers of his cloud host until they reach the attestable he has rented for this exchange, att_B. The attestable, the router in front of it, and even the whole cloud hosting environment can all be abstracted down to just att_B, as we see in Figure 5.15.

This emphasis on the particulars of Bob's setup is somewhat unusual. We have done it here to be able to clearly delineate the trust that Alice and Bob must have in each of the communication arrows in the diagram, which we do in the next section. In general, Bob's side of this diagram would mirror Alice's side, and we would not distinguish between a cloud-based attestable and a local one. For the remainder of the book, we employ abstractions that are as aggressive as possible, unrolling them only where necessary to highlight particular details.

5.3.2   *Communication guarantees*

There are a number of communication guarantees implied by, and required by, these diagrams.

The owner of an environment needs a guarantee that all the messages sent and received within their environment are under their control. Not that this does not extend into nested environments, but it does apply both to communication between immediate children and also to communication between children and external parties.

Each arrow has a sender and a receiver. The sender must believe it can send messages to the receiver, and the receiver must believe it can receive messages from the sender.

Note that for a sender that is not an IM environment, its receiver must believe it can receive a message, but there is no guarantee the appropriate message will be sent. It is critical that a lack of liveness in such an arrow does not lead to a lack of fairness. Only with arrows with an IM environment as a sender or receiver can the loss of liveness lead to a loss of fairness (and even in those cases, generally the disruption must continue for an extended period).

Both the sender and the receiver must believe that any environments crossed by an arrow between them, including the environment of the open Internet as represented by the blank space between their boxes, will be unable to snoop on their traffic due to appropriate use of encryption between their endpoints. For instance, attestables communicate with each other through messages encrypted under a shared symmetric key, and communication between the dependent environments and the PBB is conducted through secure channels built on the basis of the TLS protocol.

Chapter 6

The Fundamental Limits
of Fair Exchange

We have met the five necessary operations of a fair exchange, examined the environments those operations can be performed within, categorized items that can be exchanged, and considered the properties that a fair exchange protocol (FEP) may have, such as its strength and symmetry.

It is perhaps not immediately obvious that these elements would be so intimately connected, but in fact the environment that an operation is performed within puts limitations on the properties of that FEP and the categories of items it can exchange.

These limitations are very strong, and apply to every possible fair exchange protocol. Merely diagramming a FEP is enough to reveal its limitations. Consider Figure 6.1, which shows the operational diagram of FEWD. Figure 6.2 expands on this to highlight the results of applying Table 6.1 to the diagram.

Table 6.1 expresses each operation/element pair as a limitation on the FEPs that employ it. We speak of limitations here because running an operation in a particular environment is no guarantee that the possible advantages of doing so will be obtained.

For instance, in a FEP where the synchronize operation is run in a dependent environment, it is impossible to achieve strong fairness. The best that can be achieved is weak fairness. However, that particular protocol may fail to even achieve weak fairness, because of some flaw that prevents accurate evidence from being assembled.

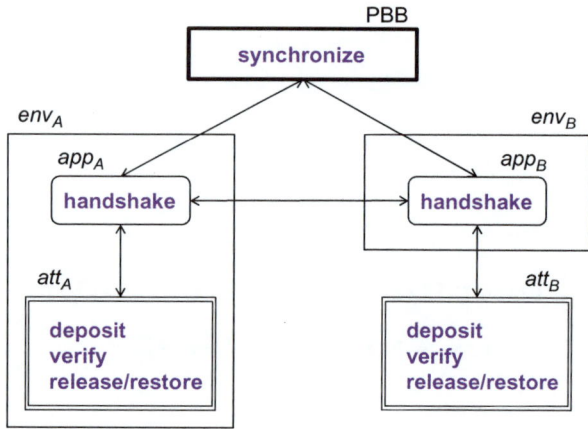

Fig. 6.1.   Execution of basic operations in FEWD.

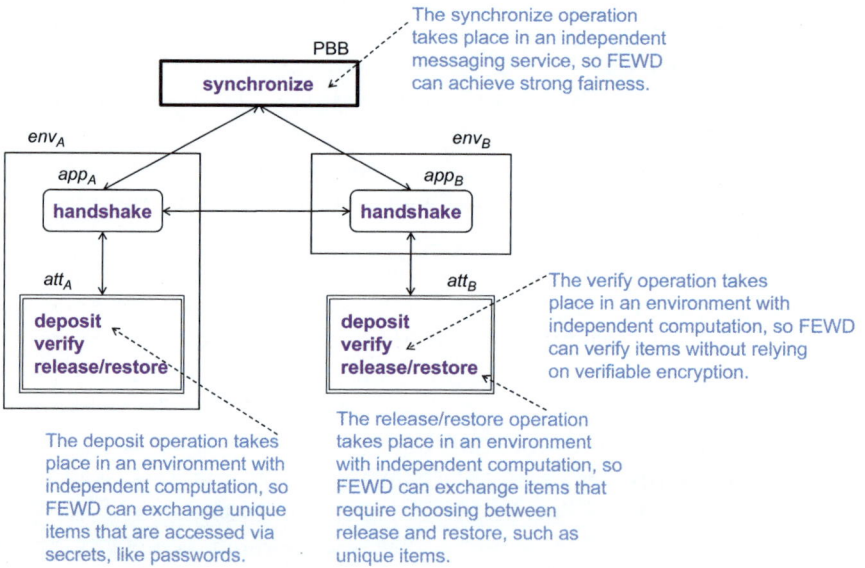

Fig. 6.2.   Execution of basic operations in FEWD and consequences.

Likewise, a FEP whose deposit operation is in an independent messaging (IM) environment may not provide the capacity for exchanging unique items. It is not limited by its operational environment, but the capacity is also not available.

Table 6.1.   The limits of fair exchange.

	Dependent	Independent Storage	Independent Compute	Independent Messaging
Handshake	Asymmetric	Asymmetric	Asymmetric	Symmetric
Deposit	None	No accounts	All	All
Verify	None	Vercrypt	All	All
Synchronize	Weak	Weak	Weak	Strong
Release/Restore	Copyable	Copyable	All	All

As the table illustrates, the environments have inclusive relationships with respect to these limitations. Anything that can be done in a dependent environment can also be done in the other three environments. Independent compute (IC) and IM can both perform any operations that can be performed in an independent storage (IS) environment. And an independent messaging environment can include an independent compute environment.

On the other hand, the respective costs and risks of these environments increase from left to right across the columns of the table, so it is generally advisable to choose the least powerful environment for each operation that still achieves the minimum necessary functionality for the resulting FEP. In this way, this framework provides guidance on generating fair exchange protocols that are fit for purpose.

The remainder of this chapter unpacks Table 6.1, clarifying each of the entries.

6.1   Handshake in D/IS/IC

An inherent asymmetry exists in any protocol where the handshake operation is performed in an environment without independent messaging.

The handshake operation solves two different problems, as noted earlier. First, it aligns the participants' expectations and establishes the rules of the exchange, so that Alice and Bob both agree on what they are getting and giving. And second, it gives the exchange a unique identifier, so this particular exchange won't be confused with some other exchange by any of the parties involved.

Each operation after the handshake makes use of the unique identifier it provides, and ensures that all of its inputs match with the identity of the exchange attempt to which they are bound.

Alice and Bob face a synchronization challenge whenever there are no trusted third parties (TTPs) involved in their exchange, as described in the synchronize section of Chapter 3. There will obviously be an asymmetry in protocols of that type, because one of the parties must message the other first, and for each operation and interaction during the protocol this remains true.

However, this inherent asymmetry also affects their interactions with third parties in that exchange. Without an independent messaging environment to provide synchronization, there is no way to guarantee that Alice and Bob will both have fair access to the exact same handshake document (one signed by both parties, for instance). This introduces a fundamental asymmetry into any protocol that runs its handshake in an environment without independent messaging.

This is not an insurmountable issue. The FEP can state that its participants are to be treated differently by the trusted third party, and that this asymmetry extends to the material required to activate the TTP in the first place. In other words, Alice and Bob have different standards on what constitutes a valid handshake document, depending on the role they are playing within that exchange process. While this is manageable, it does add complexity, both to the protocol as well as to the interactions with the TTP.

On the other hand, protocols that can provide a strong fair exchange guarantee have no need for a back-end FEP, and as a result do not have to bear as much of the burden of additional complexity cost from performing the handshake outside of IM. For example, FEWD provides both Bob and Alice with explicit cancellation tokens within the handshake document, guaranteeing strong timeliness even if there is a period when Alice could post her sync token while Bob could not. Weaker protocols that require a strong back-end pay a higher price for their handshake asymmetry, requiring the TTP to provide multiple different entry points for the back-end protocol.

6.2   Handshake in IM

No restrictions are placed on a protocol where the handshake operation is performed in an environment with independent messaging.

Performing the handshake in an environment that offers independent messaging can alleviate the complexity introduced to combination protocols by asymmetric handshake documents. The IM environment allows full synchronization to occur over the handshake document, so Alice and Bob are guaranteed either to both have access to it, or that neither of them do.

A classic escrow exchange, where the TTP handles everything, is the definitive example of the handshake operation performed in IM. In this case the TTP must insist that Alice and Bob both agree to the exchange before they proceed. Alice and Bob want to do this anyway, because depositing their items without an agreement in place can lead to unfair outcomes. On the other hand, even if Alice has a full agreement in place with the TTP, Bob's acceptance of the handshake document has to go through the full synchronization process in the TTP before the synchronize operation can begin — the only alternatives are unfairness, or asymmetric interfaces that treat Alice and Bob differently. Doing synchronization over the handshake document essentially amounts to a miniature fair exchange protocol that kicks off the escrow-based fair exchange protocol.

However, a full escrow-based protocol is not the only way to provide an IM environment for the handshake operation. Armed with this knowledge, we can conceive of a version of an escrow protocol that uses a lightweight synchronization mechanism like a public bulletin board (PBB) as part of the handshake operation, guaranteeing that if Alice has access to a valid handshake agreement, then Bob does as well. This can reduce the complexity and fragility of a combination protocol, like an optimistic FEP, at the cost of adding an interaction with a mutually trusted public bulletin board at the beginning of the exchange.

6.3 Deposit in D

Nothing may be exchanged in a protocol where the deposit operation is performed in a dependent environment.

Alice cannot deposit D_A in Bob's dependent environment without violating the *no peeking* condition of the deposit operation: clearly if D_A is exposed in Bob's dependent environment, then he can fully access it. This results in an unfair outcome for Alice, since Bob now has D_A and can stop participating in the exchange. Since the deposit step occurs before the sync step, Alice has no evidence that Bob ever committed to this exchange, and no chance to have the unfair outcome corrected.

It is important to note that parts of D_A may well be amenable to being exposed to Bob's dependent environment as a natural part of a fair exchange protocol. If D_A is a unique item, for instance, then Bob will already have access to all the aspects of it that are public, and that may well include everything except control aspect of D_A (the password or secret key). This kind of access does not fulfill any of the requirements of the deposit operation, and should not be regarded as a form of deposit.

It is tempting to imagine Alice sending D_A to Bob during an optimistic FEP as a kind of deposit, but actually the deposit step must happen well before Alice is prepared to release D_A to Bob. Optimistic fair exchange protocols are explored in detail in Chapter 10, and present an interesting and sometimes counter-intuitive example of deposits.

6.4   Deposit in IS

Only copyable items and assets (i.e., items that are not accounts) may be exchanged in a protocol where the deposit operation is performed in an independent storage environment.

Recall the guarantees that must be offered by the deposit operation for copyable items.

- Alice cannot modify or destroy D_A (no takebacks),
- Bob cannot access D_A (no peeking),
- unless the exchange completes successfully (releasable).

An independent storage environment offers all of these. Once Bob has an encrypted copy of D_A in his dependent environment, Alice can no longer modify or destroy that copy. Since D_A is deposited within an independent storage environment, Bob cannot access it. And if the exchange releases successfully, then the release function can send Bob the key to decrypt D_A. Therefore, copyable items can be exchanged within a protocol that deposits in an independent storage environment.

Recall that unique items require the deposit operation to offer two additional guarantees.

- Alice cannot access unique D_A (no access),
- unless the exchange completes unsuccessfully (restorable).

Assume all the operations other than deposit are performed by a trusted third party in an independent messaging environment. If that trusted third party has the access control information, then they are able to provide it to Alice upon restore, in the same way they could provide it to Bob upon release. Therefore, as long as the TTP has access to the unique item, the protocol can achieve the *restorable* guarantee while depositing in an independent storage environment.

Alice can guarantee this in several ways. She could encrypt D_A with the TTP's key, for instance. Alternatively, she could transfer the unique item into the trusted third party's control, prior to depositing it.

This is possible with an asset where Alice is able to change the access control associated with an asset to something she does not know. For instance, the TTP could publish a public key for this express purpose. Alice changes the public key of D_A to the TTP's and sends it to Bob. On release, the TTP receives encrypted D_A from Bob, changes its public key to Bob's, and then returns the modified, unencrypted version to him. The same occurs for Alice on restore.

Since Alice can change the control of D_A without knowing the new control information (the new secret key, in the example above), she can deposit that asset by changing its public key and then sending it directly to Bob. This seems like deposit in a dependent environment at first glance, but critically, Alice has associated D_A with a secret key that is known only to the TTP. The TTP could publish an encrypted version of that key, which Alice could include in her deposit to Bob, although they would only do that for the expository purposes.

An account, on the other hand, has a control system that cannot be modified by Alice without her knowing the new secret (recall that this is a defining characteristic of account type unique items). The only way she can deposit an account while maintaining the *no access* guarantee is with the help of a trusted third party. Independent storage is insufficient.

6.5   Deposit in IC/IM

No restrictions are placed on a protocol where the deposit operation is performed in an environment with independent compute or independent messaging.

Depositing an account D_A requires Alice to associate a new key with D_A, as we have just seen. She must be able to prove she can no longer access D_A, while also proving that access is still possible, so that D_A can eventually be released or restored.

This makes depositing an account-type unique item in an independent storage environment impossible. However, in an independent compute environment Alice can deposit D_A, because she can fulfill the two requirements: *no access* and *restorable*.

The independent compute environment provides the *no access* guarantee, by definition, because IC environments follow the rules faithfully and do not allow peeking. As a result, Bob can be satisfied that D_A is properly deposited if Alice's independent compute environment, whose program Bob knows, tells him that it has done the work of changing the key to something Alice does not know.

Conversely, Alice will be satisfied that the account D_A will be restored to her if the exchange is cancelled, because she knows her independent compute environment will faithfully follow the established rules with respect to release and restore following the synchronize operation of the exchange, as defined in the handshake document (which is part of the program that is loaded into the independent compute environment).

6.6   Verify in D

Nothing can be exchanged in a protocol where the verify operation is performed in a dependent environment.

If Bob can verify D_A in his dependent environment, then he has access to D_A before he has performed the synchronize operation. Until synchronization occurs, Bob can cancel the exchange and walk away, leaving Alice with an unfair outcome.

This mirrors the case for deposits in dependent environments, including that Bob may be able to verify a great many things about D_A in his dependent environment. If there are aspects of D_A that are public knowledge, then those can all be examined directly to ensure they conform to Bob's expectations of D_A.

Sometimes almost all aspects of the unique item are known to both parties ahead of time: exchanging a domain name, for instance, or a TODA file, or a stock sale, where Bob can examine the unique item thoroughly before agreeing to make the exchange with Alice. However, the control of D_A, which for accounts is generally expressed as a secret, must still be fairly exchanged (including full deposit and verify steps) separately from such side channels of information and analysis.

6.7   Verify in IS

Only items that are verifiable under encryption may be exchanged in a protocol where the verify operation is performed in an independent storage environment.

To verify items in an independent storage environment, the participants must interact with the encrypted items without being able to learn more about them than the protocol and handshake document dictate. This is generally expressed as one or more operations that Alice may perform on D_B in order to confirm that it contains the kind of structures she is interested in. Checking to ensure that a particular message is signed with a valid cryptographic signature for some public key is a common use case.

Performing the verify operation in independent storage is often used in protocols like gradual release (Chapter 11), which eschew trusted third parties in favour of the participants directly managing the exchange.

Only items that are verifiable under encryption can be verified this way, by definition. Note that while many different kinds of properties are arguably verifiable under encryption the resulting programs can be quite slow. For instance, various techniques for fully homomorphic encryption or garbled circuit compilation create an exponential increase in size. This is an area that is undergoing rapid progress, and the class of items that are pragmatically verifiable under encryption can be expected to grow over time.

6.8   Verify in IC/IM

No restrictions are placed on a protocol where the verify operation is performed in an environment with independent compute or independent messaging.

Environments with independent compute can perform any kind of computation without exposing either the results of that computation or any of the intermediate steps to achieve it. This means that sensitive items like secrets can be safely verified within an environment that supports independent compute (which independent messaging environments do implicitly).

Care must still be taken: the verifications performed must be explicitly agreed to within the handshake document by both parties. If this were not the case, Alice could ask for the output of the identity function over D_B as a test result, and thereby leak the entire item. Even if test results are limited to booleans, Alice could still leak D_B by asking for each consecutive bit as an independent test result. Mitigating this kind of risk is an important part of designing a concrete implementation of a fair exchange protocol.

6.9   Synchronize in D/IS/IC

A strong fair exchange guarantee is unavailable in any protocol where the synchronize operation is performed in an environment without independent messaging.

Without an independent messaging environment, Alice and Bob can only communicate with each other. This introduces an adversarial version of the Two Generals Problem, as described in the synchronize section of Section 3.4.1, which does not yield a deterministic solution.

Without a deterministic solution to the synchronization problem, there is always a chance that an unfair outcome will result — in other words, that D_A will be released to Bob but D_B will also be restored to him, or some other variation. This unfair outcome can occur without any of the trust assumptions of the protocol having been violated, and so protocols that do not synchronize in an independent messaging environment must be characterized as weak fair exchange protocols.

Various FEPs try to overcome this by making it less likely that a violation of fairness will occur. Gradual release protocols accomplish this by making it difficult for either party to tell when a favourably unfair outcome can be achieved (Chapter 11 introduces the concept of "marginal fairness" to formalize this idea). Oblivious transfer protocols increase the cost of attempting an unfair outcome, by punishing cheaters.

It is also worth noting that multiparty versions of FEPs do not change this fundamental limitation. If Alice wants to exchange with Bob, it might be tempting to involve more parties in that exchange, with the idea that they can use a consensus protocol to synchronize themselves.

However, Alice either trusts those parties, in which case they are a trusted third party, or she doesn't. The same holds true for a consensus system formed from those parties: she either trusts it, making it a TTP, or she doesn't, in which case the guarantee is weak. No protocol she runs with those untrusted parties, who may be colluding with Bob, will guarantee they provide a trustworthy independent messaging environment.[1]

Performing consensus with untrusted third parties is still just as weak as synchronizing directly with Bob, from a fair exchange standpoint. The FEP Alice is using must explicitly treat the consensus system as a TTP if it is to provide a strong fair exchange guarantee when used as the environment for the synchronize operation.

---

[1]Given a world where each party is operating its own dependent messaging environment, and there is no way to limit back-channel communication between the other group members, this is obviously true. It remains true even if back-channels are eliminated, assuming the other nodes have prepared ahead of time, even if they've never met before but are merely part of a collusion club that can recognize soft signals like hash parities and message timing. Like betting in bridge, soft signals are powerful and inescapable.

6.10   Synchronize in IM

A strong fair exchange guarantee is possible in a protocol where the synchronize operation is performed in an environment with independent messaging.

Given an independent messaging environment, it is possible for Alice and Bob to achieve perfect synchronization every time, up to the trust assumptions of the protocol. This allows that protocol to provide a strong fair exchange guarantee.

Note that every environment with independence requires explicit trust assumptions to be added to the FEP. Where these are parameterized — for instance, by allowing Alice and Bob to make choices about which third parties they mutually trust, or which cryptographic primitives they will trust — those parameters must be explicitly agreed to within the handshake document.

In the case of an independent messaging environment, the trust assumptions are quite significant: both parties must trust it to be able to receive their messages, to be able to send them messages, to follow all of the rules of the fair exchange protocol and the handshake document faithfully, and to not leak confidential information. An IM environment generally has the guarantees of IS and IC environments, in addition to its messaging.

However, computation and confidentiality are not strictly necessary for the synchronize operation. In FEWD, for instance, a public bulletin board is used for the synchronize operation. Its requirements are simpler and more specific than a TTP: it merely produces a signed ordered list of posts. Synchronization does not require a heavyweight TTP with a large trust burden, and correspondingly large cost and risk burdens. It merely requires independent messaging.

6.11   Release/Restore in D/IS

Only copyable items are exchangeable in a protocol where the release/restore operation is performed in a dependent or independent storage environment.

A copyable item can only be released, never restored. (This is even true for anti-items, as we saw earlier.) This greatly simplifies the release/restore operation for copyable items, because the choice is between releasing both items or doing nothing. In particular, the "do nothing" option applies both to cancelled exchanges as well as to ongoing exchanges, whereas there are three possible states when exchanging unique items: release, restore, and do nothing.

Alice can release D_A to Bob merely by sending it to him, as she might do in an optimistic protocol. She can also be the release mechanism for D_B, as in a gradual release protocol when the synchronize operation has yielded Bob's key to her. These examples show it is possible for Alice to perform the release operation for copyable items in a dependent environment without violating fairness.

However, in neither of those examples does Alice concern herself with restoring the item. Once she has seen it, she cannot be forced to forget it, and neither can she force Bob to do so. He may have already written down the sensitive information from D_A on a piece of paper, or glanced at it and remembered it — there is no way for Alice to know.

It is not immediately obvious whether the release/restore operation requires independent compute. The key insight is that if Alice was able to do all the computation for release/restore herself, then she could compute both branches, thereby gaining access to both D_A and D_B. The computation must have access to both items, but the participant must not have access to both items.

Alice could receive a key from the environment hosting the synchronize operation, and use that to release D_B, but whatever sent her the release key had to also be capable of sending the restore key, and that information must live inside an independent compute environment (in this case the same environment as the synchronize operation).

This is the major distinction between copyable items and unique items: a copyable item can be left in the deposit box when the exchange is cancelled, but a unique item must be restored in order for fairness to be maintained.

6.12   Release/Restore in IC/IM

No restrictions are placed on a protocol where the release/restore operation is performed in an environment with independent compute or independent messaging.

Unique items require independent compute for their release, as we've just seen, because there is a choice to make: Alice's item must either be released to Bob, or restored to her, but not both. Furthermore, the choice that is made for Alice's item must match the choice made for Bob's item: either they are both released, or they are both restored. This requires access to compute that is not within the control of Alice or Bob.

However, it does not require much computing. For instance, a FEP may be described that encrypts the control secrets for D_A and D_B under two keys, l for release and t for restore, and ensures that Alice has $\{D_B\}_l$ and $\{D_A\}_t$ and that Bob has $\{D_A\}_l$ and $\{D_B\}_t$, and that they do not have each other's encrypted data. Then the release/restore operation can be run in an environment that reads the PBB, and posts either l or t on the PBB, as dictated by the outcome of the sync operation over the PBB output.

An even simpler version has the sync value fed into it from a trusted source. One branch point, two possible outputs: about as simple a computation as one could imagine. This puts more pressure on the other operations, but modeling the minimal necessary for these operations is a useful exercise.

6.13   Inaccessibles

We return now to digitally inaccessible items, armed with our understanding of the fundamental limitations imposed upon fair exchange protocols by their choice of environments in which to perform their operations.

As mentioned in Section 2.3, an inaccessible item may be a copyable item, like a spoken-word secret or a printed market report, or it may be a unique item, like a signed photograph or a jug of milk. It may even combine both aspects: a secret treasure map, for instance, may be valuable both as a historical artefact and also on account of the information it contains.

As we have seen, different protocols are able to accommodate different types of items, so if we want to exchange inaccessible items, we first need to understand what class of item they belong to, and then ensure we choose a protocol that supports that class of items. This is not always entirely trivial. In the case of a printed market report, for instance, it might be that the copying cost is not effectively zero, as it is for making a digital copy or for a spoken-word secret, but actually tens of dollars, if the report is fancy enough.

On the other hand, that same report might sell for thousands of dollars, meaning the copyable portion of it makes up the vast majority of its value. Its authors may then be able to consider it as a copyable item, and make use of a protocol suitable for copyable items but not for unique ones. For instance, they might deposit it in a special deposit box that will incinerate it if the payment isn't made in time. As long as they sell more market reports than it burns, they might write this off as a cost of doing business.[2]

Whatever protocol they choose for exchanging this marketing report, we know that it must need independent storage. The deposit box we described earlier has that: it does not make any decisions (no compute), but it does keep the report in isolation, preventing Bob from accessing it, preventing Alice from modifying it, and is able to release it to Bob if the exchange is successful (and able to destroy it if the exchange is cancelled).

Their protocol will also need independent compute for verification, as a physical item cannot be verified under encryption. This independent compute almost certainly comes in the form of a trusted human being. This might be a mutually trusted, fully independent escrow agent, or it might be an agent working for Bob, who Alice believes is constrained by the nature of the deposit box system (perhaps it is guarded), but whom she does not need to trust. Note that this verifier is probably very different from Alice's chosen verifier for Bob's item, as they need different specialities.

Alice and Bob can choose whether they want to sync weakly, or to use a strong sync mechanism with independent messaging. Note that if they are both in the same place, such a mechanism can be purely mechanical, requiring no external energy source. For instance, Alice and Bob could be in separate rooms, each with the other's deposit box, perhaps viewing each other through a glass wall. They each have two coins, a sync coin and a cancel coin. There is a coin slot adjacent

---

[2]The total cost, including the wasting of resource and the resulting pollution, is harder to ignore. Self-incinerating deposit boxes, like self-destructing memos, are fun to fantasize about, but probably a terrible idea in reality.

to each box. If they both put their sync coins in before either puts in a cancel coin, then the boxes open. Otherwise, the boxes stay closed, and self-incinerate either after a predetermined timeout, or if one of them puts in their cancel coin before putting in their sync coin.

This describes a purely mechanical mechanism that provides a strong fair exchange guarantee. It is an independent messaging environment, but one powered only by the participants. Note also that it provides an independent messaging for the release/restore operation. With a small modification this same exchange protocol works for unique items: simply have the deposit boxes straddle both rooms, with a door on each side. Opposite pairs of doors open depending on whether both sync coins have been entered, or a cancel coin was first entered. The mechanical force of the coins rolling down the slot may well be enough to power the whole mechanism, with no external energy supply needed.

Interestingly, the same cost dynamic is possible with digital exchanges as well. Alice and Bob could each send a laser pulse containing their sync token up to a small unpowered satellite, which would then use that energy to synchronize and send the proof of success or cancellation back down to each participant. It could also serve as a means of deposit, verify, and release/restore — although as we will see in the next chapter, such additions are unnecessary. Alice and Bob can manage their own independent compute agents within their dependent environment. As long as they have an external source of independent messaging for the synchronize operation, they can build any type of exchange using attestables.

Chapter 7

Attestables

Attestables provide independent computation. In fact, the attestable interface described in this chapter is the minimal interface for providing independent computation.[1] It can be fulfilled in several ways: through judicious use of trusted hardware; by a trusted service provider; via a decentralized system, maybe by using fully homomorphic encryption; and perhaps one day even directly through software. It is a lightweight interface, with a simple API that makes minimal demands on the provider.

It is also, though, a very restrictive interface. It doesn't need to do much, but there are three things it must not do: it must not reveal any data except through its API; it must not change the program it is running; and it must not communicate with anyone except its owner (or parties explicitly authorized by its owner, in some cases).

Perhaps surprisingly, the effect of these restrictions is not to limit what a user can do with their device, but rather to reveal a new ability that we have long lacked: the power to compel our devices to perform our bidding in the future, even if we change our minds. We may rant and rave, like Ulysses lashed to the mast, but once we commit ourselves, our faithful crew carries on, ears plugged against our onslaught.

---

[1] It also provides a minimal interface for exfiltration-resistant computing, which can be broader than independent computation, because it allows for messaging and cross-system concerns.

7.1   The Attestable Interface

The four aspects of attestables are as follows:

(1) the attestable follows a fixed set of rules (faithful agent),
(2) the attestable leaks no information (black box),
(3) the owner completely controls input/output (no trojans), and
(4) the attestable can attest to the above points (pinky swear).

An attestable must be a *faithful agent*. Once it has been loaded with a program, the resulting process can never be changed. The owner may evaluate that process to completion, at which time it will likely self-destruct, eradicating all the information inside itself. They may choose to destroy the process early, likewise eradicating all of its information.

However, the owner of an attestable may not under any circumstances be allowed to alter the process that is running in that attestable. Messages can be sent to the attestable, which the process will accept or reject based on the API expressed by its program. However, if there is any capacity for changing the running code, loading additional code, or removing some but not all of the running process, then that thing has failed to be a faithful agent and is not an attestable.

Each attestable must be a *black box*, with no observable output beyond the messages its process sends. This is probably the most difficult requirement. New ways of leaking information through side channels appear quite frequently. Direct observation of the attestable is another threat. Potential techniques for mitigating these risks include using exactly constant-time algorithms and tamper-resistant packaging.

One small advantage that attestables have is that their use cases, particularly those of interest to fair exchange protocols, are primarily transient, so no persistence is necessary. This reduces the surface area of attack, and may mean that powering off the device zeros all of its data.

These first two properties are also the requirements for exfiltration-resistant computing, a more general model of computation that resists attempts to examine the data or change the process. Exfiltration-resistant computing is the core of an Independent Compute (IC) environment. Roughly speaking, an IC environment hosted by a trusted provider is equivalent to an IM environment with exfiltration-resistant computation.

Attestables must have *no trojans*. It is imperative that the owner completely controls the inputs and outputs of the device, rather than some other party (the manufacturer, for instance, or the host of the attestable). Anything that is capable of sending or receiving messages without the owner's permission represents an unacceptable risk, and is not an attestable. Conversely, there are certainly cases where the owner of an attestable may want to delegate the ability to send and receive messages to someone else. If Alice were to rent a hosted attestable, for instance, and share with Bob the ability to communicate with it, and gave up the ability to destroy the attestable before the rental period was over, then if Bob trusts the host, they could use that attestable in their exchange as a PBB.

Finally, attestables must be able to attest,[2] or *pinky swear*, that they are a good and proper attestable. This is typically done in the form of a signature over a document. It is up to the participants to decide whether to trust a given attestable, based on its attestation.

7.2   API of an Attestable

Attestables generally support the following three functions:

- **LOAD**
  - **input**: A program, including all its configuration parameters.
  - **output**: Destroys the previous program and all of its states, then loads the new program into the attestable. Return the hash of the new program.

- **ATTEST**
  - **input**: Nonce.
  - **output**: A message signed by the attestable, containing its certificate tree, ephemeral public key, program hash, and the nonce.

---

[2]Attested executions are discussed in a variety of places, including Pass *et al.* (2017), which focuses on the identification and separation of the basic abstractions that compose trusted services, as seen, for instance, in Chun *et al.* (2007) and Levin *et al.* (2009).

- **PROCESS**
    - **input**: Encrypted message containing input data, program hash, component public key, remote public key.
    - **output**: Error if decryption fails or the program hash or component public key do not match, otherwise run the program on the input data and return a message encrypted for the remote public key containing the program's output.

Loading a program may take additional security steps to delete the previous program, including zeroing out the component's memory. It may also return an attestation, in which case a separate attestation function may not be strictly necessary. Bob does not send Alice's attestable a nonce in this case, but he does know that the attestable is loaded with the program and handshake document that they just produced.

Additionally, all the communication Bob sends to Alice's attestable is encrypted. Alice may destroy her attestable at any time, but once she destroys it, she has no way to make use of Bob's messages, or to send him messages using their attestables' shared keys.

7.3   Interaction With Attestables

Alice remains in full physical and logical control of her attestable throughout its lifecycle. Logical interaction with the attestable is mediated by Alice's application. Once Alice has loaded a program into her attestable, there are three things she is able to do:

(1) **Deliver**: Alice can deliver an input message to the attestable. No message can reach the attestable without Alice's consent. A message sent from another party to the attestable is received by Alice's application, which decides whether to forward it to the attestable or to block it.

(2) **Dispatch**: Alice can dispatch an output message from the attestable. Every message generated by the attestable goes exclusively to Alice's application. If a message is addressed to another party, Alice's application decides whether to forward it or to block it.

(3) **Destroy**: Alice can destroy the attestable at any time during its operation. Calling the component's load function, for instance, with a no-op program, is generally sufficient to fulfill this requirement. In cases where the load function is not sufficiently robust, it may be necessary to have a separate destroy function.

Note that Alice's application cannot read the messages sent or received by her attestable, since they are encrypted.

7.4 Attestables in Action

Anything that fulfills the above requirements can be an attestable: a module on a chip, like a secure enclave, or on a device, like a discrete tamper-proof chip in a phone; a plug-in system like a USB key; a second device on the same network; a third-party service; a device hosted by a cloud provider; a decentralized system; or even a satellite in low Earth orbit.

Wrapping these diverse systems in a common interface allows the participants to choose from the maximum set of possible trusted points when engaging in activities like a fair exchange process. Additionally, the attestable interface eliminates almost all of the functionality these services typically offer, leaving the trust surface small and allowing them to be plugged into precisely designed parts of the protocol. This reduces the trust burden considerably.

As long as Alice believes her attestable will be a faithful agent and has no back doors, and Bob believes it will be a faithful agent and a black box, then they can use it within their exchange.

Alice may have a nuanced view of particular types of attestables, beyond simply trusting one type fully and not trusting another at all. This can be characterized by saying she believes there is a risk represented by a certain device: for example, a 1% chance that Bob will compromise it during the execution of the protocol and break the fairness by extracting D_A after cancelling the exchange; or a 5% chance that her own device will fail during the exchange, breaking fairness by preventing her from retrieving D_B during a successful completion.

Risk mitigation techniques over both of these risk scenarios are provided in Chapter 17. Alice may force Bob to use multiple different devices, for example, three different devices, where two of them would have to be compromised to expose D_A. This provides Alice with her desired level of compromise tolerance.

Alice may also replicate her own devices, providing her with the desired level of crash tolerance. The combination of these techniques can allow Alice and Bob to assemble an acceptable ensemble of attestables without forcing them to make use of expensive, highly trusted services or devices.

Part 2
Protocols Old and New

Chapter 8

Categorization of Fair Exchange Protocols

A wide variety of fair exchange protocols (FEPs) have been produced by scholars over the years, and nearly as many different criteria for categorization. In this chapter, we categorize them by their approach to handling disputes, leading to two broad classes: the strong FEPs, and the weak FEPs (see Figure 8.1).

Remembering the definitions from Chapter 1, we say that a FEP is strong if it always completes to produce a fair outcome that is either success or cancel. A completion in success implies that the participants have exchanged their items, that is, the exchange leaves Alice in possession of Bob's item and Bob in possession of Alice's item. When the exchange completes in cancelled, it leaves Alice in possession of her item and Bob in possession of his. We say that a FEP is weak if it does not guarantee completion in a fair outcome.

The most valuable feature of strong FEPs is that they prevent the occurrence of disputes. They are able to observe this property thanks to the inclusion of a trusted third party (TTP) that provides an execution environment with independent messaging (IM) for the execution of the synchronize operation. It is worth clarifying that strong FEPs guarantee fair outcomes only under the trust assumptions placed on their hardware and software components (see Section 1.3).

There are several implementations of strong FEPs, which perform their synchronize operation in an IM environment. These can be categorized into two main groups: escrow-based and attestable.

In escrow-based protocols, the TTP is centralized and implemented as a escrow service that is responsible for mediating the whole execution of the protocol. This service gets involved from start to completion and provides the infrastructure to execute the five basic operations within its premises. Crucially, it provides an execution environment with IM (see Section 5.1.4) for the execution of the synchronize operation. This property is fundamental because it guarantees that the two participants have the same view of the final state of the exchange (success or cancel). Escrow-based protocols are widely used in current online shopping, for example, they are deployed by Amazon (Amazon Pay, 2019), Alipay (AliPay, 2020; Werker, 2017) and PayPal (PayPal, 2019).

In attestable-based protocols, the monolithic TTP of escrow protocols is split into three different pieces: a public bulletin board and two attestables, one for each participant. These two attestables are the environments for the execution of the deposit, verify, and release/restore operations. The public bulletin board is the environment for the execution of the synchronize operation; therefore, it is trusted to provide an execution environment with IM. Again, it is crucial to guarantee that the two attestables have the same view of the final state of the exchange (release or restore). In Chapter 13, we return to the discussion of these protocols by introducing FEWD, the first attestable FEP.

Weak FEPs generally do not use a TTP to synchronize the exchange. In the absence of a TTP, these protocols have no access to execution environments with IM to execute the synchronize operation; consequently, they cannot guarantee fair outcomes. As shown in Figure 8.1, weak FEPs can be further categorized into three classes: optimistic front-end, gradual release, and oblivious transfer.

In FEP with optimistic front-ends, the participants send the items under exchange in single send operations executed directly against each other. The participants take an optimistic approach in the sense that they assume that the exchange is likely to complete in success, and deploy a back-end protocol that is activated to resolve disputes when the optimistic front-end completes unfairly. In Chapter 10, we isolate the front-end and back-end of optimistic protocols, such as Asokan's protocols discussed in Asokan *et al.* (1998) and Asokan (1998).

Strong
- Unfair outcomes are impossible, up to the trust assumptions of the protocol.

Escrow-based
- Alice and Bob deposit D_A and D_B with the escrow service, which executes all five operations.

Attestable-based
- Alice and Bob deposit D_A and D_B with their attestables, which execute the deposit, verify, and release/restore operations.

Weak
- Unfair outcomes are possible because the execution environment of the synchronization operation does not have IM.

Optimistic frontend
- Alice sends D_A to Bob and then Bob sends D_B to Alice.

Gradual release
- Alice and Bob exchange segments and can pay a cost to generate missing segments.

Oblivious transfer
- Alice and Bob exchange messages which either guarantee unlock or have a chance to destroy.

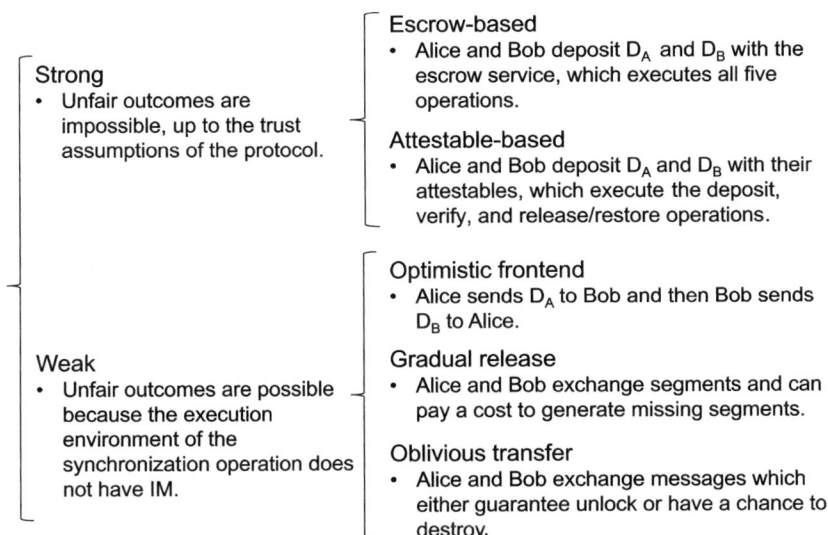

Fig. 8.1. Categorization by strength of the FEP.

In gradual release protocols, the participants first encrypt their items and next they send the encrypted items to each other. They verify each other's encrypted items, and if satisfied, they gradually dole out their decryption keys bit by bit. The fundamental limits of fair exchange (Chapter 6) state that these protocols can only achieve weak fairness, and can only exchange copyable items that are verifiable under encryption. Gradual release protocols are described in Chapter 11.

Chapter 9

Escrow-based Fair Exchange Protocols

Escrow-based fair exchange protocols (FEPs) involve a trusted third party (TTP) responsible for running the entire protocol. The TTP is activated at the start of the exchange and mediates the exchange of messages between the two participants (Alice and Bob) until the completion of the exchange.

The TTP executes the five basic operations of FEPs and prevents the occurrence of disputes. To ensure a fair outcome, the Finite State Machine (FSM) must have only two possible outcomes: either both parties are left in possession of each other's items or neither party has access to the other's items.

We use FSM models to explain the operations of these protocols (see Figure 9.1). The double-lined circles represent the final states of the machine. The FSM models the most important property of escrow–based protocols: it always terminates in one out of two possible states, either release or restore. Release corresponds to successful exchange and restore corresponds to the cancellation of the exchange. There are no final states for disputes like in the FSM shown in Figure 10.1.

- **Handshake** is executed within the TTP and triggers the execution of the protocol. It drives the FSM to the state where the deposit, verification, and synchronization operations are executed.
- **Deposit, verify, and synchronize** are executed by the two participants. Successful execution of each operation produces

a success event, which progresses the machine to the release
state, on the contrary, a failure in the execution of one of the
operations produces a cancel event which leads the FSM to the
restore state.

- **Release** the items are released to the participants (D_A to Bob
  and D_B to Alice) if the FSM reaches this final state, which
  represents a successful exchange.
- **Restore** the items are restored to their original owners
  (D_A to Alice and D_B to Bob) if the FSM reaches this final
  state, which represents the cancellation of the exchange.

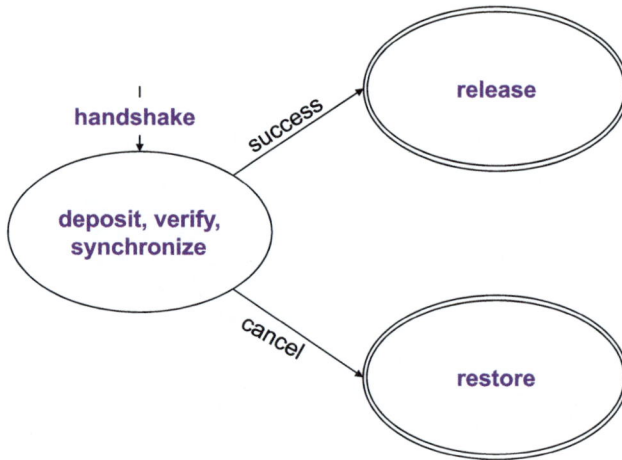

Fig. 9.1.   FSM executed by the TTP in an escrow-based fair exchange.

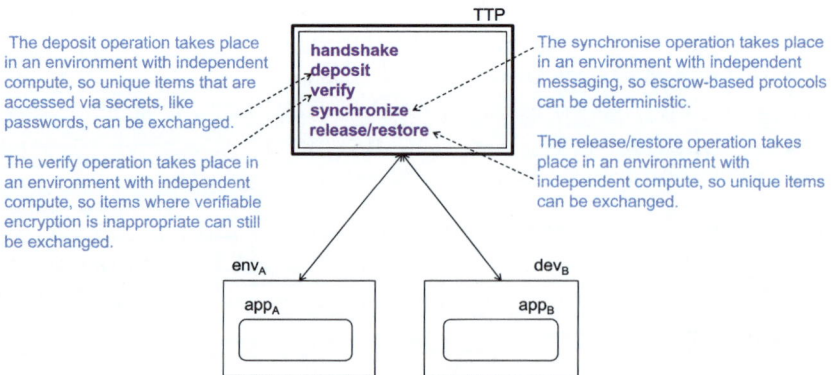

Fig. 9.2.   Execution of basic operations in escrow-based protocols.

The two most prominent features of the escrow-based model are: First, the role of the TTP is intrusive, it always gets involved to mediate and control the exchange. Second, the implementation of the TTP is monolithic, it executes all the five operations within itself (Figure 9.2). This approach provides security and fairness, but also introduces a single point of failure and can increase costs and risks.

9.1   Drawbacks of Resolution-based Fair Exchange Protocols

FEPs that rely on dispute resolution suffer from several significant drawbacks, many of which stem from the TTP's monolithic implementation.

- **Some disputes are hard to solve**: These protocols assume that disputes can always be solved by the TTP. While this may be true in some applications, it is not always the case. In some situations, resolving a dispute may require actions (such as item return, rollback, revocation, compensation, penalties, etc.) that are too costly or time-consuming, or are simply impossible to execute (Asokan *et al.*, 1997).
- **The TTP is stateful and gathers sensitive information**: In order to solve disputes, the TTP must store some of the states of the protocol's execution. As a result, the TTP has access to and collects sensitive information about the application. This makes the TTP vulnerable to external malicious attacks, such as hacking, and internal temptations, such as collusion with one of the participants or absconding with collected information.
- **In dispute resolution, the TTP becomes central**: When disputes occur, the TTP becomes a central component of the exchange and must be available to facilitate the dispute resolution process. This means that the TTP must be reachable and free from technical failures.

Fair exchange protocols in this category can be effective for use cases that can tolerate these drawbacks. Note though that the costs and risks introduced by the TTP during dispute resolution are often hidden until things go wrong.

Chapter 10

Optimistic Fair Exchange Protocols

In an optimistic fair exchange protocol (FEP), Alice releases D_A directly to Bob. This is really the hallmark of optimistic fair exchange: in other types of FEPs, the release/restore operation for D_A is performed without Alice's involvement.

This central distinction also serves as our path into the heart of optimistic protocols. Starting here and working our way out, we find all the essential properties of optimistic protocols. Alice releases D_A directly to Bob. What does she need to believe in order to do this? She must believe that if Bob does not release D_B to her, then the trusted third party (TTP) will.

That means that Bob must have deposited D_B with the TTP, and Alice must have verified this. In fact, these are exactly Alice's deposit and verify operations in an optimistic FEP. Bob sends Alice the evidence of his deposit with the TTP, and she verifies that an item matching the description of D_B from the handshake document has been properly deposited with the TTP.

Alice must also have some way of convincing the TTP to release D_B to her. To do this, she must prove to the TTP that Bob agreed to the terms of their exchange of D_A for D_B, and also that the exchange process has reached a point where D_A could have been released to Bob. In other words, the synchronize operation has been performed and resulted in a successful exchange instead of a cancelled one.

The handshake document presents the terms. The synchronize operation is where Alice and Bob agree to those terms, and move the document forward. So Alice must present the TTP with the handshake for the exchange, and also with sufficient evidence to prove there was a successful synchronization.

So before Alice can safely send D_A to Bob, she must have:

- Proof that Bob deposited D_B with the TTP.
- Bob's sync token over the handshake, so she can go to the TTP and recover D_B if Bob does not send it.

Once Alice has those, she can send D_A to Bob without fear of an unfair outcome.[1] Conversely, at this point Alice may go directly to the TTP and collect D_B. There is no way for the TTP to know whether Alice has sent D_A to Bob or not, because they are operating in dependent environments — for the TTP to verify that Bob has access to D_A would require posting it to an independent messaging (IM) environment.

This means Bob must also be able to go to the TTP and collect D_A, otherwise he may experience an unfair outcome. Bob can't collect D_A from the TTP if Alice hasn't deposited it. Interestingly, because of the asymmetry of the protocol, she doesn't actually have to deposit it before beginning the exchange: it is enough that she deposits it before the synchronize operation with the TTP. This means that Bob does not need to confirm that Alice has made the deposit before he proceeds.

Bob also needs to know that the TTP will release D_A to him if it releases D_B to Alice. He must be able to authenticate with the TTP as Alice's counterparty in this exchange. This might be tied to Bob's deposit of D_B with the TTP, or Alice could provide him with an authentication token earlier in the exchange. It could also be explicit in the handshake document itself: for instance, Bob's public key from the handshake could be used to sign a nonce from the TTP in order to authenticate him to receive D_A.

Before Bob can safely send his sync token to Alice, he must know:

- that D_A will be deposited with the TTP, and
- that the TTP will release D_A to him if it releases D_B to Alice.

---

[1]As usual, up to the trust assumptions of the protocol, like the TTP being trustworthy, the deposit mechanism being secure, and so on.

There is a deep interplay between the nature of Bob's deposit of D_B with the TTP, the manner of Bob's authentication with the TTP to receive D_A, and the way Bob synchronizes with Alice before she can send D_A to him.

10.1 General Model

As a result of this requirement that a TTP can release an item to Alice if Bob fails to deliver D_B to her, optimistic protocols are limited to the exchange of *instruments.*

There are techniques for transforming any copyable item into an instrument, with varying degrees of efficiency, as described in Chapter 2. These instruments come in two different flavours: a generatable version of D_B can be released to Alice by the TTP; or the anti-item D_A^{-1} can be released to Alice by the TTP, thereby nullifying her item D_A that was sent to Bob. Note that there is no restore operation in optimistic FEPs, only a release operation.

It is important that these instruments be deposited correctly with the TTP. Just as it is unsafe for Alice if Bob holds the ability to release D_A, it is also clearly unsafe for Bob if Alice holds the ability to release D_A^{-1}. In both cases, these items need to be deposited with the TTP.

We frequently speak of the "front-end" of an optimistic protocol, which is a protocol that provides weak fairness. This is coupled to the "back-end" of the optimistic protocol, a strong FEP, by the evidence that is generated during the execution of front-end protocols.

The FSM of a generic optimistic protocol is illustrated in Figure 10.1.

In the example shown in the figure, Alice is the initiator, that is, the party that releases its item first to its counterpart, to Bob, in this example. Let us examine the weak front-end first, which produces one out of three possible events: *success, cancel,* or *activate dispute resolution.*

(1) Alice's device initiates the execution of the weak front-end directly against Bob's device, possibly after some setup such as a key exchange.
(2) Message exchange between Alice and Bob takes place.

(3) Hopefully the message exchange produces a *success* event, which leads to the *release* state where Alice is left in possession of D_B and Bob is left in possession of D_A.

(4) Another possibility is that the message exchange produces a *cancel* event that drives the FSM to the *cancelled* state where the items D_A and D_B remain with their original owners (Alice and Bob, respectively) and nobody has been financially hurt.

(5) A less desirable alternative is that the message exchange produces an *activate dispute resolution* event. This encourages Alice to trigger the execution of the strong back-end protocol to resolve the dispute with the assistance of a TTP. Note that this is the only outcome that triggers the involvement of the strong back-end protocol.

The back-end protocol relies on a TTP (not shown explicitly in the Figure 10.1) that is responsible for restoring.

(1) The TTP is provided by Alice (the party that resulted offended from the execution of the weak front-end) with evidence of the dispute.

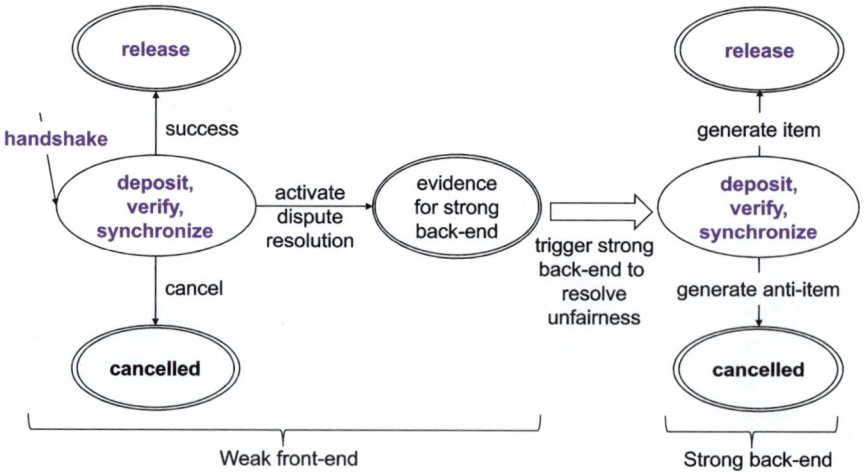

Fig. 10.1. FSM executed by the participant that initiates an optimistic fair exchange.

(2) The TTP produces one out of two possible events:

- *generate item*: the TTP generates D_B and releases it to Alice. The FSM progresses to the final *release* state that represents a successful exchange.
- *generate anti-item*: the TTP generates D_A^{-1}, that is, an anti-item of D_A and releases it to Alice. The FSM progresses to the final state that represents the cancellation of the exchange.

The conceptual separation of the optimistic fair exchange model into front-end and back-end allows us to consider different models for front-ends and back-ends. We explore this idea later, with both gradual release protocols (an optimistic front-end can be thought of as a gradual release protocol where only a single message is sent) and with FEWD (which can function as a back-end for an optimistic front-end).

Optimistic front-ends are run entirely in dependent environments. Applying the fundamental limits of fair exchange from Chapter 6, we find that the front-end will always be asymmetric (due to the handshake in D), can have at most weak fairness (due to the synchronize in D), and can exchange at most copyable items (due to the release/restore in D).

Note that if the deposit and verify operations were performed in a dependent environment, it would not be possible to achieve fairness, even weak fairness. The key to achieving fairness in an optimistic protocol is that D_B is not deposited with Alice, it is instead deposited with the TTP. What Alice verifies is not D_B, but the proof that D_B was correctly deposited with the TTP (along with the handshake document and Bob's sync token).

The back-end of an optimistic protocol provides strong fairness by synchronizing in the IM environment of the TTP. It reuses the handshake document (and operation) from the front-end, which forces the back-end to also be asymmetric. It is still limited to only exchanging instruments, since the front-end can only handle instruments. Depending on how those instruments are generated, there may be additional limitations imposed on the items — many optimistic protocols are limited to instruments that are verifiable under encryption, for instance.

Chapter 11

Gradual Release Fair Exchange Protocols

Sometimes there are no mutually trusted third parties (TTPs) that Alice and Bob can rely on for their exchange. It is reasonable to ask whether there are any protocols that might let them find fairness in this situation, and what tradeoffs must be made in order to do so. Gradual release protocols provide an answer to those questions.

Their first thought might be to gradually exchange little pieces of their items directly, like pixels from a photo, or letters from a text, or bytes from a file. Suppose D_A is a treasure map, and D_B is a text file containing directions to a different treasure. Bob receives pixels from D_A, and Alice receives letters from D_B. It may happen that Alice receives enough words that she can reconstruct the rest of the document, but Bob still has no idea where Alice's map is showing. She can stop sending pixels, and Bob will have an unfair outcome.

Note that this hinges on Alice being able to reconstruct D_B from partial information. This is what allows her to have an unfair outcome, but it is also critical for gradual release: without this ability, when Alice sends her last message to Bob, he can refuse to send his last message to her, and now he has D_A but she cannot reconstruct D_B.

What is needed is an ability to measure how much work must be performed to reconstruct the document, so that amount can be distributed fairly between the participants. If the work required by Alice to reconstruct D_B is the same as the work required by Bob to reconstruct D_A, then they have a much better chance of a fair outcome.

Fortunately, verifiable encryption provides exactly this ability. Alice encrypts D_A under a key K_A and sends it to Bob. Then she sends him bits of K_A. As long as Bob can verify that D_A matches its description in the handshake document, and can verify that each bit really is from K_A, then he also knows how much work remains to brute force the unknown bits of K_A.

Note that Alice and Bob now have two different ways of synchronizing themselves to achieve release. One is through sending these *segments* back and forth, which generally contain a bit of their key and its proof of correctness. If Alice receives all of Bob's segments, she can assemble K_B and use it to release D_B.

However, if Bob stops sending segments, then Alice can perform some amount of work — in particular, she can brute force the last few bits of K_B — to release D_B.

Note that this segment exchange is entirely peer-to-peer, so Alice and Bob send their segments directly to each other without requiring any intermediaries. Alice, who plays the *initiator* in this chapter, sends her first segment to Bob, who is playing the *responder*. Once initiated, they each only send a segment after they have received one.

As a result, either party could decide to stop sending segments at any time, stopping the synchronization of the exchange. That makes it important that an intractable amount of work is required at the beginning of the exchange. Without that, Bob could extract D_A without sending even one segment to Alice.

It is also important that a negligible amount of work remains at the final segment, otherwise Alice may pay a high cost for being the initiator. This steep gradation of work from the beginning of the exchange to the end creates additional opportunities for unfair outcomes, which we explore in Chapter 11. First, however, we look at gradual release from an operational perspective, and then spend some time understanding the implications of having two different paths to synchronization.

11.1 Operational Model

When Alice and Bob engage in a gradual release fair exchange, they go through a sequence of actions, such as the following:

(1) Alice and Bob agree to exchange D_A for D_B.
(2) Alice encrypts D_A under a fresh secret key, K_A. Bob does the same with D_B and K_B.
(3) Alice sends Bob her encrypted document $\{D_A\}_{K_A}$. Bob sends her $\{D_B\}_{K_B}$.
(4) Alice verifies $\{D_B\}_{K_B}$. Bob verifies $\{D_A\}_{K_A}$.
(5) Alice transforms K_A into $N/2$ segments. Bob does the same.
(6) Alice sends k_{A1} to Bob. Bob sends k_{B1} to Alice.
(7) Alice checks the proof of k_{B1}. Bob likewise checks k_{A1}.
(8) The previous two steps are repeated until k_{AN} and k_{BN} have been exchanged. (Alternatively, use work to generate the remaining segments.)
(9) Alice recovers K_B from the segments received from Bob. Bob does the same with K_A.
(10) Alice uses K_B to decrypt $\{D_B\}_{K_B}$. Bob uses K_A to decrypt $\{D_A\}_{K_A}$.

These actions can be mapped to the operational framework by associating them each with one of the five operations of fair exchange. The sequence of operations, which take place entirely in the participant's dependent environments, is shown in Figure 11.1.

Handshake incorporates action 1. The participants agree to the particulars of this exchange. This is executed outside of the online protocol, for instance, via email, but the item classifications, verifiable encryption scheme, and other particulars must match the supported parameters of the specific gradual release fair exchange protocol (FEP) used for the exchange.

Deposit incorporates actions 2 and 3. The participants deposit their items with each other in independent storage (IS). For example, Alice encrypts D_A under K_A and sends this $\{D_A\}_{K_A}$ to Bob.

Verify incorporates action 4. Alice uses verifiable encryption to ensure that Bob's deposit $\{D_B\}_{K_B}$ matches its description in the handshake document.

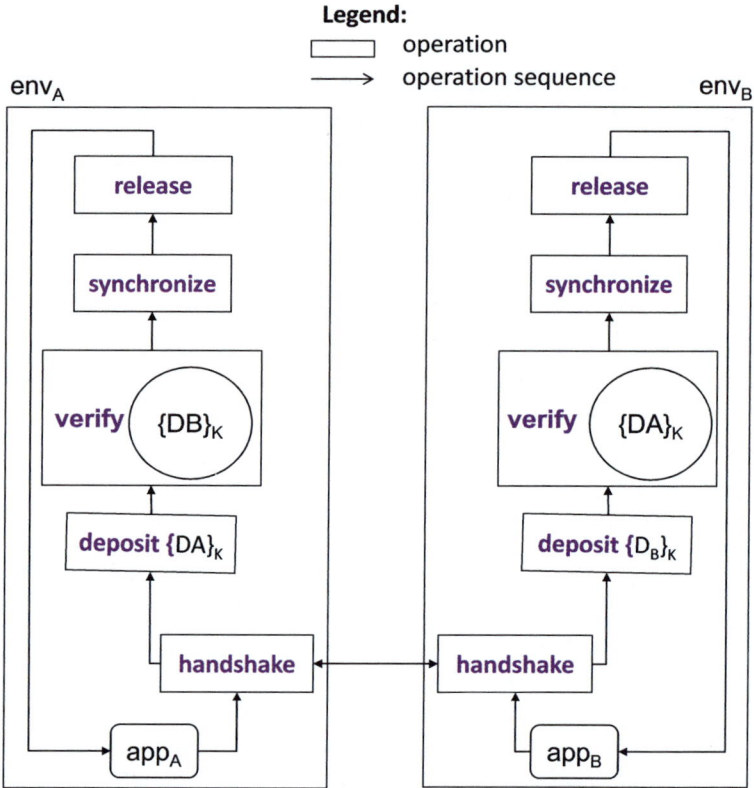

Fig. 11.1.   Operations in gradual release protocols.

Sync incorporates actions 5, 6, 7, and 8. This operation is the topic of the next section. In brief: Alice transforms K_A into $N/2$ segments, each containing a bit of K_A and a proof of correctness. She sends one to Bob, checks the one she gets back from him, and continues until either she receives them all or she decides whether to do work to make up the remainder.

Release/restore incorporates actions 9 and 10. Alice uses K_B to release D_B from its IS environment $\{D_B\}_{K_B}$. Restore does nothing, as is always the case in the absence of independent compute (IC).

The restrictions imposed by the fundamental limits of fair exchange in Chapter 6 define boundaries on the properties of gradual release protocols and the kinds of items they can exchange. These are listed as follows, and also noted in Figure 11.2.

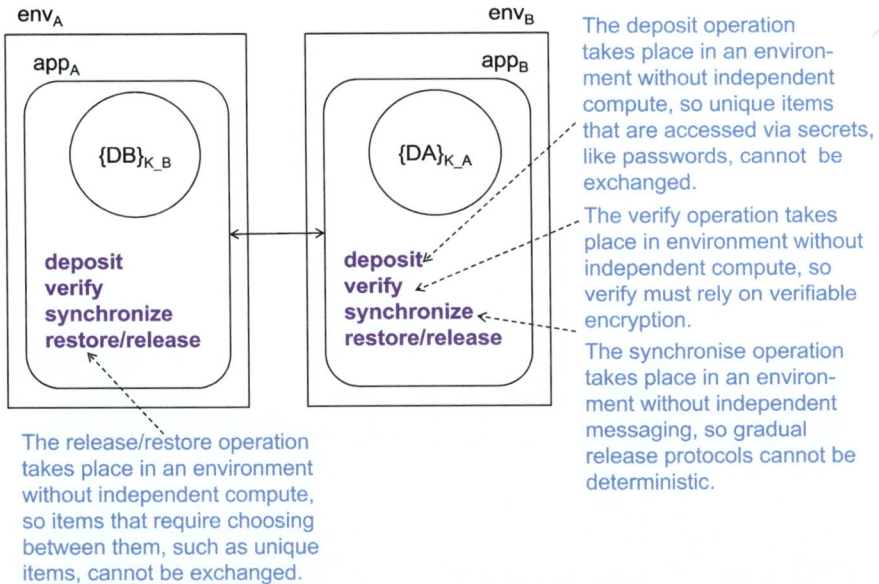

The deposit operation takes place in an environment without independent compute, so unique items that are accessed via secrets, like passwords, cannot be exchanged.

The verify operation takes place in environment without independent compute, so verify must rely on verifiable encryption.

The synchronise operation takes place in an environment without independent messaging, so gradual release protocols cannot be deterministic.

The release/restore operation takes place in an environment without independent compute, so items that require choosing between them, such as unique items, cannot be exchanged.

Fig. 11.2. Execution of basic operations in gradual release protocols. Explanation.

- Handshake is in a dependent environment, so gradual release protocols are inherently asymmetric and one participant must follow different rules from the other (Section 6.1). In particular, gradual release protocols have an initiator and a responder.
- Deposit is in an IS environment, so gradual release protocols cannot exchange accounts, because Alice cannot prove to Bob that she does not know the new account password (Section 6.4).
- Verify is in an IS environment, so in gradual release protocols, only items that are verifiable under encryption can be exchanged (Section 6.7).
- Synchronize is in a dependent environment, so gradual release protocols cannot offer a strong fair exchange guarantee: unfairness is always possible without violating the trust assumptions (Section 6.9).
- Release/restore is in a dependent environment, so gradual release protocols are limited to exchanging copyable items, because they cannot fairly choose between release and restore (Section 6.11).

11.2   Synchronization in Gradual Release

The important differentiation in gradual release from other FEPs is its synchronize operation. The other operations are all fairly bog-standard for vercrypt items, as we've just seen: deposit your item in an IS environment through encryption, verify your desired item under encryption, and procure a key to release the item from IS.

The individual elements are laid out in Figure 11.3. Note that synchronization in gradual release is like a zipper, with Alice and Bob's synchronization activities strictly interleaved. It is critical for Alice's fairness that she not send multiple segments to Bob before receiving a valid segment from him.

This is very unlike escrow-based FEPs, where Alice can send messages to the escrow service completely independently of Bob's messages. It is also, as we will see, very different from attestable-based

Legend:
g_A : function that returns D_A
g_B : function that returns D_B
S_{iA} : Alice's ith segment
S_{iB} : Bob's ith segment

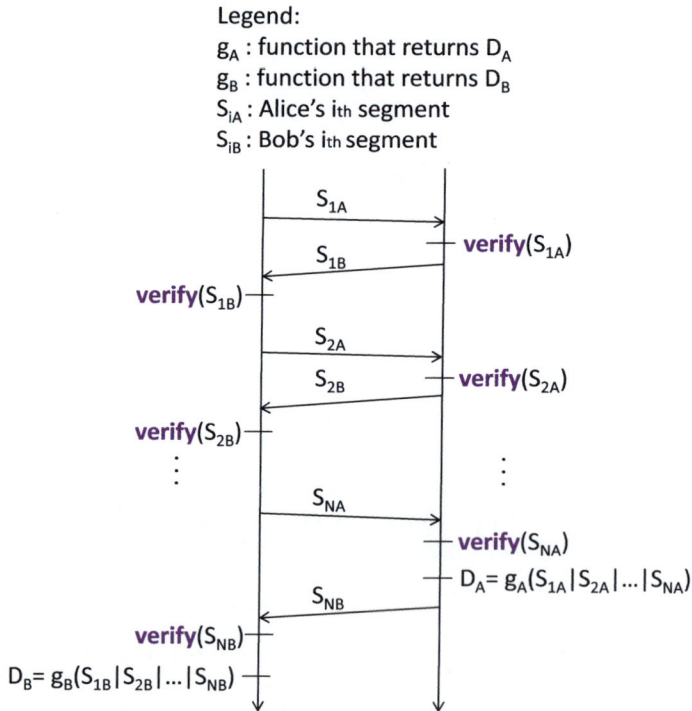

Fig. 11.3.   Sync steps in gradual release.

FEPs, where Alice can post her sync and cancel tokens on the public bulletin board (PBB) at any time, regardless of what Bob is doing, without risking fairness.[1]

As a result of this zipper sync, Alice might be stuck waiting for Bob indefinitely, unable to complete the exchange: she cannot send her next segment until she receives one from him, but because there is no trusted party, there is also no way for Alice to cancel the exchange.

In fact, the situation is somewhat worse than that, because this exchange of segments is only half of the synchronization story in gradual release. Bob does not have to wait for Alice to provide her segments. He can apply work to generate those segments himself.

This means that Alice refusing to send more segments does not cancel the exchange: Bob can still complete it on his own by applying work. It also means that Bob could stop sending segments to Alice, knowing that he can release D_A, while forcing Alice to do the work to release D_B.

Whether this yields an unfair outcome depends on whether Alice is willing to do that work. If Alice receives D_B and Bob receives D_A, then we judge the exchange to have been fair. But let us assume that Alice is a rational agent, and that she will not do the work if the value of D_B is less than the cost of the work.

First, we need the following values:

- v_A, the value to Alice of D_B;
- v_B, the value to Bob of D_A;
- w_A, the cost of work for Alice; and
- w_B, the cost of work for Bob.

Note that Alice and Bob both divided their keys into $N/2$ segments earlier. This gives a total of N segments to be transferred, with Alice transferring the odd segments S_{2t+1} and Bob transferring the even segments 2_{2t}.

---

[1]PBBs are typically used for "asynchronous sync" to provide strong timeliness to the participants, but they can also be used for lockstep synchronization like gradual release's zipper sync. The trick is just to hash chain the postings, so each must reference the previous, with the canonical successor to a post being the first, and all later successors rejected as invalid.

Then Bob has some threshold segment S_b he receives from Alice, which is the first segment where it is worth it for him to do the work of releasing D_A if he receives no more segments from Alice. In particular, S_b is the first segment where the following inequality holds true[2]:

$$v_B > w_B * 2^{(N-b)/2}$$

Likewise, Alice has some threshold segment S_a she receives from Bob, the first segment where the following inequality holds true:

$$v_A > w_A * 2^{(N-a)/2}$$

It is definitely the case that S_b does not equal S_a, as they are sent by different parties.[3] Therefore, a party can always act maliciously to cause an **unfair outcome** for a rational counterparty in a gradual release exchange. There are two reasons this does not happen every time a gradual release exchange occurs. First, doing so often harms the malicious actor; and second, the values listed above are generally not known precisely.

It is relatively obvious that the best outcome for both parties in the model above is to send all their segments (except perhaps Bob's final segment to Alice), since sending a segment opens the possibility of receiving another segment, which will cut the cost of acquiring the item in half. So rational actors should be expected to complete the exchange (again, modulo the last segment, which has a very small cost to Alice). However, note that this model ignores an important cost, which we consider in the next section.

Alice may have a good understanding of v_A and w_A, but it is likely that she does not have exact figures for those, let alone for v_B and w_B. Additionally, brute forcing a key is random, so while $w_A * 2^{(N-t)/2}$ provides an upper bound on the cost of work Alice needs to do to complete the work from segment S_t, the actual work may be anywhere from 1 to that upper bound.[4]

---

[2]This is a simplified form that does not account for the discrete jumps where t in segment S_t is odd or even. The complete picture is given in the next section, which also considers the cost of knowledge.

[3]Note that Alice sends her segment first, so in general she has an extra factor of two in work that must be done, meaning S_b will often come before S_a.

[4]The expected value is half this upper bound, as one may have expected.

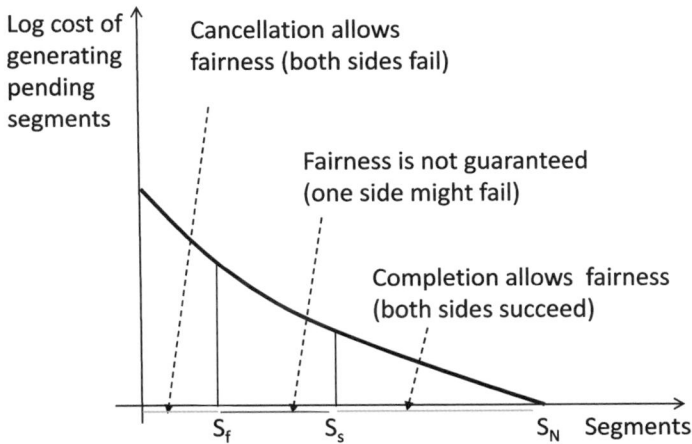

Fig. 11.4.   Safe intervals in gradual release fair exchange.

This creates a "region of confusion" shown in red in Figure 11.4, and presented as a finite state machine (FSM) in Figure 11.5.

Alice conservatively chooses some s, for success, where the cost of work for segment S_s for Alice is much less than v_A. She will definitely put in the work to release D_B from this point forward, and if she receives S_s from Bob, then she considers the exchange to have succeeded, regardless of what happens afterwards. This requires that the last few segments of the exchange have a negligible cost of work associated with their completion.

Alice also conservatively estimates some f, for failure, where the cost of work for segment S_f for Bob is much greater than v_B. Alice believes that if she stops sending segments before segment S_f, then the exchange will definitely fail: neither side will do the work required to release the other's item. This depends on the cost of work for the release from the early segments being intractable, otherwise Alice could have an unfair outcome from sending her first segment, and the exchange would never get started.

It also depends on Alice being unsure which segment is actually S_f. If she knew that segment S_f is definitely the first segment for which Bob would do the work to release D_A, but also knows that she will not do the work to release D_B until she receives more segments, then by sending S_f she is allowing Bob to cause an unfair outcome for her. And as it turns out, Bob might have a very good reason for doing that.

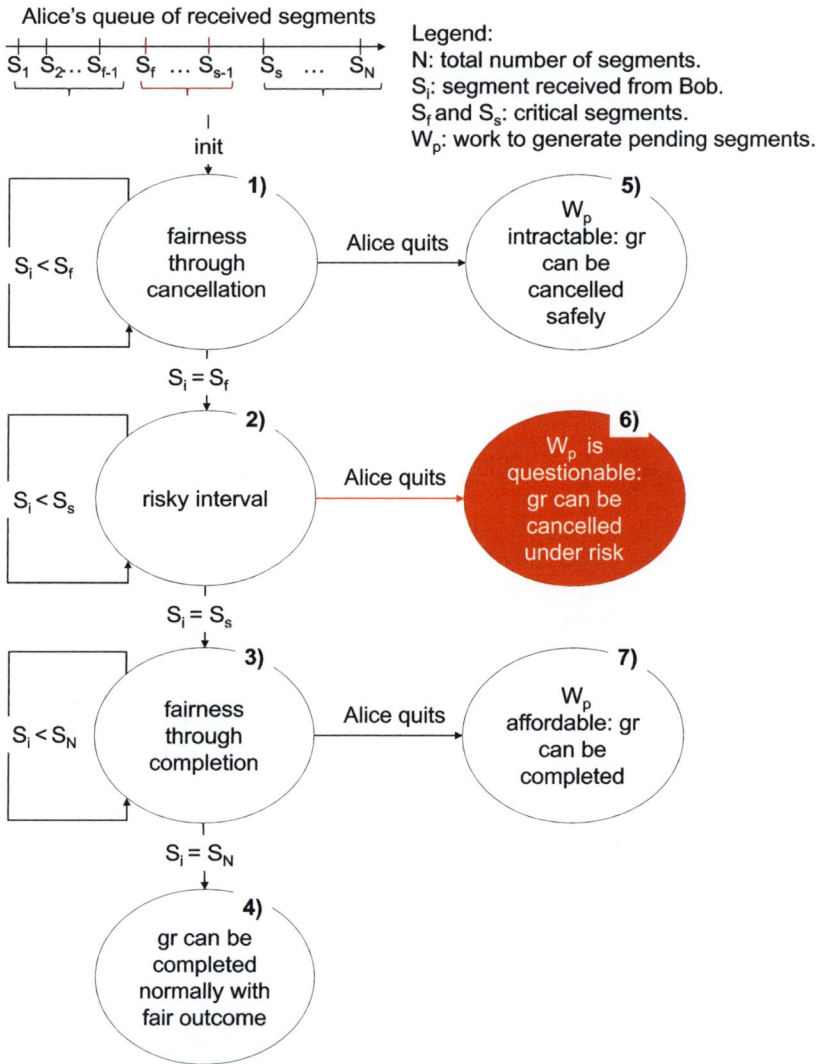

Fig. 11.5.   FSM with risky intervals in gradual release.

11.3   Marginal Fairness

So far we have only considered cases where Alice sharing D_A with Bob has no cost to her. This is very rare: if there was no cost for sharing, the document would typically be public already.

We now consider those cases where Alice experiences some cost for sharing her document with Bob, and vice versa.

We define Alice's **marginal value** as the total value received after the completion of the exchange, taking into account the value of D_B to Alice, the cost of the work required to open D_B, and the cost of Bob receiving D_A.

Given this definition of marginal value, we can then define **marginal fairness** for gradual release protocols. We consider a particular use of a gradual release FEP to have marginal fairness if the exchange completes with neither party having negative marginal value.

In this section, we show that in the presence of perfect knowledge and reasonable costs, many gradual release exchanges fail to achieve marginal fairness, resulting in an unfair outcome for one of the participants.

There are six values that Alice and Bob both need to know to have perfect knowledge of the exchange.

- v_A The value to Alice of D_B.
- v_B The value to Bob of D_A.
- c_A The cost to Alice of Bob knowing D_A.
- c_B The cost to Bob of Alice knowing D_B.
- w_A The cost of work for Alice.
- w_B The cost of work for Bob.

To calculate Alice and Bob's marginal values M_A and M_B, respectively, at time t, we use the following formulas:

$$M_A(t) = v_A - w_A 2^{T-\lfloor (t-1)/2 \rfloor} - c_A \theta(v_B - w_B 2^{T-\lfloor t/2 \rfloor})$$
$$M_B(t) = v_B - w_B 2^{T-\lfloor t/2 \rfloor} - c_B \theta(v_A - w_A 2^{T-\lfloor (t-1)/2 \rfloor})$$

where

- t is the current step in the exchange,
- T is the last step in the exchange, and
- θ is the Heaviside step function.

Note that Alice only steps on odd numbers, and Bob only steps on even. An exchange involving both participants sharing 256 bits would require 512 steps, with t ranging from 1 to 512.

These formulas make a number of simplifying assumptions.

(1) Alice always goes first.
(2) Each segment contains exactly one bit.
(3) The cost of work is a constant multiplier.
(4) Participants consider any positive marginal value to be fair.
(5) Participants act rationally to maximize their marginal value.

These assumptions are not onerous: letting Bob go first is isomorphic. Including more bits, or fewer bits, in a segment changes the base of the exponent from 2 to something else, but does not change the dynamics of the system. Cost of work changing with amount of work is overwhelmed by the exponential factor, unless it is also exponential, which seems somewhat unrealistic. Alice can easily obtain a profit by giving her valuation of D_B a haircut in the above formula. And we already noted in the previous section that if the participants act irrationally and maliciously, one of them can always produce a marginally unfair outcome for the other.

To determine whether a given exchange has marginal fairness requires checking $M_A(t)$ and $M_B(t)$ for each $0 \leq t \leq T$. Let Alice's maximum marginal value be $M_A(t_A)$, and Bob's be $M_B(t_B)$. Without loss of generality suppose $t_B < t_A$, so that Bob achieves his maximum marginal value within the exchange first. If $M_A(t_B) < 0$, then this exchange does not provide marginal fairness for Alice, because for Bob to achieve his best outcome, he must stop sending segments at a time when Alice must pay more to release D_B than it is worth to her.

This is quite unlike fairness definitions in other types of FEPs. Gradual release introduces an extra cost variable into the synchronize operation. This cost needs to be considered when Alice is deciding whether to accept a proposed exchange with Bob, but she must consider it for each segment sent and received, since the costs change at each step.

Conversely, it is also clear why this is the case in gradual release: if Bob can gain D_A without Alice being able to gain D_B, this clearly maximizes his profit. So Bob will be willing to do work equal to almost all of c_B (his cost of Alice releasing D_B) to prevent that from happening.

If Alice and Bob have a good sense of these values, they can check whether their proposed exchange provides marginal fairness

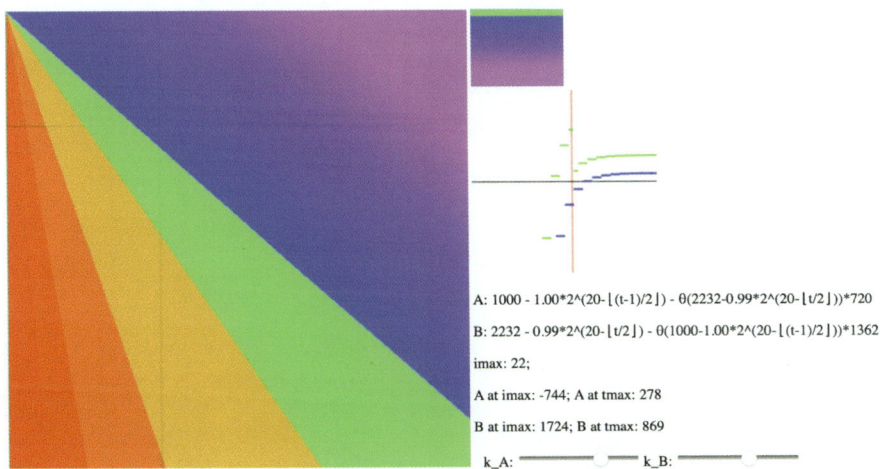

Fig. 11.6. Exploration of marginal fairness. Green is fair, cooler is unfair for Alice, hotter is unfair for Bob.

before entering into it. We have created an interactive tool for exploring marginal fairness in gradual release exchanges, as seen in Figure 11.6.[5] We hope you will find it useful for engaging in mutually satisfying gradual release exchanges.

---

[5]Available online at https://inatree.net/fewd/grtool/.

Chapter 12

Attestable-based Fair Exchange Protocols

Fair exchange protocols (FEPs) that make use of attestables are known as *attestable-based protocols*. Attestables serve as an abstraction layer for independent compute (IC) environments.

In particular, attestables capture the idea that we may wish to commit ourselves to following certain rules in the future, such that our future selves are unable to break those rules. Far from restricting our use of our devices, this ability to bind the device's future operation to a particular set of rules provides us with the freedom to do something new: running computations others can trust, even if they do not trust us (the owners of the computations).

Of course, our future selves can always destroy the device, or cut it off from the network. These abilities, inherent to our possession of the device, are reflected in the requirements of attestables, which include the device owner having explicit control over all input and output messages to the attestable, as well as the ability to terminate the component at any time.

Conversely, once the rules have been established, it is important that the device owner cannot go back on their word, so isolation of the processing is equally essential. Concealment of the data is also essential for our use cases, which include exchanging information that must be kept confidential until the exchange has been finalized.

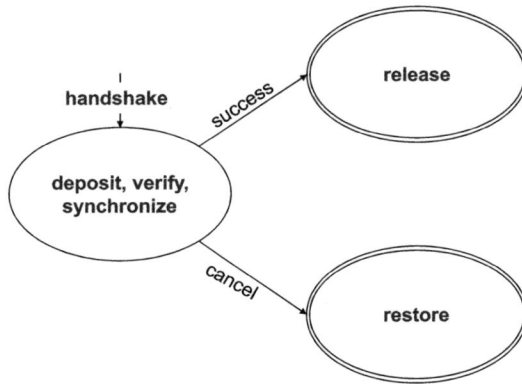

Fig. 12.1.   FSM executed by a participant in an attestable-based FEP.

The Finite State Machine (FSM) model of attestable–base protocols is shown in Figure 12.1. A comparison of this FSM against that of escrow-based protocols (see Figure 9.1) will reveal that they are exactly the same. This should not come as a surprise since both protocols guarantee the same outcomes: both complete either in success or cancel. This property is expressed in the FSMs. They have only two final states: either release or restore. Release corresponds to successful exchange and restore corresponds to the cancellation of the exchange. There are no final states for disputes like in the FSM shown in Figure 10.1.

Attestable-based protocols combine the convenience of escrow-based protocols with the efficiencies of optimistic protocols. To recap, escrow-based protocols can be used to exchange any category of item and provide strong fairness guarantees that prevent the occurrence of non-performance disputes in the exchange. However, they are plagued by high costs and risks introduced by the centralized trusted third party (TTP) that is used for holding the items in escrow and driving the exchange. Attestable-based protocols do not need a centralized TTP, therefore, they are not afflicted by the risks and costs that they inevitable introduce. Figure 12.2 illustrates the components of an attestable-based protocol and the places where five basic operations of FEPs are executed.

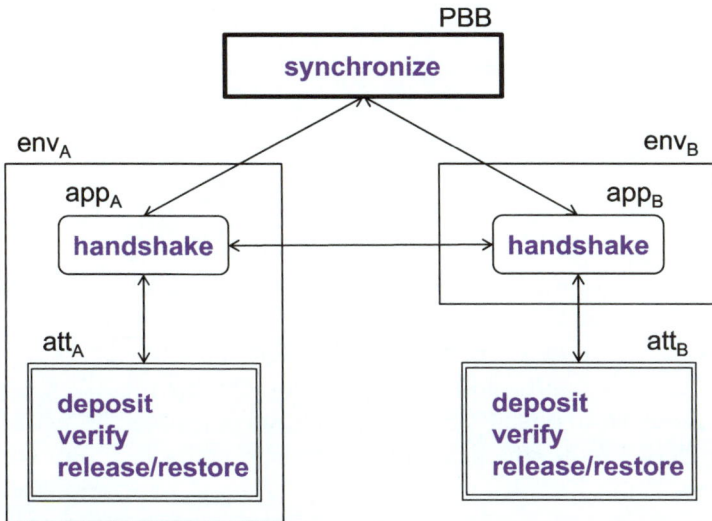

Fig. 12.2. The five basic operations of fair exchange implemented in an attestable-based protocol.

12.1 Stateless Split TTPs

Attestable-based protocols depart from a monolithic stateful TTP in favour of a stateless split TTP. The TTP is still a mediator, but it is implemented as the aggregation of two components:

- **Attestable**: one for each participant. In the figure, Alice is in possession of att_A and Bob is in possession of att_B. This component of the TTP provides IC (see Chapter 5) and is responsible for storing the state of the protocol.
- **Public bulletin board**: this component of the TTP provides independent messaging (IM) (see Chapter 5) and nothing else in the sense that it is stateless. It does not participate with any computation. In fact, it is not aware that it is being used to run a FEP.

Attestable-based protocols gain modularity. The split of the TTP enables to split responsibilities rather than allocating all of them to the TTP. Also, the split approach makes the implementation more flexible, the attestable and Public bulletin board (PBB) can be implemented separately.

12.2   Adversary Model

We assume the adversarial participant is able to subvert and control all of their components of the figure other than their attestable.

We assume that the communication channels that communicate the attestables with each other, the PBB, and possibly with other remote devices are asynchronous and unreliable, and can delay, duplicate, or lose messages. These properties emerge from the depending environment that physically and logically separates the attestables. In this dependent environment, a malicious participant can gain control of the channels and partially disrupt or completely stop communication.

12.3   Operational Steps

The split TTP allows the designer to separate the basic operations into three groups.

- **Handshake** is executed between Alice's and Bob's applications, app_A and app_B, respectively. The applications provide only a dependent environment.
- **Deposit, verify, and release/restore** are executed in the attestables that provide an independent computing.
- **Synchronize** is executed in the PBB that provides IM.

Chapter 13

FEWD: Fair Exchange Without Disputes

We present fair exchange without disputes (FEWD), an attestable-based fair exchange protocol (FED) with desirable qualities. FEWD provides strong fairness, eliminating the possibility of non-performance disputes, and allows elimination of the major sources of cost and risk from trusted third parties (TTPs).

The basic insight in FEWD, as in all attestable-based protocols, is to put the deposit, verify, and release/restore operations into an independent compute (IC) environment in the control of the participant. Alice's attestable takes deposit of D_B, verifies it, and releases it on successful completion, or restores D_A if the exchange is cancelled. Bob's attestable does the same for D_A. The synchronize operation is performed in the independent messaging (IM) environment of a public bulletin board (PBB), providing strong fairness.

We show a version of FEWD that achieves strong fairness on copyable items, and a different version of FEWD that achieves strong fairness over any class of digitally exchangeable items. There are further variants for specific situations, including where Alice has a copyable item but lacks access to an attestable, and Bob has both an attestable and any kind of digitally exchangeable item (Chapter 14).

FEWD provides strong timeliness along its whole execution timeline, without relying on synchronized clocks to implement timeouts. It is also an invisible and non-invasive protocol for the class of copyable items, allowing it to layer over other protocols transparently.

The abstraction barriers imposed by separating the environment of the synchronize operation from the attestables simplifies component replication as well, providing a clean approach to mitigating the risk of attestable crashes, attestable compromises, and PBB faults of any kind. This allows appropriate balancing of cost and risk for a wide range of use cases, including both those involving very high-value items and those exchanging low-value items. Chapter 17 describes these protective measures in detail.

Our goal for FEWD is a working system usable in industry. A proof of concept architecture and implementation has been designed alongside the work that lead to this book, and further applications and pending work are described in Chapter 19. FEWD is part of the TODA Project (Coward and Toliver, 2022), and provides open exchangability across the full gamut of digital items.

13.1   Initial Setup and Setup Document

The setup document that Alice and Bob agree upon consists of several parameters:

- **Public bulletin board**: Specifies the uniform resource locator (URL) and transfer layer security (TLS) certificate of the PBB that Alice and Bob agree to use.
- **Device keys**: Specifies the keys and certificates that are used for the attestation of Alice's and Bob's trusted components.
- **Documents**: Describes the documents that Alice and Bob are exchanging, D_A and D_B, respectively. It contains three sub-parameters: *setup_values*, *module*, and *certificate*.

An example of such a setup document can be seen in Listing 13.1.

Listing 13.1. Example of a full setup document.

```
1  { public_bulletin_board: {
2      pbb_url:   PBB_url
3      tls_cert:  PBB_certificate }
4
5    device_keys: [
6      { // Alice's attestable
```

```
7     AIK:   A_pubkey      // Attestation Identity Key
8     EPID:  A_EPID_pk     // Enhanced Privacy ID
9     cert:  A_certificate }
10
11    { // Bob's attestable
12      AIK:   B_pubkey      // Attestation Identity Key
13      EPID:  B_EPID_pk     // Enhanced Privacy ID
14      cert:  B_certificate } ]
15
16  documents: [
17    {                                // Alice's document D_A
18      setup_values: [parameters]              // P_A
19      module: {                 // certified module M_A
20        setup_values_types: [types]           // S_A
21        doc_values_types:   [types]           // T_A
22        verify_function:    [hash, url]       // V_A
23        gatherer_function:  [hash, url] }     // G_A
24      certificate: [hash, url] }        // over M_A
25
26    {                                // Bob's document D_B
27      setup_values: [parameters]              // P_B
28      module: {                 // certified module M_B
29        setup_values_types: [types]           // S_B
30        doc_values_types:   [types]           // T_B
31        verify_function:    [hash, url]       // V_B
32        gatherer_function:  [hash, url] }     // G_B
33      certificate: [hash, url] }        // over M_B
34    ] } }
```

We examine Alice's document description in the following. Any notation introduced is symmetrically applied for Bob as well, e.g., M_A is the module in Alice's document description, and M_B is the module in Bob's.

- **setup_values**: The list of setup values that Alice's document is expected to satisfy to be accepted by Bob. At static analysis time, Bob's application ensures that the types of the values included in the list *setup_values* match the types specified in the list *doc_value_types*. We use P_A as a shorthand notation to refer to the *setup_values* associated with Alice's document.

- **module**: The certified verification module that Bob's attestable uses in the verify operation to ensure that D_A satisfies the values included in *setup_values*. We use M_A to refer to the verification module. The module contains four parameters:

  - **setup_values_types**: the list of the types of the values included in *setup_values*. We use S_A as a shorthand notation to refer to the *setup_values_types* associated with Alice's document.

  - **doc_values_types**: the list of types $t_1, \ldots, t_m$ of the list of values ($X_A = \{x_1 \ldots, x_m\}$) associated with Alice's document. We call X_A the list of *doc-values*. The values included in *doc-values* are gathered by the gather function; some of them are gathered directly from Alice's document and others from the environment through the Internet. We use T_A as a shorthand notation to refer to the *doc_values_types* associated with Alice's document.

  - **verify_function**: the verifier function. It takes *setup_values* from the setup-document and the *doc-values* list gathered by the gather function as input and produces a boolean: true if the values in *setup_values* match the values in *doc-values*. True and false represent, respectively, the acceptance and rejection of D_A. We use V_A as a shorthand notation to refer to the *verify_function* used to verify Alice's document.

  - **gather_function**: a function run during the verify operation that accepts D_A as input and gathers the list of *doc-values*, that is, $X_A = \{x_1 \ldots, x_m\}$. If the types of the values in X_A match the types listed in *doc_values_types*, the gather function outputs X_A, otherwise it outputs an error, which cancels the exchange. We use G_A as a shorthand notation to refer to the *gather_function* used for gathering the list of *doc-values* associated with Alice's document.

- **certificate**: the certificate of the module that ensures its provenance and integrity.

The descriptions of Alice's and Bob's documents contain all the information needed to verify the documents. The setup document also includes the information needed for conducting static analysis before run-time to assess the risk of getting false positives. We discuss this issue in Chapter 15.

FEWD can be executed within a legal context that involves the negotiation and agreement of a letter of intention over a channel outside FEWD, for example, over email or phone. Such a letter would include a section with a description of technical parameters to set up the execution of the protocol, written in a machine readable format. Possible legal implications of the setup document are discussed in Chapter 16.

13.1.1 *Example of a handshake description*

Alice and Bob are arranging an exchange of items under FEWD. Alice expects to receive a train ticket for travel to Paris, Rome, or Madrid that must be valid between March 27 and April 16. The pseudocode shown in Listing 13.2 shows the list of setup values and setup value types, P_B and T_B, respectively. It also shows the functions verify and gather, V_B and G_B, respectively. This example includes a mutable type, *proofNotBanned*, and a complex type, *3capitals*, in order to demonstrate that the list T_B can include arbitrarily complex types.

Listing 13.2. Pseudocode.

```
1   P_B=[ // setup-values for D_B
2        "Paris"          // p_1 of type s_1
3        2021-03-27       // p_2 of type s_2
4        2021-04-16       // p_3 of type s_3
5        ]
6
7   M_B { // verification module for train tickets
8
9    S_B=[ // setup-values types
10          let 3capitals= [Paris,Rome,Madrid]
11          3capitals  // s_1
12          date       // s_2
13          date       // s_3
14          ]
15
16   T_B=[ // doc-values types
17          3capitals  // t_1
```

```
18        date           // t_2
19        date           // t_3
20        proofNotBanned // t_4 /* mutable type */
21        today          // t_5
22        ]
23
24   function G_B(D_B) // gatherer function
25   {
26    x_1 = D_B.destination
27    x_2 = D_B.start_date
28    x_3 = D_B.end_date
29    x_4 = getProof('interpol.gov/bad_tix/'+D_B.id)
30    x_5 = getTodaysDate()
31    return [x_1, x_2, x_3, x_4, x_5] // X_B
32   }
33
34   // the verify function
35   function V_B( p_1 : s_1      // Paris | Rome | Madrid
36                 p_2 : s_2      // 2021−03−27
37                 p_3 : s_3      // 2021−04−16
38
39                 x_1 : t_1      // D_B.destination
40                 x_2 : t_2      // D_B.start_date
41                 x_3 : t_3      // D_B.end_date
42                 x_4 : t_4      // interpol.gov result
43                 x_5 : t_5 )    // today's date
44   {
45       if (x_1 !== p_1)   return false
46       if (x_2 >=  p_2)   return false
47       if (x_3 <=  p_3)   return false
48
49       // ensure the Interpol proof is valid for today
50       if (invalidProof(x_4, x_5)) return false
51       return true
52   }
53
54   } // end verification module M_B
```

13.2 Post of Sync and Cancel Tokens

There is a stage during the execution of FEWD when Alice and Bob need to post their tokens to the PBB and retrieve them, as we will see in Section 13.3.

A potential approach to implementing the interaction between the attestables and the PBB is to program the application to bridge the interaction. Only the application interacts directly with the PBB and it is responsible for driving the attestable–PBB communication. It drives the communication with the attestables as well.

We discuss this idea only from Alice's perspective, but as this is a symmetric protocol, Bob follows the same procedure.

The code that deals with the interaction with the PBB, including the verification of the Certificate Authority (CA) certificate of the PBB, is programmed in the application. A disadvantage of this approach is that it requires that the PBB offers an application programming interface (API) that prevents the applications from altering the content or the order of the tokens.

A significant advantage of this approach is that the code deployed within the attestable is independent of the API of the PBB. Only the code of the application needs to take into account the particularities of the API of the PBB that Alice and Bob agree to use.

We will use the finite state machine (FSM) shown in Figure 13.1 to explain the idea. Note that the FSM is only an example protocol. Other similar protocols can be devised — the protocol shown in the figure aims at simplicity; but those are details, the distinguishing feature of the figure is that the application is responsible for posting tokens s_A and c_A to the PBB when it receives them from its attestable. The application is also responsible for retrieving the tokens from the PBB and forwarding them to its attestable, which uses them to unlock D_B.

- **state 1**: The state machine enters state 1 when Alice's attestable receives $D_B K_{A,B}$ from Alice's application. This message is originally produced by Bob's attestable and includes

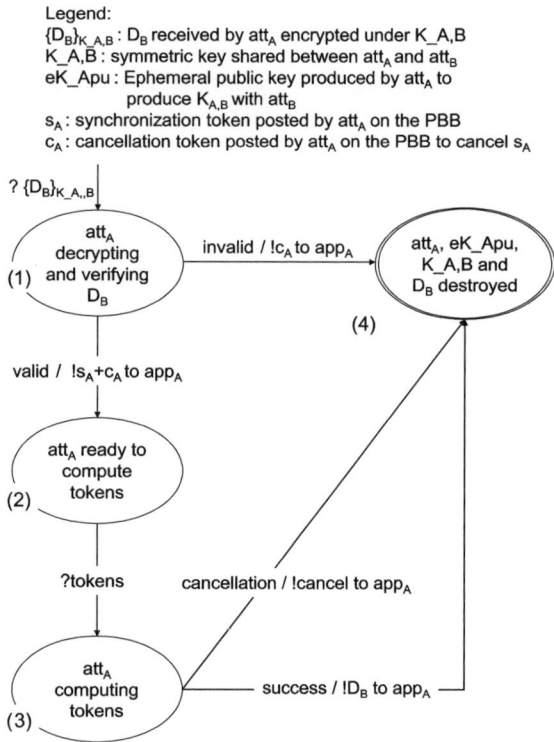

Fig. 13.1.   Alice's attestable processes Bob's D_B.

Bob's D_B document encrypted under $K_{A,B}$, that is, under the key that the attestables have previously agreed on. In this state, Alice's attestable decrypts the document and verifies that it meets the properties stipulated in the description of the document and produces either *invalid* or *valid*. If the outcome of the verification is *invalid*, the attestable sends a cancel token c_A to its application and progresses to the final state 4. Upon receiving c_A, the application posts it to the PBB. Alternatively, if the outcome of the verification is *valid*, the attestable sends two tokens to its application (s_A and c_A) and progresses to state 2. Note that the possession of s_A and c_A within the application gives Alice the freedom to either continue with the execution of the protocol that leads to a successful exchange or to a cancelled exchange. Alice can instruct her application to post either s_A or c_A.

- **state 2**: Alice's attestable progresses to this state when it is ready to request the tokens from Alice's application. Eventually, it issues a token request *tokens* against Alice's application, retrieves the tokens, and progresses to state 3.
- **state 3**: In this state, Alice's attestable computes the tokens, that is, analyses the record of tokens retrieved by Alice's application from the PBB, to determine if it indicates whether the exchange is *successful* or *cancelled*. If it is *cancelled*, Alice's attestable sends a *cancel* message to Alice's application to notify it of the outcome, and progresses to the final state 4. On the contrary, if the outcome is *success*, Alice's attestable uses the tokens to release D_B, sends it to Alice's application, and progresses to the final state 4.
- **state 4**: This is the final state where the attestable is destroyed (torn down) along all the sensitive data such as the ephemeral key associated to Alice's attestable (eK_{Apu}), the symmetric key that Alice's attestable and Bob's attestable share ($K_{A,B}$), and the copy of D_B left within Alice's attestable.

13.2.1 *Sync tokens with cancellations*

FEWD assumes that during the setup time, Alice and Bob agree on the following rules to post and retrieve tokens.

(1) There are two **sync tokens**, s_A and s_B, that can be posted with the intention of progressing the exchange towards successful completion. Also there are two **cancel tokens**, c_A and c_B, that can be posted with the intention of cancelling the exchange.

- s_A and c_A can be posted to the PBB only by Alice's attestable.
- s_B and c_B can be posted to the PBB only by Bob's attestable.

(2) Alice's attestable and Bob's attestable are free to post their respective sync and cancel tokens at an unspecified and arbitrarily long time after initiating FEWD.

- For example, Alice's attestable is free to post a sync token s_A to try to progress the exchange or a cancel token c_A to try to it at any time.
- A cancel token c_A always succeeds in cancelling the exchange if Alice's attestable has not previously posted s_A.
- If Alice's attestable has already posted s_A, the cancel token c_A succeeds in cancelling the exchange only if it is posted before Bob's attestable posts s_B.

(3) The same cancellation policy is followed by cancel tokens c_B posted by Bob's attestable.
(4) FEWD does not impose restrictions on the attestables to post or retrieve tokens from the PBB. Incidentally, there is nothing to stop Alice's attestable to resend a token to the PBB, for example, after failing to receive a post confirmation; as a result, tokens on the PBB might be duplicated. FEWD delegates the responsibility of dealing with duplicated token to the attestables.

Note when we say that Alice or Bob post a token, we mean that they instruct their attestables to post the tokens. We clarify that the attestables might not interact directly with the PBB (to post and retrieve tokens) but through their applications as explained in Section 13.2.

The implementation of this agreement relies on the ability of the PBB to order the posted token following a *happened before* policy; for instance, the PBB can rely on timestamping for ordering the tokens, but there are other mechanisms.

The FSM model of Figure 13.2 shows how each attestable is expected to post and process tokens after retrieving them from the PBB. All the tokens shown in the FSM belong to a single execution of FEWD between Alice and Bob.

In the figure, the labels on the edges represent posts, thus s_A means that s_A has been posted by Alice's attestable. The initial state of the FSM is activated from the previous stage of FEWD. The FSM includes two final states. The *FEWD cancelled* state represents the cancellation of the exchange. However, the s_A *and* s_B *posted* state represents progress to the next stage of the exchange, namely, to

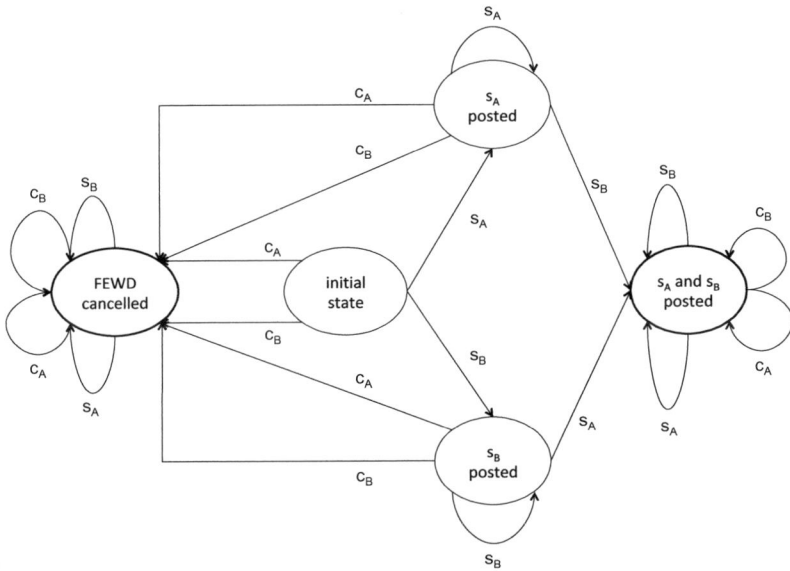

Fig. 13.2. FSM of sync and cancel tokens.

the stage where the tokens can be retrieved from the PBB and the documents released from the attestables.

The execution of the FSM results in several arbitrarily long sequences of posts that are initiated either by Alice's attestable or Bob's attestable. To appreciate the impact of cancel tokens, let us analyse the potential sequences that can be initiated by Alice's attestable. To simplify the discussion, let us focus only on the first three posts of each sequence under the assumption that each token is posted only once, that is, there are no repeated tokens. Figure 13.3 shows the sequences graphically. We do not show or analyse the sequences initiated by Bob's attestable because they are similar. In the figure, we use a circle with a star ($*$) to represent s_A, s_B, c_A, c_B, or no token, that is, no token posted. If posted, this token is irrelevant; its has no effect on the final state of the FSM.

- seq 1 is the only sequence that progresses the exchange to the next stage. It includes the post of s_A immediately followed

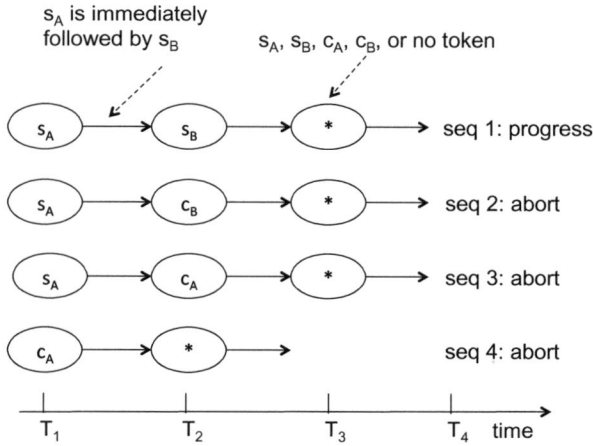

Fig. 13.3.   Sequences of tokens initiated by Alice's attestable.

by s_B. If there is a token to the right of s_B, it does not influence the final state of the FSM.

- A feature shared between seq 1, seq 2, and seq 3 is that all of them show the initial intention of Alice's attestable to progress the exchange. Note that after posting s_A, Alice's attestable is uncertain about the outcome of the exchange: it can either be completed successfully by Bob, or he cancelled by Bob or by Alice. In this regard, the three sequences have their particularities:

  o seq 1: Bob progresses the exchange by means of posting s_B with the assistance of his attestable.
  o seq 2: Bob uses the power of the cancel token. He cancels the exchange by means of posting s_B.
  o seq 3: Alice changes her mind and succeeds in cancelling the exchange by means of posting c_A.
  o seq 4: Alice uses the power of the cancel token. She cancels the exchange immediately by means of posting c_A.

The impact of the normal tokens (s_A and s_B) and the cancel tokens (c_A and c_B) are different. Posting s_A or s_B opens a window of uncertainty about the future development of the exchange for the poster. Let us assume that Alice's attestable has posted s_A and that it is waiting for Bob's attestable to post, hopefully s_B. If Alice becomes impatient and decides to complete the exchange, she needs to post c_A, retrieve the relevant records from the PBB, and examine them. If the examination reveals that s_A is followed by either c_A or c_B, Alice's attestable can safely cancel the exchange. However, if the examination reveals that s_A is followed by s_B, Alice's attestable must continue to the next stage where the documents are released. In contrast, if s_A has not been posted yet, the cancellation effect of c_A is immediate and categorical: Alice's attestable can post c_A at any time and cancel the exchange without further interaction with the PBB.

13.3 Core Functionality

In this section, we describe the core functionality and building blocks of the protocol. We make the following assumptions:

- D_A and D_B are copyable items.
- The PBB and the attestables of the participants are free from threats of accidental technical failures.
- The PBB offers time-stamping facilities.
- Alice's app and Bob's app can be subverted by their owners to manipulate computation and communication.
- Channels $chan_{AB}$, $chan_{AP}$, and $chan_{BP}$ are unreliable from the attestables' perspectives, because Alice's app and Bob's app may delay messages, reorder them, or drop them completely.

In subsequent sections, we will enhance the protocol with additional mechanisms to cover situations where these assumptions are unacceptable. For instance, we will account for potential failures of the attestables and for the exchange of unique items.

FEWD relies on posting and retrieving tokens from a PBB. Here we focus on the application-driven approach, in which the applications are responsible for posting and retrieving the tokens from the PBB (explained in Section 13.2). Another potential approach uses the attestables to post and retrieve the tokens (this is covered further in the online supplemental material).

13.3.1 *Handshake*

FEWD starts with the attestation of the attestables initiated by the applications in Alice's and Bob's dependent environments.

Figure 13.4 shows the main idea. The appraiser shown in the figure is a piece of code designed to attest a remote attestable. Alice and Bob have their own appraisers deployed within their respective applications. The attestation of Bob's attestable is initiated by Alice's appraiser when it sends an attest request, shown as (1) *attest*. Reciprocally, the attestation of Alice's attestable is initiated by Bob's appraiser when it sends an attest request, shown as (2) *attest*. A successful attestation produces a symmetric $K_{A,B}$ shared between att_A and att_B.

Note that there are no technical difficulties to prevent the deployment of the appraiser within the attestables. However, to minimize the size of the code that the attestables run, the figure suggests that the appraiser deployed within the apps.

A successful completion of the reciprocal attestation protocol leaves Alice's and Bob's attestables in a position to begin the execution of the stage b of the protocol.

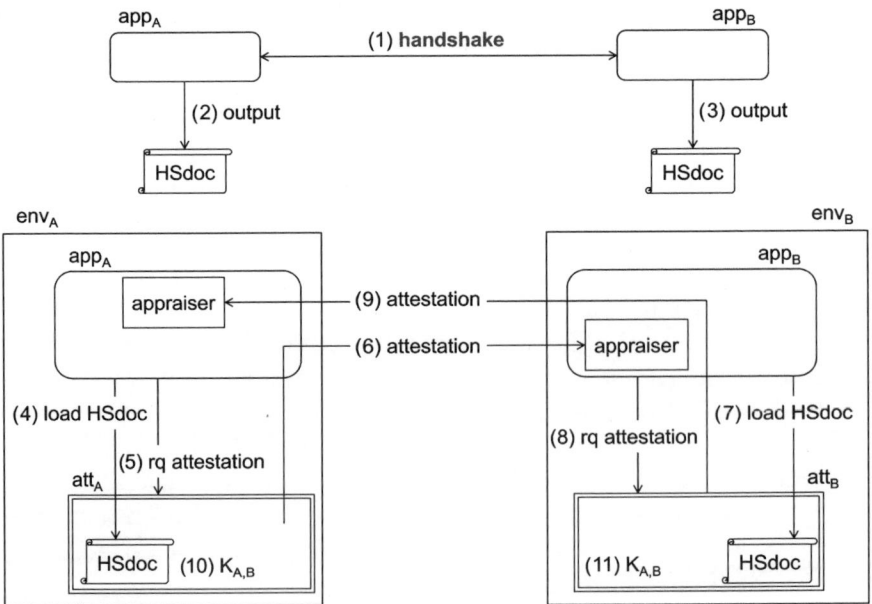

Fig. 13.4. **Handshake** followed by reciprocal attestation.

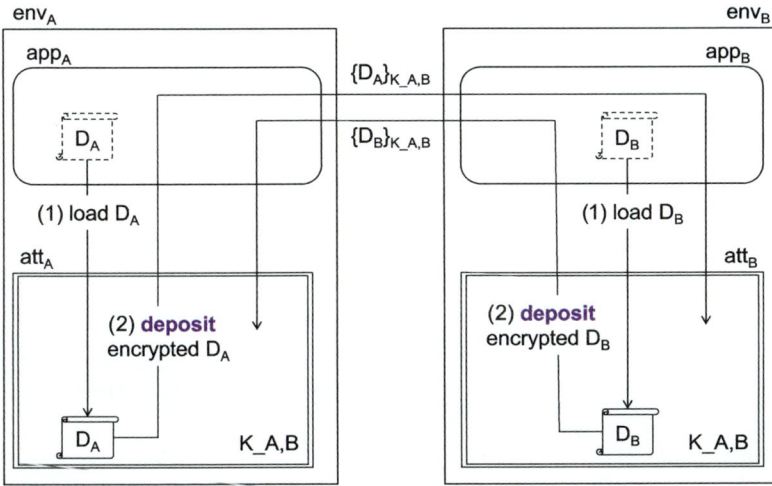

Fig. 13.5.   Attestables **deposit** documents.

13.3.2   *Deposit*

The second stage is shown in Figure 13.5 and deals with the deposit of the documents D_A and D_B. Dashed boxes of the documents represent the sources, while the boxes of solid lines represent the destinations. We will describe the steps from Alice's perspective:

(1) input D_A: Alice's app sends the document D_A to its attestable.
(2) encrypt and send D_A: Alice's attestable encrypts D_A under $K_{A,B}$ and sends the encrypted version $\{D_A\}K_{A,B}$ to Bob's attestable. $K_{A,B}$ is the symmetric key agreed upon between att_A and att_B in the previous (1) step.

From this stage onward, Alice's attestable and Bob's attestable work independently: they do not communicate directly with each other, but only by means of posting tokens and retrieving tokens from the PBB.

13.3.3   *Verify*

In the third stage (Figure 13.6), the documents $\{D_A\}K_{A,B}$ and $\{D_B\}K_{A,B}$ are decrypted and verified, and the sync tokens s_A and s_B are produced.

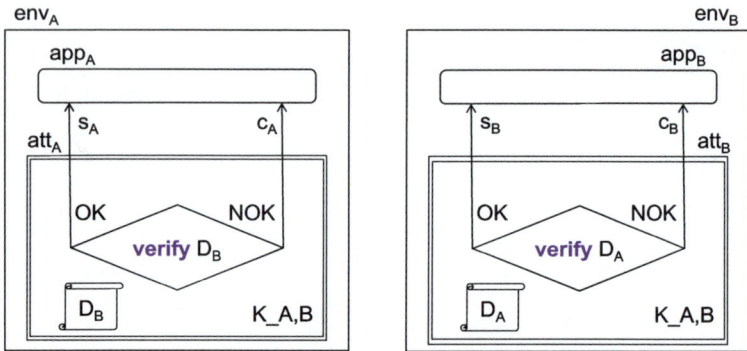

Fig. 13.6.   Attestables **verify** documents and produce tokens.

The following procedure is used by Alice's attestable:

(1) It uses $K_{A,B}$ to recover D_B from $\{D_B\}K_{A,B}$.
(2) It uses the certified verification module M_B to verify D_B.
(3) It produces s_A if M_B successfully verifies D_B.

13.3.4 *Synchronize*

The fourth stage is shown in Figure 13.7 and deals with the posting of the sync tokens to the PBB.

On Alice's side, the following steps are executed:

(1) send s_A to app: Alice's attestable sends s_A to its application.
(2) post s_A: Alice's establishes channel $chan_{APBB}$ on the PBB and uses it to post s_A to the PBB.

Channels $chan_{APBB}$ and $chan_{BPBB}$ are conventional communication channels.

Figure 13.7 suggests that Alice's application posts its token first, yet it is possible that Bob's application takes the lead.

Once posted to the PBB, the tokens need to be retrieved. On Alice's side, the following steps are executed:

(1) $chan_{APBB}$: Alice's application establishes the channel $chan_{APBB}$.
(2) **retrieve** $[s_B + s_B]K_{PBB}$: Alice's application uses the $chan_{APBB}$ channel to retrieve tokens s_A and s_B from the PBB. Note that

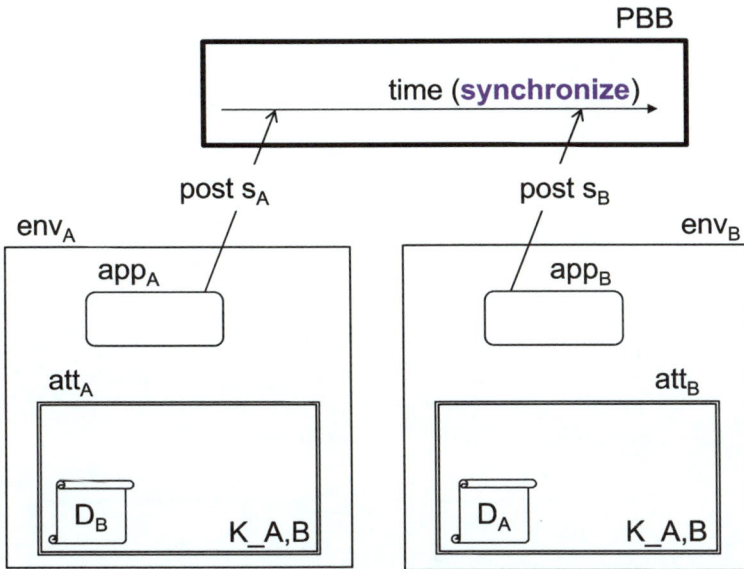

Fig. 13.7.   Attestables use PBB to **synchronize**.

the retrieval is a message that contains the two tokens and is signed under key K_{PBB}.

(3) **forward** $[s_B + s_B]K_{PBB}$: Alice's application forwards $[s_B + s_B]K_{PBB}$ to its attestable, which, with the help of K_{PBB}, verifies the integrity and provenance of the message.

(4) TC_A **has** $[s_B, +s_B]K_{PBB}$: Alice's attestable is now in possession of s_A and s_B.

The precise mechanisms to retrieve tokens from the PBB depend on the implementation of the PBB and the operations supported by its API. For example, if the PBB were implemented on IPFS, the attestables would need to send specific content identifiers as part of their query.

13.3.5   *Release/restore*

In the fifth step (see Figure 13.8), the attestables release or restore the documents to their respective applications.

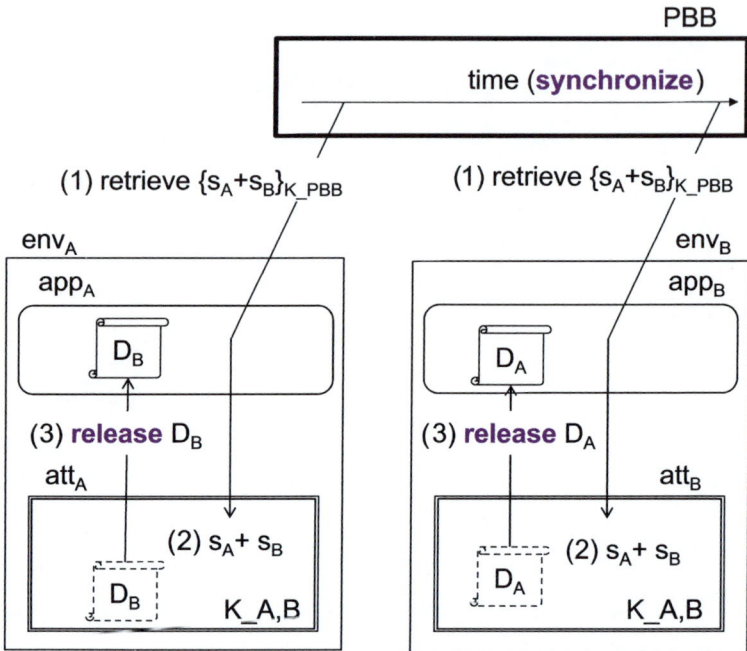

Fig. 13.8. Attestables **release** documents to their applications.

Alice's attestable releases D_B to app_A only if the release conditions are met for s_A and s_B. For instance, Alice's attestable requires that the tokens be retrieved from the PBB, rather than merely produced locally by Alice's app. This involves verifying the authenticity of the PBB, via a CA certificate or equivalent.

Additionally, Alice's attestable verifies that s_B was posted by Bob's attestable, which involves verifying the signature of att_B. Bob's attestable follows a similar procedure to release D_A to app_B.

Chapter 14

The Family FEWD

The framework described in Part 1 is generative, and applying it to fair exchange without disputes (FEWD) allows the development of new fair exchange protocols (FEPs) that efficiently fit particular use cases.

This chapter highlights several such protocols, variants of FEWD made by mixing and matching in the operational model. We show how different sets of operations impact different classes of items and environments, and how more efficient versions of protocols can be developed when handling items that can be exchanged within more limited environments.

14.1 Exchange of Unique Items

FEWD can be used for exchanging a unique items in return for another unique item.

We present an example where Alice gives Bob a unique item in return for another unique item. The protocol makes the following assumptions:

- Alice's item is I_A and is stored on the server S_A under the key K_{appA}, which is initially known only to Alice's application, which is represented by app_A.
- Bob's item is I_B and is stored on the server S_B under the key K_{appB}, which is initially known only to Bob's application, which is represented by app_B.

- Alice's application uses key K_A to access Bob's item if the exchange completes in success.
- Bob's application uses key K_B to access Alice's item if the exchange completes in success.
- Alice's attestable and Bob's attestable are programmed to send keys K_{attA} and K_{attB} to their respective applications only if they retrieve the pair of sync tokens s_A and s_B from the public bulletin board (PBB).

14.1.1   *Successful exchange of unique items*

The time line of an execution that completes in success is shown in Figure 14.1.

- T_1 and T_2: Alice's application app_A and Bob's application app_B have their items I_A and I_B, stored on servers S_A and S_B, under K_{appA} and K_{appB}, respectively.

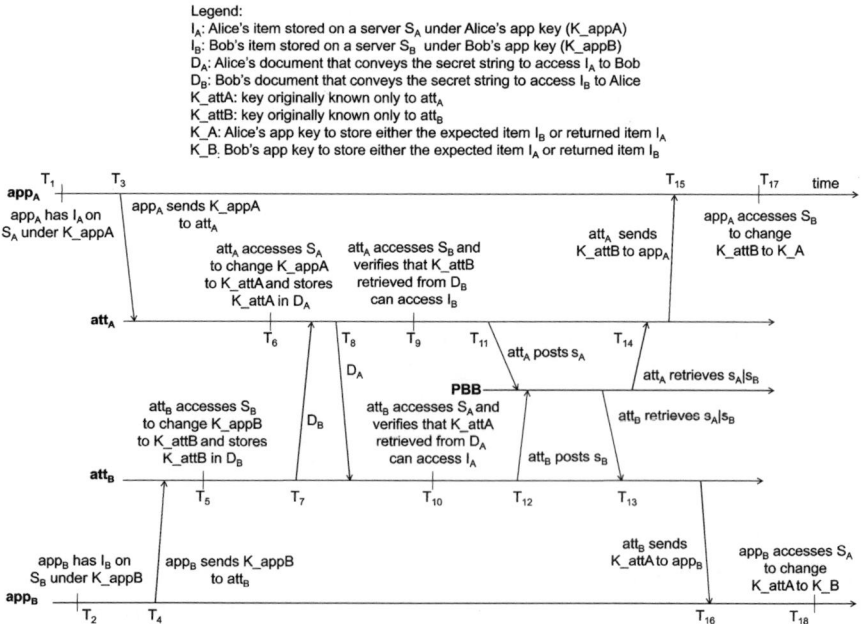

Fig. 14.1.   Successful exchange of unique items.

- T_3 and T_4: app_A and app_B send their keys K_{appA} and K_{appB} to their respective attestables att_A and att_B.

  ○ Now app_A and att_A both have access to I_A, and on Bob's side both app_B and att_B have access to I_B.

- T_5: att_B creates the key K_{attB}, changes K_{appB} to K_{attB}, and includes the latter in D_B.

  ○ Only att_B can access I_B.

- T_6: Alice does the same: att_A creates the key K_{attA}, changes K_{appA} to K_{attA}, and includes the latter in D_A.

  ○ Now only att_A can access I_A.

- T_7 and T_8: att_B and att_A exchange D_B and D_A.
- T_9: att_A verifies D_B by connecting to S_B and confirming K_{attB} can access I_B.
- T_{10}: att_B also verifies D_A by connecting to S_A and confirming K_{attA} can access I_A. Assume these verifications were both successful.

  ○ Now att_A and att_B both possess key K_{attA} for accessing I_A and key K_{attB} for accessing I_B.

- T_{11} and T_{12}: att_A and att_B post their sync tokens s_A and s_B to the PBB.
- T_{13} and T_{14}: att_A and att_B retrieve both sync tokens (s_A and s_B) from the PBB.

  ○ In the figure, retrieval is shown as a single operation that retrieves the concatenation of the two tokens $s_A|s_B$.

- T_{15} and T_{16}: att_A sends K_{attB} to app_A; on the other side, att_B sends K_{attA} to app_B.

  ○ Note that att_A, att_B, and app_A all have the key for I_B, but app_B does not, and likewise app_A does not have the key for I_A.

- T_{17} and T_{18}: app_A changes K_{attB} to K_A, which is known only to app_A, and app_B does the same with K_B.

Note that upon successful completion of the exchange, stale keys K_{appA}, K_{appB}, K_{attA}, and K_{attB} are left inside the attestables. Steps T_{17} and T_{18} are not necessary for security (up to the attestable assumptions), but may be convenient.

Legend:
K_appA: Alice's app key to store I_A on server S_A
K_appB: Bob's app key to store I_B on server S_B
K_A: Alice's app key to store either the expected item I_B or returned item I_A
K_B: Bob's app key to store either the expected item I_A or returned item I_B
——— att_A and app_A can complete the protocol without further communication
◯ att_A and app_A need to communicate with third parties to complete
the protocol

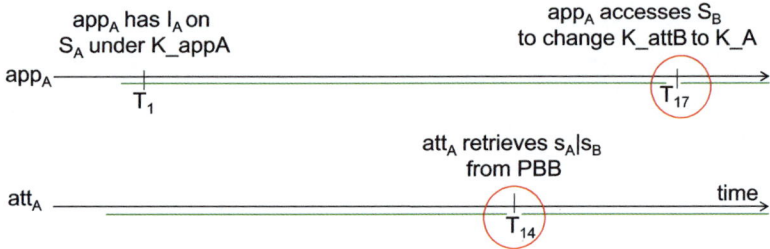

Fig. 14.2.   Timeliness in the exchange of unique items.

Strong timeliness of the protocol: In Figure 14.1, both Alice's and Bob's attestables observe a strong timeliness: they can complete the exchange independently, that is, without communicating with each other and without compromising fairness. The strong timeliness of the protocol are illustrated by the green lines of Figure 14.2. The red circles indicate the points where, to complete the exchange, the attestables need to communicate with third parties.

For example, to complete the exchange in T_{17}, Alice's attestable needs to communicate with the S_B server to change K_{attB} to K_A. Similarly, to complete the exchange in T_{14}, Bob's attestable needs to communicate with the PBB to retrieve the tokens $s_A|s_B$. External communication is also required from Alice's side in steps T_6, T_9, and T_{11} of Figure 14.1.

14.1.2   *Cancelled exchange of unique items*

The timeline of a cancelled exchange is shown in Figure 14.3.

We begin with step T_{10}, where this figure diverges from the earlier one where verification was successful.

- T_{10}: The verification of D_A fails: att_B cannot use K_{attA} to access I_A on S_A.

Legend:
I_A: Alice's item stored on a server S_A under app_A key (K_appA)
I_B: Bob's item stored on a server S_B under app_B key (K_appB)
D_A: Alice's document that conveys the secret string to access I_A to Bob
D_B: Bob's document that conveys the secret string to access I_B to Alice
K_attA: key originally known only to att_A
K_attB: key originally known only to att_B
K_A: app_A's key to store either the expected item I_B or returned item I_A
K_B: app_B's app key to store either the expected item I_A or returned item I_B

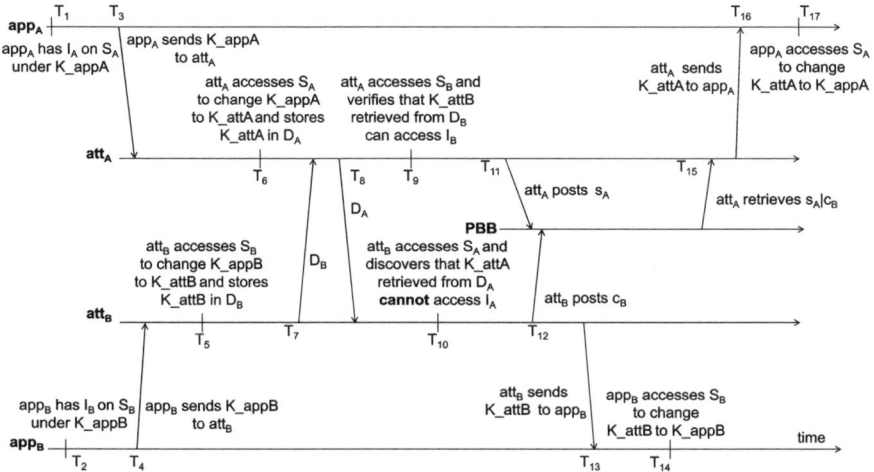

Fig. 14.3.   Cancelled exchange of unique items.

- T_{11}: att_A posts its sync tokens s_A to the PBB.
- T_{12}: att_B posts a cancel token c_B to the PBB, and collects $s_A|c_B$ from it.
- T_{13}: att_B proceeds to return access to I_B to its application: it sends key K_{attB} to its application.
- T_{14}: app_B changes K_{attB} to K_{appB} (the original key of I_B), which is known only to app_B and att_B.
- T_{15}: att_A retrieves the tokens $s_A|c_B$ from the PBB, which indicates that the exchange has been cancelled.
- T_{16}: att_A returns access to I_A to its application: it sends key K_{attA} to app_A.
- T_{17}: app_A changes K_{attA} to K_{appA} (I_A's original key), which is known only to app_A and att_A. Alternatively, the application can use a fresh key that is known only to the application.

One of the important properties of this protocol is its strong timeliness, which means either participant can independently drive the exchange to completion at any time. Figure 14.2 shows

Alice's timeliness. However, note that the protocol assumes that the PBB is available (T_{14}) for token retrieval; to reduce the risk, the designer can incorporate replication of the PBB. A stronger assumption is that the S_B server is expected to be available (T_{17}) to Alice's app to change the password from K_{attB} to K_A; this risk is more difficult to minimize as the functionality of S_B is not under FEWD control.

14.1.3   *Failure of the attestables*

The Fairness of the protocol shown in Figure 14.1 is vulnerable to fail-stop failures that might impact the attestables. We will use Figure 14.4 to show the risk intervals when the exchange terminates in success.

As indicated by the green and red lines, the risk interval of the two attestables is similar. The green lines before T_5 and T_6 indicate that a failure of the attestable has no impact on the fairness of the protocol. The risk interval is marked with a red line and starts when

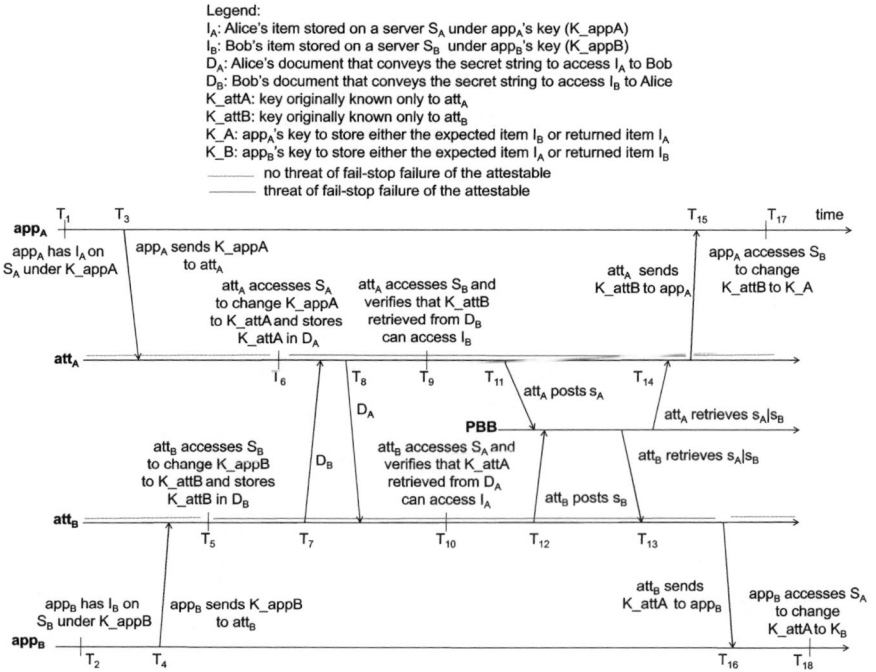

Fig. 14.4.   Threats of fail-stop failures in a successful exchange of unique items.

Bob's attestable and Alice's attestable gains exclusive access to the items, at points T_5 and T_6, respectively. During this interval a failure of Alice's attestable would result in the loss of the K_{attA} key and, therefore, of the means to access Alice's item (I_A) on the server S_A. Similarly, Bob is exposed to the risk of losing K_{attB} if his attestable fails.

As indicated by the green line, the risk interval ceases when the attestables send the keys K_{attB} and K_{attA} to their respective applications at points T_{15} and T_{16}. From then on, the applications are responsible for providing access to their items.

Fairness of the protocol shown in Figure 14.1 is vulnerable to fail-stop failures that might impact the attestables. We will use Figure 14.5 to show the risk intervals when the exchange is cancelled.

As shown in the figure, the risks for Alice (marked with green and red lines) are the same as in Figure 14.4. However, the risk intervals for the attestable that cancels the exchange (Bob's in the example of the figure) is slightly shorter since it does not need to retrieve sync tokens from the PBB.

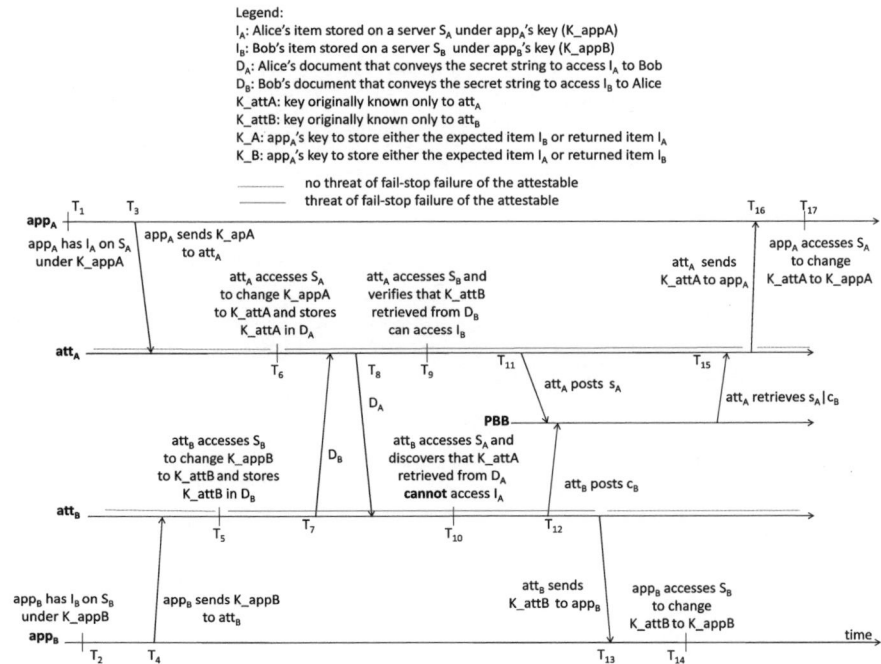

Fig. 14.5. Threats of fail-stop failures in an unsuccessful exchange of unique items.

14.2   Exchange of Copyable and Unique Items

The items exchanged in a FEP are not necessarily of the same class. In this section, we show the exchange of a unique item for a copyable one.

To illustrate the point, Figure 14.6 shows the documents created when exchanging a copyable item for a unique item. Alice creates copyable D_A as usual, and Bob creates a document D_B that includes his credentials to access his account on the server.

14.2.1   *Successful exchange of a copyable and unique item*

A development of events that leads to a successful exchange is shown in Figure 14.7. This protocol is a simplified version of the protocol shown in Figure 14.1 that results from the fact that Alice's item is copyable and as such it is located within Alice's applications rather than in a server.

The figure assumes that Alice and Bob have already agreed on the exchange: Alice is willing to give a copy of her item D_A; in return, Bob is willing to give his item I_B to Alice, which is located in a

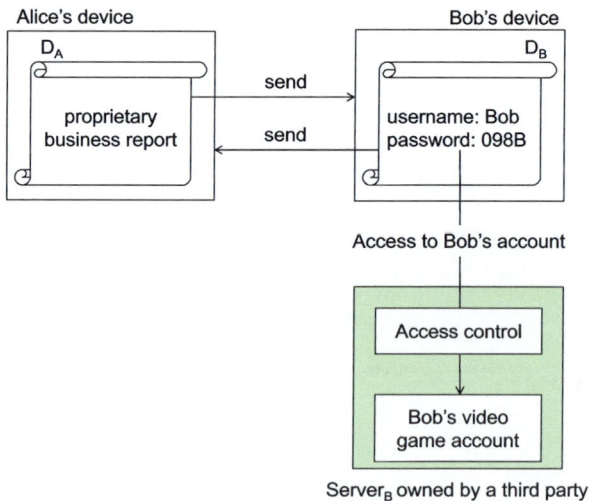

Fig. 14.6.   Example: Exchange of copyable D_A for unique D_B.

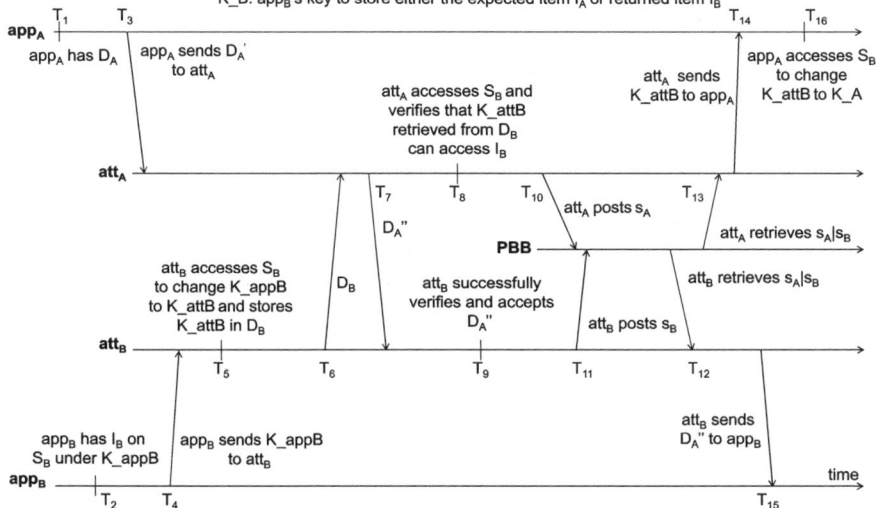

Legend:
D_A: Alice's copyable item; D_A': copy of D_A; D_A'': copy of D_A'
D_B: Bob's document that conveys the secret string to access I_B to Alice
I_B: Bob's item stored on a server S_B under app_B key (K_appB)
K_attB: key originally known only to att_B
K_A: app_A's key to store the expected item I_B
K_B: app_B's key to store either the expected item I_A or returned item I_B

Fig. 14.7. Successful exchange of a copyable and unique item.

server S_B. If the exchange succeeds, Alice will give to Bob a copy of D_A, and in return, Bob will reveal to Alice the secret string that grants access to I_B. Alice and Bob have already accepted each other's attestables, so that exchange of messages is not shown in the figure.

- T_1: Alice's application has Alice's copyable item D_A.
- T_2: On the other side, Bob has his unique item I_B stored on the server S_B under the key K_{appB}. The key is known to Bob's application.
- T_3: Alice's application provides Alice's attestable with a copy of D_A; it is shown as D_A'.
- T_4: Bob's application discloses key K_{appB} to Bob's attestable.
- T_5: Bob's attestable accesses server S_B, changes K_{appB} to key K_{attB}, and stores K_{attB} in D_B. K_{attB} is known only to Bob's attestable.
  - At this stage, only Bob's attestable knows the key to access I_B.
- T_6: Bob's attestable sends D_B to Alice's attestable.

- T_7: Alice's attestable makes a copy of D'_A (shown as D''_A) and sends it to Bob's attestable.
- T_8: Alice's attestable retrieves K_{attB} from D_B and accesses server S_B to verify that key K_{attB} grants access to I_B. This figure shows Alice's attestable is satisfied.
- T_9: On the other side, Bob's attestable att_B verifies D''_A to be certain that it is what Bob is expecting. This verification can be conducted with the assistance of function $desc()$ as explained in Chapter 13. Bob's attestable is satisfied.
- T_{10}: Alice's attestable posts its sync token s_A to the PBB.
- T_{11}: Bob's attestable posts its sync token s_B to the PBB.
- T_{12}: Bob's attestable retrieves sync tokens s_A and s_B from the PBB.
- T_{13}: Alice's attestable retrieves sync tokens s_A and s_B from the PBB.
- T_{14}: Having successfully retrieved the two sync tokens, Alice's attestable sends the key K_{attB} to Alice's application.
- T_{15}: Having successfully retrieved the two sync tokens, Bob's attestable sends D_A to Bob's application.
- T_{16}: Alice's application accesses server S_B to change K_{attB} to K_A, which is known only to Alice's application.

  o The exchange completes successfully at this point: Alice's application has gained exclusive access to I_B and Bob's application has a copy of D_A.

14.2.2 *Unsuccessful exchange of copyable and unique items*

The execution of the protocol shown in Figure 14.7 might be cancelled by either Alice or Bob. Figure 14.8 shows an example of an exchange cancelled by Bob.

Up to T_8 the exchange runs like shown in Figure 14.7, therefore, we exclude these steps from the discussion.

- T_9: Bob's attestable verifies D''_A to ensure it meets Alice's expectations. In this exchange, we assume that Bob's attestable is not satisfied and, therefore, it rejects D''_A.
- T_{10}: Alice's attestable posts its sync token s_A to the PBB.

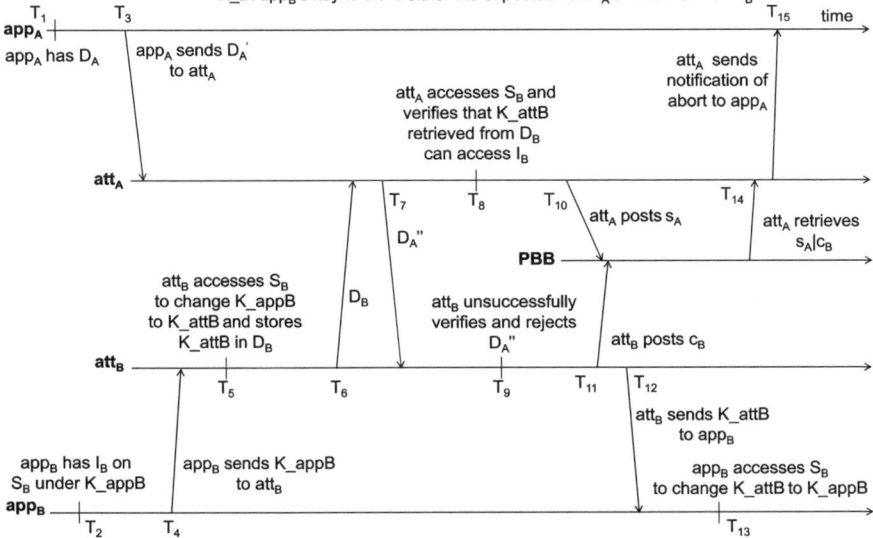

Legend:
D_A: Alice's copyable item; D_A': copy of D_A; D_A'': copy of D_A'
D_B: Bob's document that conveys the secret string to access I_B to Alice
I_B: Bob's item stored on a server S_B under app_B key (K_appB)
K_attB: key originally known only to att_B
K_A: app_A's key to store the expected item I_B
K_B: app_B's key to store either the expected item I_A or returned item I_B

Fig. 14.8. Unsuccessful exchange of copyable and unique items.

- T_{11}: Bob's attestable posts its cancellation token c_B to the PBB. This also indirectly notifies Alice's attestable that it is cancelling the exchange.

  ○ The remaining steps that Bob's attestable and Bob's application execute are aimed at returning access to I_B to Bob's application.

- T_{12}: Having rejected D_A'', Bob's attestable sends K_{attB} to Bob's application.
- T_{13}: Bob's application accesses server S_B to change K_{attB} back to K_{appB}.
- T_{14}: Alice's attestable accesses the PBB and retrieves s_A and c_B, indicating that Bob's attestable has cancelled the exchange.
- T_{15}: Alice's attestable sends a notification of the outcome to Alice's application.

  ○ Note that Alice's attestable did not send K_{attB} to her application, so she has no way to access I_B.

o The exchange is cancelled at this point: Alice's application has access to D_A; on the other side, Bob's application has access to I_B on server S_B.

14.2.3 *Failure of the attestables*

Fairness of the outcome of an exchange of a copyable item for a unique item can be impacted by fail-stop failures of the attestables. Figure 14.9 illustrates the risk intervals. The risk interval is asymmetric due to the asymmetry of the items. It is significantly shorter for the component that deals with the copyable item because its application always retains a copy of the item, therefore, a potential fail-stop failure of the attestable does not result in the loss of the copyable item.

As indicated by the green line of Figure 14.9, Alice's attestable, which deals with the copyable item, is risk-free until step T_{10}, where it

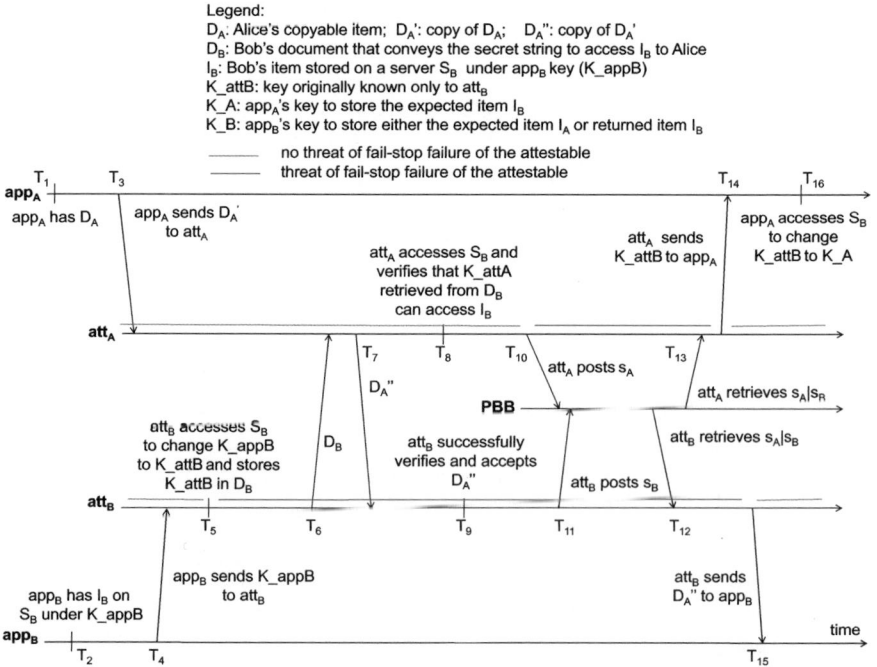

Fig. 14.9. Threats of fail-stop failures in a successful exchange of copyable and unique items.

posts its sync token s_A to the PBB. The risk starts at this point and ceases at point T_{14} where Alice's attestable, upon retrieving the two sync tokens, is enabled to send the key K_{attB} to Alice's application. This is indicated by the green line beyond T_{14}.

Potential failures that might afflict Bob's attestable before T_5 have no impact on the fairness of the exchange. This is indicated by the green line. The risk interval is marked with a red line and starts at T_5 when Bob's attestable accesses the server S_B to change the key that grants access to I_B. The risk ceases at step T_{15} where the attestable, after retrieving the two sync tokens, is enabled to send D_A'' to Bob's application. The green line beyond this point indicates that fairness is not impacted by fail-stop failures of Bob's attestable.

The risk intervals of the attestables when the exchange is cancelled by the attestable that deals with the unique item (D_B in this example) are shown in Figure 14.10.

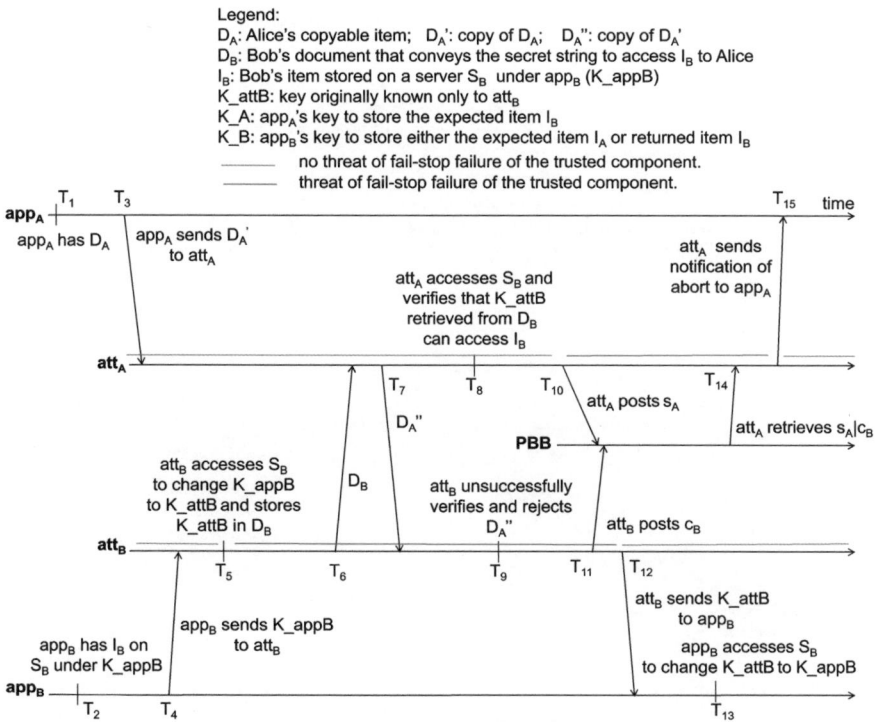

Fig. 14.10. Threats of fail-stop failures in a unsuccessful exchange of copyable and unique items.

14.3   Exchange of Digital Money for Copyable Item

Suppose Alice agrees to give Bob a secret, in exchange for Bob paying her with digital money.

Alice's secret string is a copyable item, and Bob's digital money is a unique item, therefore, Alice and Bob can use FEWD to conduct the exchange.

However, in this particular exchange, we can take advantage of the properties of digital money's architecture to simplify FEWD. In particular, we can use digital money's ledger as a PBB. The result is the protocol shown in Figure 14.11.

A challenge in this exchange is the transfer of Bob's digital money from Bob's address to Alice's address. Solving this by taking advantage of the immutable and public nature of the digital money transaction records can help simplify the resulting FEP. The execution of a digital money transaction is conceptually equivalent to posting a sync token on the PBB.

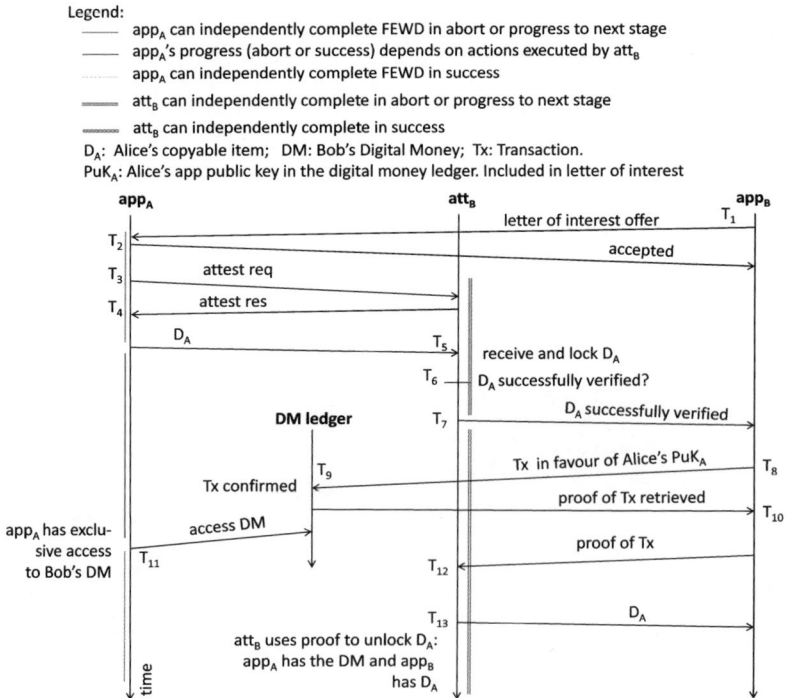

Fig. 14.11.   Successful exchange of a copyable item for digital money.

Similarly, the examination of digital money's ledger's proof structures, to learn about the status of a given transaction, is very similar to retrieving a sync token from the PBB. Regarding the properties of the documents under exchange, note that we are dealing with only a single secret string (D_A) that cannot be revealed to Bob's app unless the exchange completes in success; consequently, only Bob needs an attestable to lock D_A — Alice can run the entire exchange from her application.

14.3.1 *Successful exchange of a copyable item for digital money*

The protocol includes the following steps.

- T_1-T_2: Alice and Bob negotiate a letter of interest to take part in the exchange. The figure suggests that Alice and Bob rely on their applications to conduct the negotiation. However, the protocol makes no assumptions about what means and communication channels they use: Alice and Bob can negotiate over the email, phone, or face to face. The letter includes a handshake document with technical details, including the digital address where Alice wishes to receive Bob's digital money. The protocol assumes that the secret key for Alice's public key PuK_A is controlled by Alice's app.
- T_3-T_4: Alice's app requests and checks the attestation of att_B. The details of the procedure are explained in Chapter 13.
- T_5: Alice's app sends D_A to Bob's attestable, which locks it until Bob's application pays for it.
- T_6: Bob's attestable verifies D_A to ensure that it is the document that Bob is expecting. During the verify operation, Bob's attestable uses the V_A verifier extracted from the M_A certified verification module as explained in Chapter 13. In this diagram the verification is successful, so att_B continues with the execution.
- T_7: Bob's attestable notifies Bob's application of the outcome of the verification of D_A.
- T_8: Upon receiving a positive outcome from validation of D_A, Bob's application submits transaction Tx to the ledger to transfer Bob's digital money to Alice's app public key (PuK_A).
- T_9: Eventually, Tx is confirmed on the ledger.

- T_{10}: Bob's application examines the proofs from the ledger to determine whether Tx has been confirmed.
- T_{11}: Alice's application examines the proofs from the ledger to learn about the fate of Tx. The figure assumes that Alice's application discovers that it can access Bob's digital money. From this point onwards, Alice's application can continue its execution independently. The protocol makes no assumption about the procedure executed by Alice's application. For instance, it can examine the proofs from the ledger to verify that Tx has been confirmed.
- T_{12}: Bob's application presents Bob's attestable with a proof about Tx confirmation.
- T_{13}: Bob's attestable releases D_A to Bob's application.

  o The exchange completes successfully at this point: Alice's application is in possession of Bob's digital money and Bob's application is in possession of a copy of D_A.

14.3.2   *Cancelled exchange of digital money for a copyable item*

Figure 14.12 shows an exchange that completes in cancellation because Bob's app deliberately or accidentally fails to execute Tx. Up to T_7, this exchange follows the execution described in Figure 14.11.

- T_8: Bob's app fails (either deliberately or accidentally) to place a correct transaction Tx in the ledger to transfer Bob's digital money to Alice's application's public key (PuK_A).
- T_9: Bob's application cannot retrieve a proof that Tx succeeded. The figure shows an arrow from the ledger to Bob's application, as would occur in the case of an accidental failure. However, in practice, this may be an empty operation.
- T_{10}: Alice's application examines the proofs from the ledger to determine whether Tx completed successfully, but discovers that it cannot access Bob's digital money. Consequently, Alice's application is uncertain about the future of Tx: it does not know whether Bob's attestable has abandoned the exchange or it is accidentally or deliberately delaying the execution of Tx.
- T_{11}: Bob's application is unable to send a proof of confirmation of Tx to Bob's attestable.

Legend:
———— app_A can independently complete FEWD in abort or progress to next stage
———— app_A's progress (abort or success) depends on actions executed by att_B
———— att_B can independently complete in abort or progress to next stage
— — att_B can independently complete in abort
D_A: Alice's copyable item; DM: Bob's Digital Money; Tx: Transaction
PuK_A: Alice's app public key in the digital money ledger. Included in letter of interest.

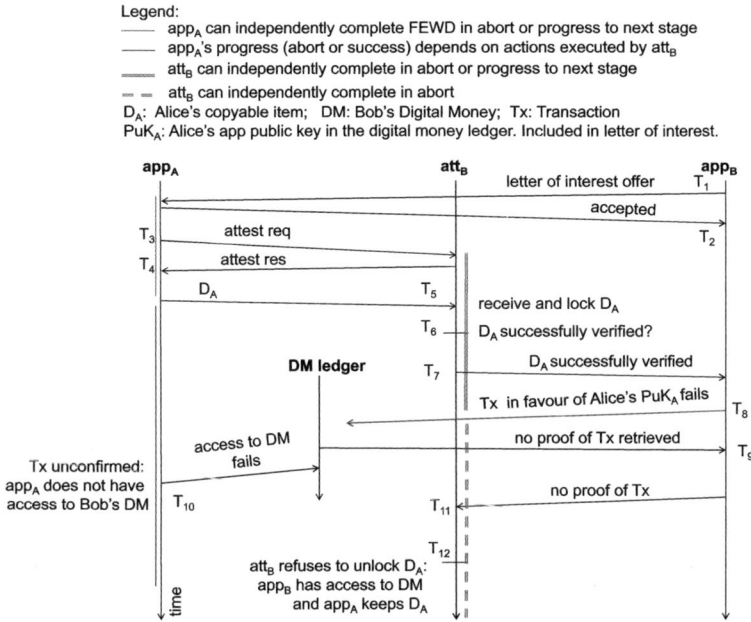

Fig. 14.12.   Cancelled exchange of a copyable item for digital money.

- T_{12}: Bob's attestable refuses to release D_A to Bob's application.

   ○ The exchange completes fairly at this point: Alice's application does not receive Bob's digital money and Bob's application does not receive D_A.

14.3.3   *Timeliness of a successful completion*

The green, blue, and red lines in Figure 14.11 mark the timeliness of the execution at different intervals when the exchange completes in success. Bob's attestable is guaranteed strong timeliness along its whole execution. Unfortunately, Alice's application is granted only weak timeliness.

Weak timeliness of Alice's application: Let us analyse the timeliness of Alice's application when the exchange completes in success (see Figure 14.11).

- $[T_1-T_5)$: The execution of Alice's application during the $[T_1-T_5)$ interval observes strong timeliness and as such it is marked with a green line. During this interval, Alice's application is able to complete the exchange independently (without further communication with Bob's attestable) by cancelling.

- $[T_5-T_{11})$: During the $[T_5-T_{11})$ interval, Alice's application observes only weak timeliness and as such it is marked with a red line. To complete the exchange either in success or cancel, Alice's application depends on the actions executed by Bob's attestable.

- T_{11}: For Alice's application, the execution of the protocol completes at T_{11}. At this point, it has Bob's digital money and can work independently. Accordingly, beyond T_{11} the execution line is marked with a blue line.

Strong timeliness of Bob's attestable

- $[T_3-T_{13}]$: Bob's attestable gets involved in the execution of the protocol at point T_3 and observes strong timeliness till its completion at point T_{13}, as shown in Figure 14.11. This interval divides naturally into two segments: $[T_3-T_8)$ and $[T_8-T_{13}]$.

- $[T_3-T_8)$: During this interval, Bob's attestable can independently (i.e., without further communication with Alice's application) complete the exchange by cancellation. This fact is emphasized by the thick green line. Until the digital money transaction is sent in T_8, Bob may choose to cancel the exchange without loss of fairness.

- $[T_8-T_{13}]$: During this interval, Bob's attestable can independently complete the exchange, either in success if Tx succeeds, or by cancelling if Tx fails. This fact is emphasized by the thick blue line. Note that during this interval, Bob's attestable depends on communication with Bob's application (see D_A *successfully verified* and *proof of Tx* arrows), which in turn depends on communication with the ledger.

14.3.4   *Timeliness during cancellation*

We now consider Figure 14.12. As before, the red and green lines mark the timeliness of the execution at different intervals when the exchange is cancelled.

Weak timeliness of Alice's application: Alice's timeline in Figure 14.12 proceeds identically to the previous example, until T_{10} is reached and the exchange is cancelled. After this point, Alice's application can consider the exchange cancelled, as the transfer is unable to take place and therefore Bob's attestable will not release D_A to him. It is important that the application does not cancel until the digital money transfer is impossible, otherwise Alice might miss the transfer, which would be an unfair result. The use of timeouts to mitigate this risk is discussed in Section 14.3.5.

Strong timeliness of Bob's attestable: Bob also proceeds as before, until step T_8, where the transaction fails. Nothing Bob does after that makes any difference, as indicated by the thick dashed green line. Once Bob discovers the transaction has failed, whether through step T_9 or because he knows T_8 was completed incorrectly, then he is free to skip steps T_{11} and T_{12} entirely.

14.3.5 *Timeouts*

To keep the protocol simple, we have not included timeouts in the descriptions of Figure 14.11 or 14.12. Consequently, there are no time constraints on Bob's attestable to complete the exchange. Though this approach does not compromise fairness, it introduces uncertainty on Alice's application's side as it has no means to know when Bob's application will execute Tx so that Alice's application has access to Bob's coin (T_{11} in Figure 14.11).

The interval between T_5 and T_8 can be arbitrarily long — it might take years, during which time Alice's D_A remains locked within Bob's attestable. If Bob cancels, for instance, by refusing to engage with the exchange after T_7, then consulting the ledger will not help Alice's application to determine the outcome of the exchange.

The absence of a time constraint on Bob's attestable might be an acceptable solution if D_A decreases in value over time. If D_A is expected to remain stable or increase in value, then this scenario is likely to be unacceptable to Alice (see Figure 17.11).

One solution is to impose a timeout on Bob's application for executing T_x. With this approach, Bob's attestable is programmed to release D_A only if the transaction T_x is executed by a certain time, say t_{out}. To prevent an unfair outcome where Alice's application has Bob's digital money and Alice's D_A is left locked inside Bob's attestable, the designer needs to set a generous timeout. It needs to be long enough to account for potential delays between T_8 and T_9.

Legend:
——————— no threats
——————— threat that att_B suffers a fail-stop failure

att$_B$ sends   app$_A$ verifies
letter of interest offer   access to Bob's bitcoin

T_1 T_{11} time

(a) Bob's application's vulnerability to fail-stop failures.

att$_B$ sends D_A successfully   att$_B$ releases
letter of interest offer   verified D_A to app$_B$

T_1 T_7 T_{13}

(b) Bob's attestable's vulnerability to fail-stop failures.

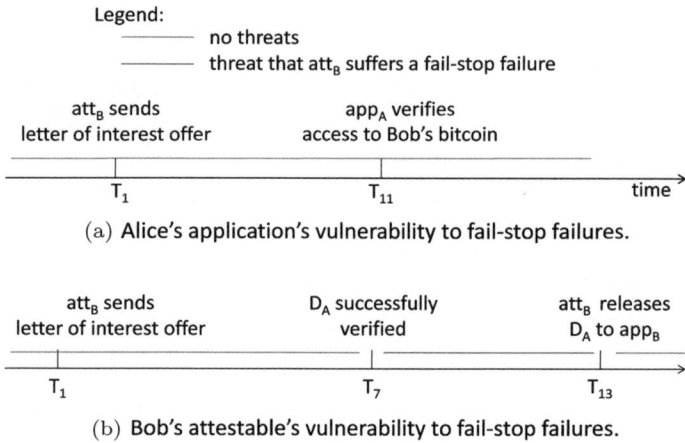

Fig. 14.13.   Threats of fail-stop failures under successful completion.

14.3.6   *Failure of the attestables*

The intervals where Alice's application and Bob's attestables are vulnerable to fail-stop failures are shown in Figure 14.13.

The green line along the whole timeline in Figure 14.13(a) indicates that Alice's application is not affected by fail-stop failures. This is because Alice's application does not store unique information.

In contrast, the green and red lines in Figure 14.13(b) show that Bob's attestable is not vulnerable to fail-stop failures in the $[T_1-T_7)$ interval. Neither is beyond T_{13} where it releases D_A to Alice's application. However, Bob's attestable is vulnerable (see red line) after it has successfully verified Alice's document (with the help of V_A verifier as discussed in Chapter 13). The reason is that after a successful verification, Bob's attestable proceeds to execute the Tx transaction in favour of Alice's PuK_A, in T_8. Since it has committed Bob's digital money, it needs to remain functional at least until it releases D_A to Bob's application.

Part 3
Real-world Fair Exchange

Chapter 15

Risk Analysis

There are a wide variety of risks that play into an exchange. In Part 1, we saw how certain strict technical risks are incorporated into the definition of strong fairness and weak fairness, and in Part 2, that framework was applied to various protocols, with sometimes surprising results.[1]

Over the next few chapters we consider additional risks that extend beyond the pure protocol level. This chapter is concerned with quantifying the participants' expectations, and examining the risks to those expectations being met. Specifically, we consider the risk of a false positive, for instance, where Alice believes she is getting one thing from Bob, but ends up with something unexpected and undesired.

In the following chapter, we look at the ways in which a legal system can benefit Alice and Bob by mitigating some of their risks in the case of an unfair exchange, and the ways in which it introduces new risks to exchanges that were otherwise fair. And in Chapter 17, we explore cases where the trust assumptions of attestable-based protocols are broken, by the crash or compromise of various components, as well as some risks and mitigation techniques that are specific to FEWD.

---

[1] Gradual release between rational actors with perfect knowledge rarely achieves marginal fairness, for instance.

15.1   False Positives

We define a **false positive** as a document that a verifier accepts, but which a human recipient would have chosen to reject.

The verifier acts as the recipient's agent, and is responsible for determining if the document meets the recipient's expectations. There are a variety of ways in which a false positive may be produced, which we have organized into six different categories of risk. These further fall into three distinct groups, depending on whether they originate with the input types, the verifier program, or an unexpected fault.

(1) **Input-type related risks**: These emerge from the types of the values that the verifier takes as input to verify a document. They can be separated into:

- **Risk due to known value changing**: To appreciate this issue, it might help to clarify that the verifier takes inputs of two types: inputs that never change their values and inputs that might change their values. The latter are problematic and sources of risk of false positives.

- **Risk due to unknown value introduced**: To appreciate this issue, it might help to separate the inputs that the verifier takes into two groups. In the first group fall inputs that are complete when the verifier is initially run. In the second group fall inputs that grow dynamically by means of appending new values to the tail of the existing ones as these new values become known. These inputs are modelled as dynamic data structures like lists and trees. The second group is problematic because a run of the verifier after the introduction of new values might reject a document that had been accepted in a previous run.

(2) **Verifier-related risks**: emerge due to the characteristics of the verifiers and the verification process and can be separated into:

- **Risk due to non-deterministic verification**: emerge from verification conducted under a non-deterministic process.

- **Risk due to probabilistic verification**: emerge from verification conducted under a probabilistic process where the actual verifier, or the gather function that gathers the values that the verifier takes as input, exhibits a probabilistic behaviour.

(3) **Fault-related risks**: emerge due to potential dormant faults that afflict the verifier, the execution environment that hosts the verifier, or both and can be separated into:

- **Risk due to a faulty verification module**: emerge from the use of a verifier with a dormant fault in its implementation.
- **Risk due to a faulty execution environment**: emerge from the use of an execution environment with a dormant fault that hosts the verifier.

These factors always represent a risk of getting a false positive. Therefore, it is convenient to offer the participants of a potential exchange a way of analyzing these risks for that particular exchange before they engage in it.

15.2   Static Analysis

The risk assessment described in Figure 15.1 is static in the sense that it is performed before committing to the exchange, based only on the information stipulated in the setup document (see Chapter 13). Note that the documents have not been transferred between attestables yet, so this analysis does not incorporate any information from D_A or D_B, and can be performed entirely by the application. The aim is to identify the risks to the fairness of this exchange before the participants commit to it.

We assume that to conduct the verify operation, Alice and Bob use certified verification modules (M_A and M_B, respectively) produced by trusted parties. We assume that the two modules are included in the setup document discussed in Chapter 13. We discuss the static analysis only from Alice's perspective, under the assumption that Bob executes a similar procedure on his side.

Note that the flowchart accounts for the six risk factors mentioned in Section 15.1. Diamonds 3 and 5 account for the first group, namely, type-related risks; likewise diamonds 7 and 9 deal with verifier-related risks, and diamonds 13 and 15 deal with fault-related risks.

Legend:
M_B: Certified module for verification of Bob's D_B. It is available from the setup document and includes V_B and T_B.
V_B: Verify function implemented for verifying D_B. It might produce false positives and false negatives. The former violate fairness, whereas the latter are harmless.
T_B: The list of types $t_1,...,t_n$ of the doc-values. The doc-values come from Bob's document (and potentially, the environment).

(1) start

(2)
M_B : import from setup document
V_B : import from M_B
T_B : import from M_B

(12) A

(3) Is any t_i in T_B mutable? — yes →
(4) Accumulate risk: V_B may produce false if run later, as the value of type t_i changes over time (known unknown).

(13) Is the implementation of M_B faulty? — yes →
(14) Accumulate risk: V_B might produce a false positive if a fault manifests in the implementation of M_B.

no

(5) Is any t_i in T_B appendable? — yes →
(6) Accumulate risk: V_B may produce false if run later, as the value of type t_i grows over time (unknown unknowns).

(15) Is the execution environment of M_B faulty? — yes →
(16) Accumulate risk: V_B might produce a false positive if a fault manifests in the execution environment of M_B.

no

(7) Verification non-deterministic? — yes →
(8) Accumulate risk: V_B might produce a false positive based on its internal process, independent of D_B.

(17) Any accumulated risk? — yes →
(18) Exchange has accumulated risk of false positives

no

(9) Is verification probabilistic? — yes →
(10) Accumulate risk: V_B will produce a false positive for a randomly selected D_B with probability p.

(19) Exchange has no risk of false positives

no

(11) A

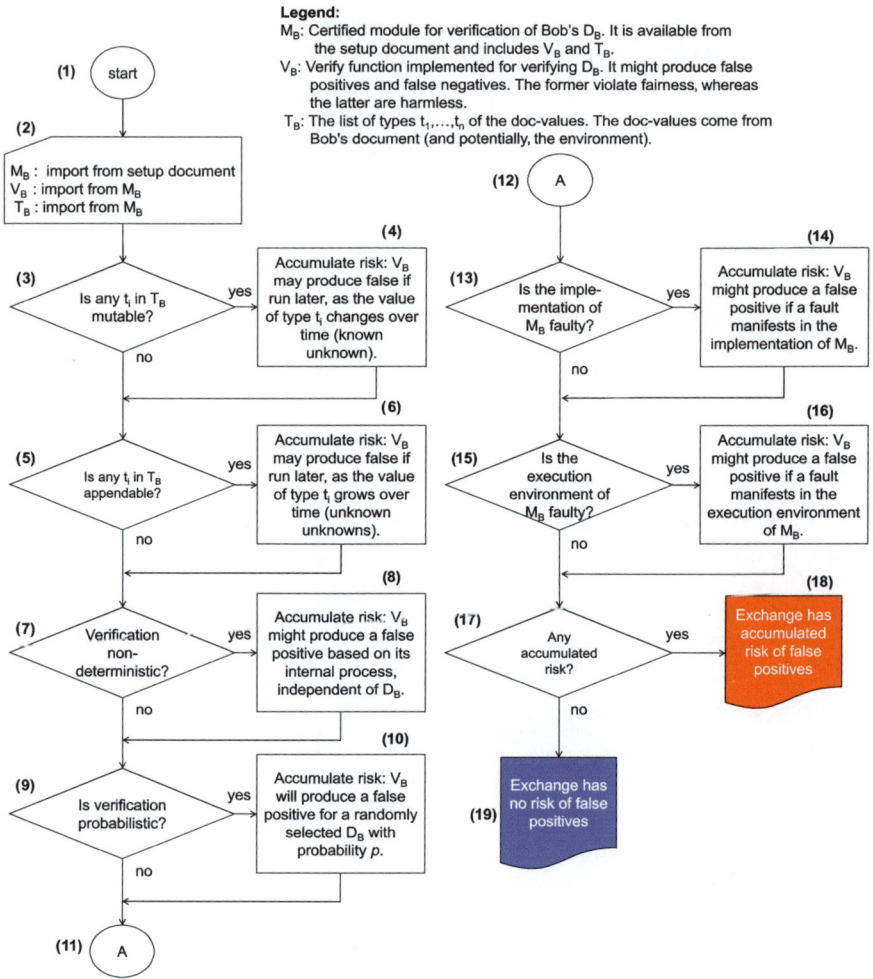

Fig. 15.1.   Static analysis of verifier false positives.

To determine the risk factors raised in diamonds 3, 5, 7, 9, and 13, the participants would need to examine the implementation of the verifier. In practice, it is likely that the party that certifies the verification module M_B is better qualified to perform this task. Therefore, we expect that they will include a risk analysis of the issues expressed in the diamonds 3, 5, 7, 9, and 13. The risk expressed in diamond 15 is of a different nature and is not under the control of the certification party or the participants. That risk can only be assessed by the manufacturers of the hardware and software components.

Ideally, participants should be presented with a rigorous quantification of the risks of all the diamonds, 3, 5, 7, 9, 13, and 17. Some risks are extremely hard to quantify however, in which case this information will not be easily available.

- **circle 1**: the start of the analysis conducted by Alice's application.
- **box 2**: the input that Alice's application uses in subsequent steps. It takes the verifier module M_B, which is assumed to be available from the setup document. The verifier function V_B and the list of types T_B are extracted from M_B.
- **diamond 3**: one or more of the types of the doc-values is mutable and changes in a manner that changes the verdict of V_B from accept to reject in a subsequent run.
- **box 4**: the accumulation of risk due to the existence of mutable types. As indicated in the box, the source of the risk is the existence of known unknowns in the sense that all the parameters that determine the acceptance or rejection of D_B are known, however, at verification time, the verifier does not know if they are going to change and how.
- **diamond 5**: one of the t_i types is an open list and as such includes values unknown when V_B is run by Alice the first time, which become known in a subsequent run.
- **box 6**: the accumulation of risk due to the inclusion of types that represent unknown values. As indicated in the box, the source of the risk is the existence of unknown unknowns in the sense that the verification process includes parameters whose existence is not known at verification time. If these unknown parameters become available in a subsequent run, the verifier might change its previous verdict from accept to reject.
- **diamond 7**: the verifier is non-deterministic.
- **box 8**: the accumulation of risk to Alice due to the use of a non-deterministic verifier. The presence of this box indicates that the implementer of the certified verification module M_B has taken the approach shown in Figure 15.2 to handle non-determinism. If he had taken the approach shown in Figure 15.3, this box would not be included and the risk would be to Bob of leaking sensitive data.

Legend:
D_B: Bob's document under verification. Received from att_B.
D^O_B: doc that result from the obfuscation of D_B.
obfuscate: a function that slightly alters D_B to conceal sensitive data.
V_B : the verification function that determines if D_B is accepted or rejected.
  It might produce a false positive due to no-determinism.

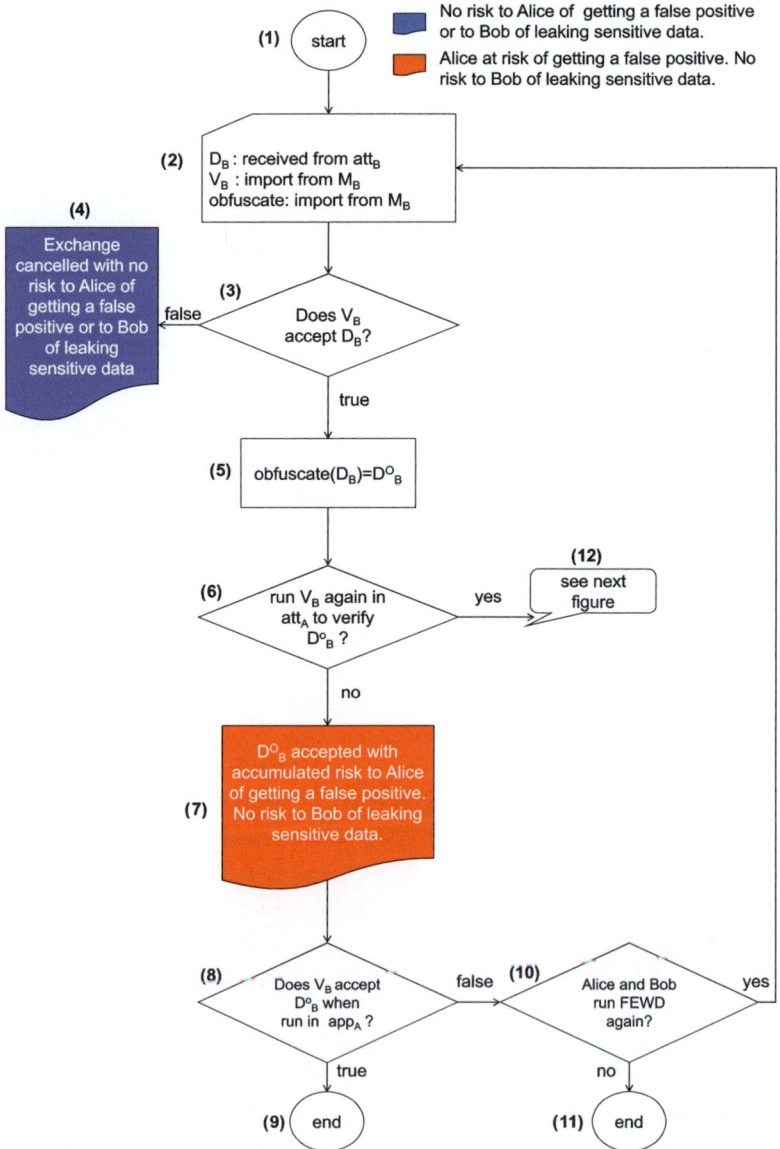

No risk to Alice of getting a false positive or to Bob of leaking sensitive data.

Alice at risk of getting a false positive. No risk to Bob of leaking sensitive data.

(1) start

(2) D_B : received from att_B
V_B : import from M_B
obfuscate: import from M_B

(4) Exchange cancelled with no risk to Alice of getting a false positive or to Bob of leaking sensitive data

(3) Does V_B accept D_B? false

true

(5) obfuscate(D_B)=D^O_B

(6) run V_B again in att_A to verify D^O_B ? yes

(12) see next figure

no

(7) D^O_B accepted with accumulated risk to Alice of getting a false positive. No risk to Bob of leaking sensitive data.

(8) Does V_B accept D^O_B when run in app_A? false

(10) Alice and Bob run FEWD again? yes

true

no

(9) end

(11) end

Fig. 15.2.   No re-run of V_B puts Alice at risk of getting a false positive.

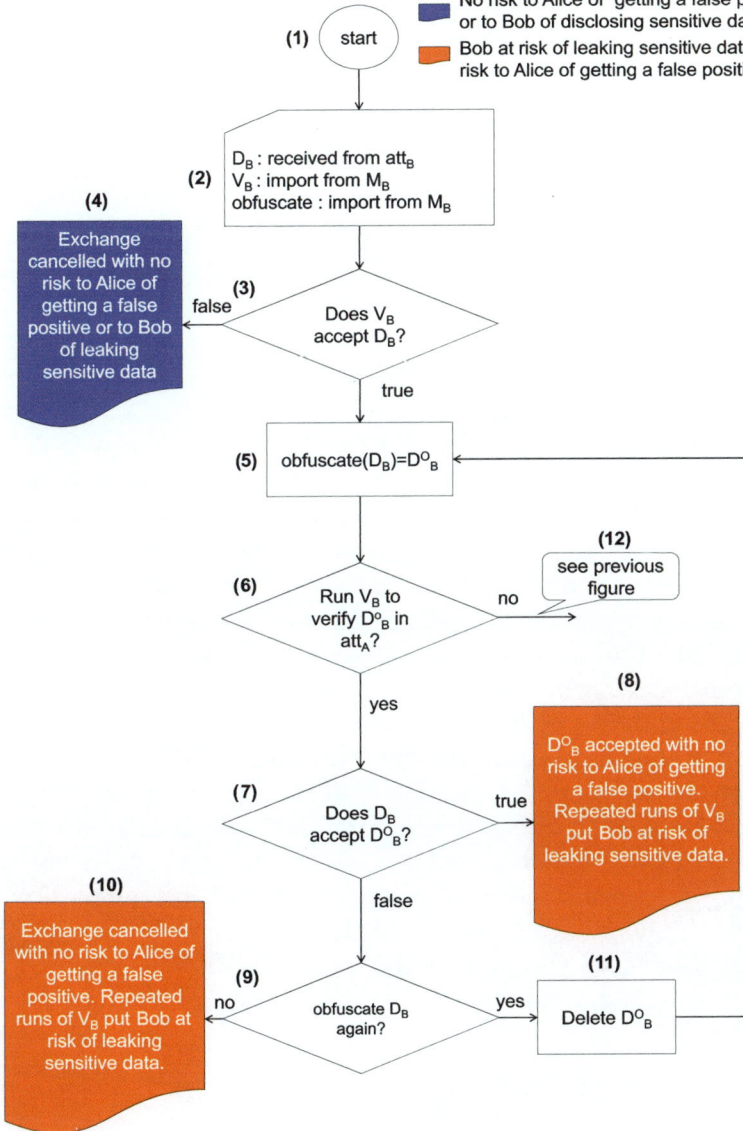

Legend:
D_B: Bob's document under verification. Received from att_B.
D^O_B: doc that result from the obfuscation of D_B.
obfuscate: a function that slightly alters D_B to conceal sensitive data.
V_B : the verification function that determines if D_B is accepted or rejected.
    It might produce a false positive due to no-determinism.

No risk to Alice of getting a false positive or to Bob of disclosing sensitive data.

Bob at risk of leaking sensitive data. No risk to Alice of getting a false positive.

(1) start

(2) D_B : received from att_B
V_B : import from M_B
obfuscate : import from M_B

(4) Exchange cancelled with no risk to Alice of getting a false positive or to Bob of leaking sensitive data

(3) false Does V_B accept D_B?

true

(5) obfuscate(D_B)=D^O_B

(12) see previous figure

(6) Run V_B to verify D^O_B in att_A? no

yes

(8) D^O_B accepted with no risk to Alice of getting a false positive. Repeated runs of V_B put Bob at risk of leaking sensitive data.

(7) Does D_B accept D^O_B? true

false

(10) Exchange cancelled with no risk to Alice of getting a false positive. Repeated runs of V_B put Bob at risk of leaking sensitive data.

(9) obfuscate D_B again? no

yes

(11) Delete D^O_B

Fig. 15.3.   Repetitive run of V_B puts Bob at risk of leaking sensitive data.

- **diamond 9**: the verifier is probabilistic.
- **box 10**: the accumulation of risk due to the use of a probabilistic verifier. The point here is that if the verifier exhibits a probabilistic behaviour, an accept verdict produced by a given run might change to reject in a subsequent run of the verifier.
- **circle 11**: a continuation of the flowchart in circle 12. It has nothing to do with the static analysis.
- **circle 12**: a continuation of the flowchart from circle 11. It has nothing to do with the static analysis.
- **diamond 13**: the implementation of the verifier is faulty and the fault manifests during the verify operation.
- **box 14**: the accumulation of risk due to the use of a faulty verifier. We assume that the fault is dormant and that it manifests unpredictably; consequently, there is a risk that an accept verdict produced by a given run might change to reject in a subsequent run due to the manifestation of the fault in either the first or second run.
- **diamond 15**: the implementation of the execution environment that hosts the verifier is faulty, and the fault manifests during the verify operation. In the execution environment, we include all the hardware and software components (with the exception of the actual verifier) such as the central processing unit (CPU), operating systems, libraries, and virtual machines.
- **box 16**: the accumulation of risk due to the use of a faulty execution environment. As in box 14, there is a risk that an accepted item might fail to meet the receiver's expectations.
- **box 17**: after conducting the static analysis, Alice is certain that the exchange has no risk of getting a false positive.
- **box 18**: after conducting the static analysis, Alice is aware that the exchange has accumulated risk of getting a false positive. The amount of the accumulated risk depends on the path taken from diamond 3 to diamond 17. The worst case scenario is that path that goes through all the boxes (4, 6, 8, 10, 14, and 16) on the on the diamonds.

15.3   Quantifying Risk

In the sections that follow, we analyse each of those six risk factors over four different parameters — quantifiability, malicious false positives, accidental false positives, and legal implications.

Table 15.1. Sources of risks of mismatched expectations.

	Quantifiable	Malicious False Positives	Accidental False Positives
Known value changing (Section 15.4)	yes	yes	yes
Unknown value introduced (Section 15.5)	no	yes	yes
Non-deterministic verification (Section 15.6)	yes	no	yes
Probabilistic verification (Section 15.7)	yes	yes	yes
Faulty verification module (Section 15.8)	no	yes	no
Faulty execution environment (Section 15.9)	no	yes	no

We define **quantifiability** as a measure (say in probability terms) that Alice will get a D_B that is a false positive, either accidentally or deliberately. Risk quantification is generally provided by the party that certifies the verification module.

Malicious false positives are possible when a participant can deliberately prepare a document that will cause a false positive.

Accidental false positives are possible if a valid document could be converted into a false positive during a post-processing phase, after being initially accepted.

Legal implications are also considered, if they exist and are relevant.

A brief summary of this analysis for the first three properties is shown in Table 15.1.

15.4 Risk: Known Value Changing

Mutable values consumed by the verifier may change after acceptance into a value that the verifier would reject. This risk is expressed by diamond 3 in Figure 15.1.

Suppose that Alice agrees to give something to Bob in return for a futures contract on oil. However, Alice wants to ensure that the value of the contract is above a certain threshold before accepting the exchange. The problem is that the value of the contract is subject to change quite rapidly, so there is a risk that the verifier V_B will accept Bob's contract, but would subsequently reject it if the value drops below the threshold.

Quantifiability: Yes. The provider of the certified verification modules can assess the risk in terms of the likelihood and impact of false positives.

Malicious false positives: Yes. If Bob is well informed about the oil market and is malicious, he can send Alice a contract that he knows will lose value.

Accidental false positives: Yes. Bob may accidentally harm Alice financially if he is not aware of the latest news about the oil market. This risk may also occur if G_B gathers outdated information or if the contract takes too long to be executed after the acceptance of Bob's contract by V_B.

Legal implications: If Bob sends Alice a contract when he knows that its value is about to drop based on inside information that is not publicly available, there may be grounds for a dispute, for instance, on the basis of Bob misleading or misrepresenting the value of the contract to Alice. If Bob made any assertions or promises about the stability of the value of the contract, there may also be grounds for a claim. However, it is possible that a dispute could arise if the contract or background information between the parties fails to convey that it is an accepted risk and that Bob is not liable for any fluctuations in the price.

15.5   Risk: Unknown Value Introduced

Documents often contain lists, trees, or other kinds of appendable values. Elements that are not present during the verify operation may have a significant impact when they become available. These appendable values introduce the risk of getting a false positive, as a value appended to an item after the verify operation accepts it might cause it to reject it if it were run again.

As an example, a "bitcoin" is a type of unique asset that can be blacklisted, for instance, by the United States Department of the Treasury. Suppose Alice receives some bitcoin from Bob as part of a fair exchange process. Alice ensures as part of the verify operation that the bitcoin she received is not blacklisted. However, this blacklist is updated regularly, and as such will be modelled as an open list in T_B. Accordingly, it is quite possible that the verifier V_B will initially accept, but would reject in a subsequent run executed after the update of the list.

Quantifiable: No. The level of risk cannot be quantified by the risk analyser because they are dealing with values that are not yet known.

Malicious false positive: Yes. The inclusion of open lists can be abused by Bob if he knows information about upcoming changes to the blacklist. Bob can deliberately send a bitcoin to Alice that he knows is likely to be blacklisted. A similar example of open lists is the certified authority (CA) certificate revocation list.

Accidental false positive: Yes. Bob can financially hurt Alice accidentally, by sending a bitcoin to her that later appears on the blacklist. Given the average latency of transactions on the Bitcoin blockchain, this may occur quite frequently.

Legal Implications: Where it is unintentional and in so far as it is a stipulated provision in the agreement and contract between Alice and Bob, namely, that the bitcoin is not blacklisted, but it turns out to be blacklisted, then the item would have not met the description agreed upon by Alice and Bob. If this is the case, then Bob has not fulfilled his obligation to ensure the bitcoin is not blacklisted. Therefore, it is likely that a dispute may arise and a claim could be brought by Alice against Bob for breach of contract on the basis that the item received by Alice does not meet a term of the contract. If, however, it is done intentionally, with full knowledge by Bob, this may give rise to other forms of disputes and potential liabilities on the grounds of fraud or misrepresentation, having mislead Alice regarding important information that is crucial to the status, and also the legality, of the exchange. Furthermore, there may be additional liability regarding the legality of the transaction itself — but that is another matter.

15.6 Risk: Non-deterministic Verification

In some situations, the documents exchanged over FEWD need to be post-processed after being accepted by the verifier and before they are released to the receiver.

If this post-processing procedure is entirely deterministic, it can be considered a standard part of the verify operation. Running it multiple times produces the same result, and causes no additional risks.

However, a non-deterministic post-processing procedure — for instance, one that introduces noise into a document to achieve a level of differential privacy — introduces a pair of related risks. Either the procedure is run exactly once, and the result accepted regardless of its outcome (despite potentially producing a false positive), or it may be run multiple times (despite potentially producing a low amount of privacy).

As an example, suppose D_B contains a medical survey that Alice wants to use for research purposes. Bob agrees to exchange D_B with Alice under the condition that what she receives is a version of D_B that achieves a sufficient amount of differential privacy to meet his needs and comply with current personal data protection regulations.

The issue is that the resulting obfuscated document D_B^o may be useless to Alice, because the added noise has pushed it outside of her verification parameters. Another way of saying this is that her verifier V_B accepted D_B, but rejects the obfuscated version D_B^o, which makes it a false positive. However, Bob has already paid the privacy cost of revealing D_B^o. Alice compensated Bob for this, but got nothing in return, yielding an unfair outcome.

The other option is that Alice's attestable could check D_B^o to ensure it passes the verifier before releasing it to her, and rerun the obfuscation procedure if it fails. However, this consumes additional privacy budget from Bob each time, and may result in substantially reducing his privacy and plausible deniability, perhaps below his comfort level or the level required by regulation.

So either Alice must accept the risk of a false positive in this exchange, or Bob accepts the risk of privacy loss. We consider each of these options in the subsequent subsections.

Quantifiable: Yes. It is possible to calculate the risk that the addition of noise to a valid document randomly selected from the expected distribution will cause it to fail verifier. It is also possible (though not trivial) to calculate the risk of rerunning the procedure and the resulting loss of privacy in a particular privacy model.

Malicious false positive: No. The non-determinism of the obfuscation process makes it difficult for Bob to select a D_B that passes V_B before obfuscation but fails it after.

Accidental false positive: Yes. Bob may send Alice a D_B that the verifier accepts before obfuscation (box 6) but which is altered substantially enough by the obfuscation procedure (box 5) that the resulting D_B^o is rejected by Alice's application (box 8).

However, the approach of Figure 15.3 eliminates this possibility because D_B^o is verified within Alice's attestable (box 6) before it is accepted by Alice (box 8) — though it trades off against Bob's loss of privacy, leading to potential legal implications.

Legal implications: It is unlikely that there is a risk for a claim to arise so long as the sender has met the obligations under the agreement regarding the items being exchanged and the execution of it. However, there may be possible liability under breaching data protection regulations, based on obligations faced by the receiver's organization, which reflect the possibility for a dispute and claims to be brought against the organization.

15.6.1 *Risk to Alice of false positive*

The steps included in the verify operation are shown in the flowchart of Figure 15.2. This approach puts Alice at risk of getting a false positive, but Bob is safe from exposing sensitive data.

(1) **box 2** required inputs are D_B, V_B and the *obfuscate* function.

(2) **diamond 3** shows the alternative results produced by V_B when executed against the version of D_B received from Bob's attestable. Note that the run takes place within Alice's attestable.

- **false**: D_B is rejected by V_B.
- **true**: D_B is accepted by V_B.

(3) **box 4** is in blue to show a safe output to Alice and to Bob because the exchange is cancelled: She is not at risk of getting a false positive and Bob is not at risk of leaking sensitive data.

(4) **box 5** D_B is obfuscated if it is accepted by V_B. The obfuscation procedure is executed within Alice's attestable att_A and produces D_B^o, the obfuscated version of D_B.

(5) **diamond 6** highlights diverging approaches — either D_B^o is verified by V_B within att_A before accepting it, or it is not. Here we assume that D_B^o is not verified before acceptance.

(6) **box 7** is in red to indicate the risk to Alice of getting a false positive, because D_B^o is not verified by V_B before it is released to Alice's application.

(7) **diamond 8** shows that from within her application, Alice executes V_B to verify whether D_B^o is accepted.

- **yes**: D_B^o is accepted by V_B.
- **no**: D_B^o is rejected by V_B.

(8) **circle 9** represents the ideal path for Alice where she has received a D_B^o that has been accepted by V_B.

(9) **diamond 11** Alice and Bob agree to re-initiate the exchange.

- **yes**: exchange is re-initiated and the verify operation re-initiated with no notion of the previous run.
- **no**: exchange is not re-initiated.

(10) **circle 11** Alice and Bob abandon the exchange.

Alice is taking a risk in this case: she knows that D_B passes her verification requirements, but the added noise might push D_B^o outside her requirements. In other words, D_B^o may fail if the verifier was applied directly to it. D_B^o would then be a false positive. See Figure 15.2, and in particular diamond 7 and box 8.

15.6.2   *Risk to Bob of leaking sensitive data*

In contrast to the previous example, this approach has Alice safe from getting a false positive, but it puts Bob at risk of the loss of privacy.

Using the earlier example of Alice purchasing an obfuscated version of D_B, a medical survey. Alice agrees to accept the obfuscated version of D_B from Bob, but only if D_B^o itself passes her verification requirements. This eliminates the risk of a false positive to Alice, because either D_B^o will pass her verifier or the exchange will be rejected.

However, it introduces a new risk, this time to Bob. Every time D_B^o is rejected by Alice's verifier, obfuscation routine needs to be run again, and fresh noise is added to D_B. This iterative process can burn up the privacy buffer and result in exposing Bob's personal information without providing him plausible deniability.

This is highlighted in Figure 15.3, where diamond 6 shows that Alice's attestable runs the verifier several times and the orange boxes 8 and 10 show the risk that Bob takes.

This figure shares many qualities with Figure 15.2. The differences are highlighted as follows.

(1) **diamond 6** D_B^o is verified by V_B within Alice's attestable (att_A).

(2) **box 7** shows the two potential outcomes produced by V_B after verifying D_B^o within att_A.

- **yes**: D_B^o is accepted by V_B.
- **no**: D_B^o is rejected by V_B.

(3) **box 8** is in orange to indicate that this is not an ideal path for Bob. Repetitive runs of V_B put him at risk of leaking sensitive data. The level of risk depends on the number of runs of V_B against different versions of D_B^o before finally a version is accepted by V_B. However, this path is safe for Alice; since D_B^o has been verified and accepted by V_B before releasing it, Alice is guaranteed that she is not getting a false positive.

(4) **diamond 9** repeating the obfuscation process produces a new version of D_B^o.

- **no**: The verify operation is abandoned.
- **yes**: A new version of D_B^o is produced to be verified by V_B.

(5) **box 10** is in orange to indicate that this is not an ideal path for Bob. Repetitive runs of V_B put him at risk of leaking sensitive data. The level of risk depends on the number of runs of V_B conducted against different versions of D_B^o before finally abandoning the exchange. However, this path is safe for Alice; since the exchange has been cancelled, she is not at risk of getting a false positive.

(6) **box 11** shows that the version of D_B^o that has failed verification is deleted. The verify operation is started with a fresh version produced in box 5.

15.7   Risk: Probabilistic Verification

We say that the verification is probabilistic when it produces false positives with a known probability. With a probabilistic verification, the probability p that a document D_B that has been accepted by the verifier V_B in one run will be rejected in a subsequent run is known.

Let us consider an exchange where Bob is expected to send a prime number to Alice. There are several applications where prime numbers are used, for example, it might be a component used to generate a cryptographic key. The number is accepted by the verifier only if the number satisfies a test of primality, for example, a statistical primality check. These tests have some small probability of producing a false positive, where a composite number is labeled as a prime in a given run.

Quantifiable: Yes. Alice can quantify the chance of receiving a false positive from some random distribution of items. Note, though, that Bob may discover an item that always produces a false positive for that verifier, or a whole family of items, depending on the nature of the verifier. Note that if Bob's attestable chooses the item, Alice may be much more assured of receiving an item that matches her expectations.

Malicious false positives: Yes. Bob can find a composite number that passes Alice's primality checker, and send it to her maliciously, generating a false positive.

Accidental false positives: Yes. Bob's primality checker may also erroneously declare a composite number to be prime — he may in fact be using the same checker that Alice is, leading to them both being duped by the false positive.[2]

Legal implications: In so far as the terms of the contract and agreement between Alice and Bob are clear with regard to the description of the item, should the item not meet it, then a claim is possible of arising for breach of contract.

---

[2]This makes it hard to determine whether Bob sent the composite number accidentally or intentionally. One way to tell is if he reuses that same composite number in other exchanges.

This is particularly clear where it is done by Bob intentionally, thereby constituting misleading and possibly fraudulent behaviour. Nonetheless, where it is unintentional or negligent, insofar as the terms of the contract and agreement are breached, then a claim may arise. Some difficulties may arise with regard to timing but also the dependence of the parties on the verifier. For example, if for whatever reason Alice and Bob include in their agreement that whatever the verifier approves they will adhere to, then it would not be possible to bring a claim *ex post* verification by the verifier. Nonetheless, the parties would be well advised to clarify in the setup document that the verifier serves specifically the role of automating the process and in no way attests to the meeting of certain contractual provisions relating to the characteristics of the item as having been met due to a defect. There may also be further issues of product liability regarding the provider or manufacturer of the verifier if it is an unexpected malfunction, or for example, where either Alice or Bob recommends its use knowing full well of its deficiency.

15.8 Risk: Faulty Verification Module

We account for the possibility that one of the components (the V_B verifier or the G_B gather function) of the certified verification module M_B suffers from dormant faults that can be maliciously or accidentally triggered by Bob's document during the verify operation.

We assume that the fault is embedded in the implementation (code) of the verifier or the gather function. To isolate the fault, let us assume that the execution environment that hosts V_B and G_B is fault-free.

As an example, suppose that Alice is expecting a picture of a cat from Bob. Alice's verifier could be maliciously abused by Bob through, for instance, a zero-day attack. A zero-day attack is a cyberattack that takes advantage of security vulnerabilities that have not been disclosed to the public yet (Bilge and Dumitras, 2013). If Bob is aware of a fault in the verifier that would cause it to accept a picture of a dog, then he can maliciously send Alice a picture of a dog. This is clearly quite a troubling outcome.

Quantifiable: No. It is hard, or perhaps impossible, to completely quantify how many bugs or exploitable faults are in the verification module. It is also difficult to quantify how likely they are to be discovered and accidentally or intentionally exploited. Verifiable software techniques are useful here, but there are limits to their application and their applicability.

Malicious false positive: Yes. A fault in the verifier could be discovered and maliciously exploited in order to cause a false positive.

Accidental false positive: No. If Bob sends Alice a document that a correct verifier would verify, then a faulty verifier cannot produce a false positive, though it might reject the document unfairly.

Legal implications: In so far as Bob sends an item that does not meet the description of the item in the agreement and setup document between Alice and Bob, then it is likely there will be a claim for breach of contract, and particularly so when it is intentional on the part of Bob.

15.9   Risk: Faulty Execution Environment

We account for the possibility that the execution environment where the certified verification module M_B runs suffers from dormant faults. By execution environment, we mean the hardware and software involved in the execution of M_B, including the operating systems, libraries, and virtual machines. To isolate the fault, let us assume that the implementation of M_B is fault-free, say, because its correctness has been formally validated and thoroughly tested.

As before, we assume that the fault manifests erratically, and that it causes the verifier to accept a document that otherwise would be rejected.

Let us revisit the example that we have used to illustrate the risk of using faulty verifiers. The risk here is the same, except that the source of the risk is the execution environment, rather than the verifier.

Quantifiable: No. The risk is not quantifiable because it is hard for the analyser to quantify how many dormant faults are embedded in the execution environment that will host M_B. Consequently, it is hard to quantify how many of these faults are likely to be accidentally triggered by Bob's document when V_B and G_B are retrieved from M_B and run. It is also hard to quantify how many of these faults will be familiar to Bob and enable him to maliciously select a document that triggers the fault and causes V_B to accept his document.

Malicious false positive: Yes. Dormant faults that afflict the execution environment could be maliciously exploited by Bob to cause the verifier to accept a false positive.

Accidental false positive: No. If Bob sends Alice a document that a correct verifier would verify, then a faulty verifier cannot produce a false positive.

Legal implications: If Bob sends an item that does not meet its description in the setup document (an agreement between the parties), then it is likely that there will be a claim. This is particularly clear where it is intentional on the part of Bob due to malicious behaviour on his part.

Chapter 16

Legal Considerations

In this chapter, we study a number of different legal issues that emerge in attestable-based fair exchange protocols (FEPs), and in particular FEWD. We do this by covering a number of areas of interest for practical applications of attestable-based FEPs. We focus on whether and to what extent they can accommodate the execution of contracts, and more importantly, whether the principles of contract under English law can apply to the use of attestable-based FEPs.

16.1 Records and Evidence

One more obvious consideration is whether FEP may act as a record of information that can be used as a definite and trusted source of information by users. Put differently, whether actions such as transactions in the form of information that has been compiled in or through the protocol or on the basis of it can be stored on it or through it. We argue that this is possible.

A second strand to this same question is whether, under English common law and potentially other legal regimes such as other common and civil law jurisdictions, information compiled and or stored by or through FEPs can be admitted and used in legal proceedings, as evidence of the rights and obligations relating to items being exchanged or transferred by means of the FEP. We argue that this is possible in certain instances and have not found any reasons for why it would not be possible.

A separate matter of concern is whether FEPs are capable of effecting the transfer of ownership of certain items, or behaving as a recognized register. There is no reason why it would be a legal register for any particular asset when it comes to transfer of title if it is not designated as such. Of course, it could theoretically be possible for a FEP to be connected to some central or distributed register that is legally recognized as a legal register for the purposes of recording transfer of title and ownership of some asset.

For those asset classes that do not require a special mechanism for transfer of title and ownership, or interaction with a specialized legal register that is not linked to the FEP being used, it is certainly plausible for attestable-based FEPs to effect the transfer of possession and ownership of an item from one party to another party, given that it can effect things like the ability to access certain items, and the possession of other items, both of which, when it comes to certain items, designates ownership.

For example, in the case of those items that are copyable including such items as images, contracts, and information, possession and ownership would be transferred between Alice and Bob in so far as it is possible to designate that what has been transferred is what has been received (it can be difficult to show if an item isn't especially unique). The same is true outside of only copyable items, for example, where Alice is exchanging digital money for Bob's digital map.

16.2   Disputes

A dispute is a problem or issue between two or more parties. The disputes of interest to us here are problems or issues that arise from the exchange of items where there is something wrong to do with the exchange of items and where one party wishes to seek recourse, whether legally through the court system, or by way of some third party to resolve the dispute relating to the exchange of items.

For the purposes of this particular section, 'disputes' refers specifically to those types of disagreements that relate to the non-performance by one party or incorrect performance of their obligations to another party. For example, the item not meeting its description.

Attestable-based FEPs are specifically geared to reducing, if not eliminating, non-performance disputes. They achieve this by alleviating reliance on a trusted third party (TTP) or an escrow service that depending on the specific protocol, is involved from the start to completion of the protocol or only when it is requested by an offended participant to resolve disputes. Thus, authentication of the item, exchange, and delivery, can all take place and be guaranteed without either party missing out. This is discussed in Chapter 9.

A correctly implemented attestable-based FEP can guarantee that non-performance disputes will never arise unless the trust assumptions of the protocol are violated such as the security of its cryptographic keys.

However, there are disputes that attestable-based protocols cannot prevent. For example, after a successful completion of the protocols, there remains the possibility for disputes to arise on the basis that an item, whose description was verified by the receiving party's attestable to match the description included in the handshake document, do not meet the expectations of the recipient.

Nevertheless, it would be possible and it would be necessary for there to be recourse by the party that has been wronged, for example, by being misled, or if the item had been misrepresented. The same is true in instances where an item that is being exchanged has an illegal provenance, for example, it had been stolen. Whether or not that recourse can be actualized is a separate matter.

16.2.1 *Types of disputes*

Disputes and dispute resolution broadly construed contain within them several presuppositions. Namely, that there is an activity of some sort that has occurred between Alice and Bob, or more participants engaged in some activity with one another. Broadly construed, what has been lacking from the study of FEPs is a clear establishment of the meaning of dispute and dispute resolution.

For example, within the activity engaged in between Alice and Bob, a dispute may arise for a variety of reasons, it may be that Alice, or Bob, has not done that which they have promised and consequently agreed to do. Alternatively, it may be that there has been some deceit at play in the actions or behaviours of either Alice or Bob.

The dispute that arises may be criminal or civil in nature, and it may have been intentional or unintentional.

Notwithstanding this bare and predominantly legal initial categorization, FEPs have inherent within them an important objective, namely, to reduce to the degree possible the likelihood for disputes to arise and thus render the necessity for dispute resolution to be otiose towards the successful or unsuccessful completion of the exchange.

This final point is critical and illuminating because, as far as we are aware, in discussions of FEPs, disputes are referenced in large brush strokes, which in reality encompass a wide variety of types of disputes. Yet, optimistic FEPs seek to accomplish one major thing, namely, bringing the dispute resolution mechanism, whose aim is to resolve the dispute between the parties conclusively and fairly, into the system and exchange, such that it is mechanically resolved between the parties swiftly, without necessity to seek dispute resolution mechanisms that exist outside of the system within which the parties interact. In doing so, the very operation activity of exchanging digital items can be decentralized without reliance on a third party.

This, however, does not refer to the type of disputes to which it is applicable. Optimistic FEPs refer to a particular type of dispute, that being disputes arising from the breach of contracts because of the non-performance of one of the parties. In so doing, one of the parties has not adhered to the terms of the exchange, either through delivery of the item exchanged or its description, such as quantum (amount) or type, each of which are depicted at the outset of the exchange between the parties.

An important goal of attestable-based FEPs such as FEWD is to eliminate the possibility for disputes that arise from breaches of the agreement or contract between the parties due to non-performance on the basis of either; (a) failed delivery and exchange; (b) quantum (e.g., amount of the item or payment amount for the item); and (c) the type and description of the item. In doing this, FEWD intends to eliminate said types of disputes. Unlike optimistic FEPs that, instead, account for the occurrence of disputes and seek to resolve them efficiently when they occur.

However, there exist caveats. For example, insofar as the software employed by the attestable, as we shall see, is capable of accurately identifying and verifying the item, the disputes we have referenced can, in principle, be eliminated. There will, however, be instances where they cannot, due to the nature of the item and the software that prevents their appropriate verification by the software. This is further explored in Chapter 15.

The types of disputes to which optimistic FEPs and FEWD do not apply includes those disputes that arise from such things as fraud, misrepresentation, and theft, the basis of which is the intention of one of the parties to engage in the exchange to take advantage of the other party. This falls outside of the intended objectives of the implementation of FEPs, including FEWD.

16.2.2 *Disputes eliminated by attestable-based FEPs*

Attestable-based FEPs seek to eliminate a certain set of disputes that arise in the context of the exchange of goods between parties. Most other protocols seek to reduce as opposed to eliminate disputes of a particular kind, whereas attestable-based FEPs are able to largely eliminate them.

The disputes in question are those fundamental terms of a contract that in the present case relate to the timing of delivery of the exchange and the properties and description of the items being exchanged that are central to the exchange taking place, to the extent that those properties are capable of being verified by the validation program, and it is those properties that had been stipulated in the handshake document. There is confidence by the parties that the validation program will run as intended and that the program will validate the properties of the items that the parties deem to be important. This characteristic of attestable-based FEPs leads to strong fairness of ownership, the validation of the properties ensures, to a degree technically capable, that the parties receive what they want, and that the parties may both conclude the exchange with a fair outcome.

In principle, so long as the properties are adequately stipulated between the parties, and the validation program can run as intended to verify said properties, then the fundamental terms to the contract will not give rise to disputes. This is because it will not be possible for disputes to arise in relation to the timing of delivery or the description of the item given the nature of attestable-based FEPs for it to be completed successfully on the basis of both the timing of completion as well as the validation of the properties of the item taking place within the protocol.

16.2.3   *Disputes not eliminated by attestable-based FEPs*

However, as discussed in Chapter 15, there is a set of potential disputes that may arise in the exchange of goods between two parties that cannot be eliminated by attestable-based FEPs. See summary of Table 15.1 and Figure 15.1.

To recap, an attestable-based FEP might fail to produce a fair outcome because of two reasons:

- **Faulty verifier**: the programs that execute the verify operations against the items suffer from faults.
- **Missing information**: the verifier is not provided with the properties to verify or with complete information to determine correctly if the items meet the expected properties.

Regarding the verification program, it may itself be faulty, and can be exploited intentionally, for example, by knowingly proceeding with a faulty validation program that produces a bug when verifying a particular property as something else, otherwise it may be due to the negligence of the party in question who should have known and it was expected for a reasonable person to have identified and thereby avoided the receipt of an item that, though the properties had been verified, it is not the item expected or described in the handshake document due to the validation program not performing as expected.

Regarding missing information, disputes may arise because one or more properties are not provided to the verifier. For example, the information required to successfully verify a property is inaccessible, such as where access to a particular database is required. There may also be properties that are provided to the verifier program but the information about the property of the item is stale. Lastly, there is also the important potential for disputes where the property of the item is simply not present at the time of the verify operation, such that the property could not be appropriately verified, such as where properties emerge in the future that are causally related to the nature of the item in question at the time of exchange, or alternatively where it is not causally related. If it were causally related, then it would also give rise to the possibility that this was intentional exploitation by the party, alternatively it may have been negligence or otherwise a mistake by the parties.

16.2.4 *Protection and dependencies eliminate disputes*

A natural question to ask is what kind of disputes can be eliminated from FEPs and what dependencies the protocol needs to satisfy. In general, we argue technology can help substantially but cannot solve the problem alone. To be effective, a technology solution would need to be reinforced by the legal system in place. Table 16.1 summarizes our understanding of the problem.

The first column of the table includes three different types of disputes: non-performance, late-delivery (delayed performance), and wrong item. Observe that each type of dispute can be eliminated with different legal and computational protections and depends (relies) on the availability of different computational mechanisms. In this order, to eliminate non-performance disputes the participants need to be protected by the legal system through a contract that clearly

Table 16.1. Dependencies that prevent the occurrence of different types of disputes.

Legal Dispute	Legal Protection	Computational Protection	Computational Dependencies	Description of Problem
Non-performance	Contractually clear roles	Strong fairness (protocol)	Uncompromised attestable or trusted third party (TTP)	Only one party receives the other's item
Late delivery (delayed performance)	Contractually clear exchange conditions	Strong timeliness (protocol)	Reliably available public bulletin board	Some party cannot complete the exchange at some time
Wrong item	Contractually clear item description	Strong verifiability (item)	Static analysis of verifiability has no accumulated risk	The recipient's expectations are not met

stipulates the roles (the privileges and responsibilities) of each participant. For example, the contract needs to stipulate what party will play the role of the initiator and of the responder, and who is entitled to cancel the execution of the protocol and at which point of the execution. Similarly, as stated in the third column, the participants need to conduct the exchange under the protection of a strong FEP (see Figure 8.1). With this protection in place, the occurrence or non occurrence of non-performance disputes depends on the correct functionality of the component that is responsible for executing the synchronize operation (the most crucial operation in a FEP), namely, the TTP or the attestables. The former is central to an escrow-based protocol, while the latter are central to attestable protocols.

16.3   Legal Rights and Obligations

An important consideration for the use of FEPs is that they are able to give rise to legal rights and obligations. Therefore, there is a connection and linkage between them and the legal system. For example, we can take attestable-based FEPs and ask whether and how their executions are able to give rise to binding legal obligations by creating a contract between parties that is enforceable as such in accordance with the terms of that contract. Other FEPs, such as escrow–based, raise the same question.

To appreciate the question, we must first understand the principles that give rise to such rights and obligations when it comes to contractual formation.

For a valid contract to be formed under English common law (which is broadly similar to some other common law jurisdictions), the requirements are as follows:

(1) offer;
(2) acceptance;
(3) consideration; and
(4) intention to form legal relations.

In our view it is certainly possible for the actions of parties (Alice and Bob) using an implementation of attestable-based FEPs to be capable of meeting these requirements. In fact, the protocols may lend themselves quite well to meeting these requirements, making it at least possible for contractual relations to be formed on the basis of using an attestable-based FEP that would give rise to binding legal rights and obligations if the requirements (1)–(4) have been clearly met.

Our analysis is to clarify the potential interpretation of the steps within the protocol as it relates to each of the parties and the requirements for the formation of contractual relations, in particular, by expounding what precisely is happening in each of the steps within the protocol. Moreover, we endeavour to highlight some of the differences that are important to highlight to help clarify how certain steps and actions within the protocol should be viewed and analysed from a legal standpoint for greater clarity of their legal implications. Of course, the analysis is only analysis and it will ultimately be a court and a judge that would conclusively apply the principles and make a finding. To rightly identify where and how legal rights and obligations may arise, we will discuss a variety of considerations that should be taken into account when considering the legal implications of FEPs.

We open the discussion with an analysis of the legal implications involved in a escrow-based FEP — the most common protocol used in current online business. Figure 16.1 presents an overview. It shows the relationship between the execution of the five basic operations (handshake, deposit, verify, synchronize and release) of FEPs and the four stages of contract formation required by the common law.

- T_1, T_2: The handshake document represents the letter of interest. It is negotiated by Alice's and Bob's applications (app_A and app_B, respectively) with the assistance of the escrow service in $T_1 - T_2$. Depending on the item, the escrow service acts as a custodian of sorts, and, depending on the item, may have legal or beneficial ownership or possession of the item in question, it may even be holding it on trust for another party in some instances.
- T_3, T_4: Alice and Bob deposit their respective items with the escrow service.
- T_5, T_6: The escrow service verifies Alice's and Bob's considerations.

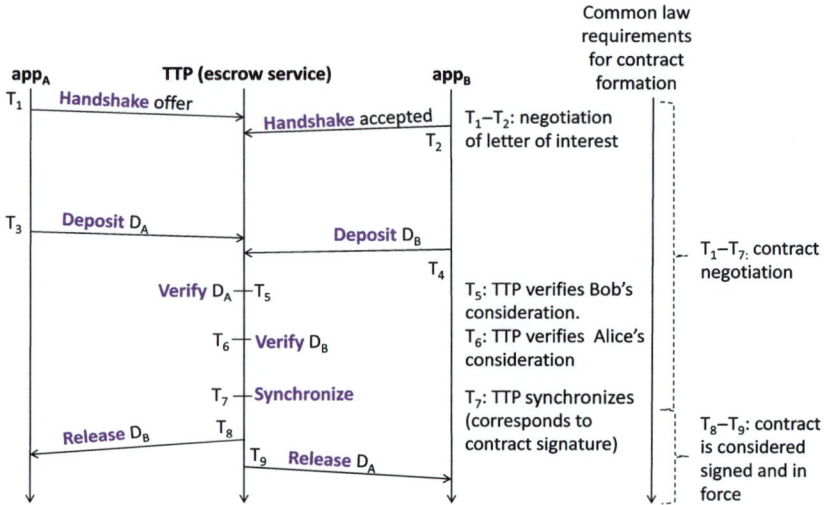

Fig. 16.1.   Legal implications of basic operations executed in an escrow service.

- T_7: If the escrow service determines that the two items satisfy the verification, it declares the exchange synchronized, which in legal concepts corresponds to contract signature. After $[T_7]$, the contract is considered signed and Alice and Bob, legally bound to the terms and conditions stipulated in the handshake document.
- T_8, T_9: The escrow service releases the documents to their new owners: D_B to Alice and D_A to Bob. The actions executed in T_8, T_9 represent the execution of the contract, and in this model, such execution is under the direct control of the escrow service. After T_9, the contract is declared fulfilled and terminated by the escrow service.

The right-hand side of the figure shows that within the common law the operations executed in T_1–T_7 would be regarded as part of the negotiation of the exchange. Also, since the contract is signed in T_7, the contracts would be considered signed and in force in T_8, T_9 and fulfilled and terminated upon the release of the last item to its new owner, in this example, upon the release of D_A to Bob.

The model shown in Figure 16.1 is widely used in current online business when it comes to ecommerce. Online shops implement it with their own small variations and simplifications, but conceptually it is the same. One example of an escrow service is where Alice, as buyer, offers (T_1) items, for example, pairs of trainers of different prices, colours, sizes, etc. Imagine that Bob, as buyer, accepts and offers (T_2). Bob uses the online application to put the trainers in their basket (T_3). Bob deposits his money (T_4) with a payment service to pay for the trainers. The ecommerce site/marketplace verifies that the trainers and payment match the offer and acceptance (T_6 and T_7). If everything is in order, the ecommerce site/marketplace approves the transfer of the payment to Alice and the delivery of the trainers to Bob, T_8 and T_9, respectively.

While the following section will look specifically at different potential implementations of FEWD (an attestable-based FEP), the underlying principles can be applied to all attestable-based FEPs. We open the discussion with Figure 16.2, which provides an overview of the legal implications of the basic operations of attestable-based FEPs.

16.4 Phases

Figure 16.2 shows the timeline execution of FEWD, which is divided into three phases: Phase I: pre-contract, Phase II: contractual formation, and Phase III: post-agreement. For simplicity, we have relabelled those three phases as follows, along with the afforded actions included within each segment, and the possible legal implications of each. Moreover, we assume that the exchange will be online.

16.4.1 *Phase I: Pre-contract*

This phase includes all actions executed between the parties, Alice and Bob, before the formation of a contract. In Figure 16.2, this phase refers to T_1-T_9. Moreover, T_1-T_9 will provide contextual and circumstantial evidence in support of the formation of a contract between the parties and be of relevance for such a determination.

Phase I is primarily concerned with three main elements:

(1) **Setup document** T_1-T_2: The first element is the creation of the setup document (also called letter of intent) between the parties. The aim of this stage is that Bob and Alice agree to the content of the setup document. This document, precisely specifies the required software, hardware, terms of service according to

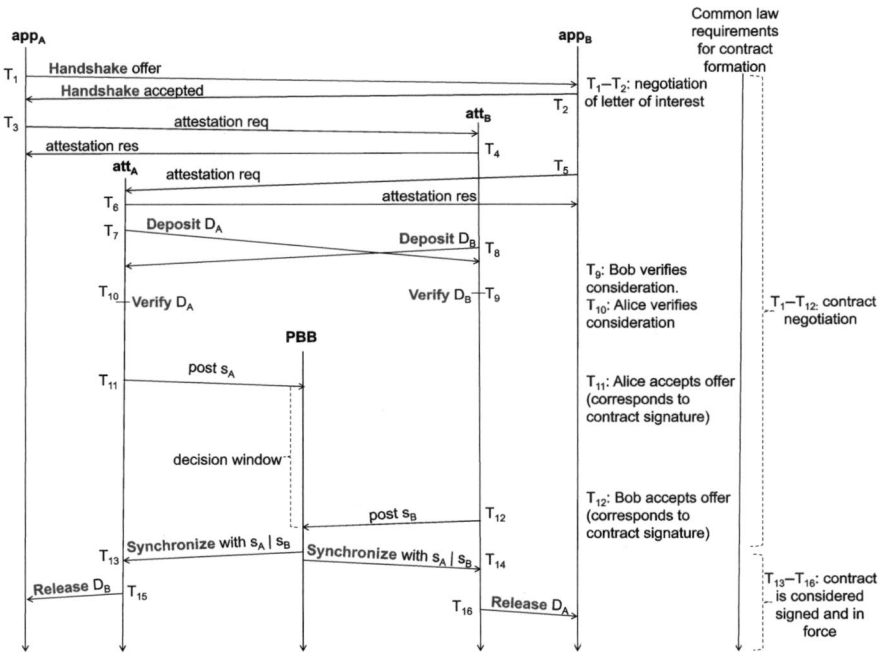

Fig. 16.2. Legal implications of basic operations executed in FEWD.

the provider along with any additional possible information. The execution of steps T_1 and T_2 provides an opportunity for each party to ascertain the intention of the other party. In the figure, the setup completes smoothly, Alice sends a handshake offer to Bob (T_1), which is accepted by Bob in T_2.

(2) **Attestables' attestation** T_3-T_6: The second element deals with the verification of the current run-time configuration of attestables to ensure that they meet the security requirements to participate in the FEP. Each party attests its counterpart's attestable. Thus, in T_3, Alice's application sends an attestation request to Bob's attestable. Reciprocally, in T_5, Bob's application sends an attestation request to Alice's attestable. The figure shows that the attestation responses from both attestables (T_4 and T_6, respectively) are satisfactory, therefore, the protocol progresses.

(3) **Deposit and verification of items** $T_7 - T_{10}$: The third element covers the execution of the first and second basic operations

of FEPs, namely, deposit and verification. Alice's attestable deposits Alice's document D_A with Bob's attestable in T_7. Reciprocally, Bob's attestable deposits Bob's document D_B with Alice's attestable in T_8. Once the documents are stored and locked inside the attestables, both participants can proceed to verify if the documents satisfy the description included in the setup document. Bob's attestable verifies Alice's document in T_9 and Alice's attestable verifies Bob's document in T_{10}. In contract terminology, the verification of a documents corresponds to the verification of the consideration (what is being exchanged) of the contract.

Phase I highlights several important features. The first is that, at any time, either Alice or Bob may decide to end the process. This is particularly important because, in our view, Phase I consists of nothing more than negotiations between the parties and no action of either party consists of anything more than demonstrating their non-binding intention to proceed with the exchange of items with the other party and verifying the validity of the item that each party is interested in.

An additional important feature of Phase I is the idea of a handshake agreement, which comprises a variety of different aspects. First, when Alice and Bob's attestables are attesting each other, they are each agreeing to the setup document. The setup document consists of a free text area, the keys for Alice and Bob, their TLS certificates, as well as a description of the items being exchanged. It also includes any terms of service the providers of the implementation would like added and any miscellaneous additions by either party. The setup document is also machine readable and is processed by each party's attestable. At T_2, Bob loads the handshake document into their attestable and at T_3, Alice loads the handshake document into their attestable.

The setup document also includes the parameters (such as what will be the TTP) of the protocol itself, which will be important for any provider of the protocol, including its availability within an application. In addition, agreeing to the setup document in Phase I may be seen and considered to be accepting the terms of service or terms and conditions of the protocol and to abide by its parameters. The setup document will also include a description of the items that are being transferred, which provides evidence for the purpose of the consideration being afforded by either party. Namely, all information within the setup document above and beyond the terms and conditions of the protocol and its rules should be viewed as a non-binding memorandum of understanding or a letter of interest/intent between Alice and Bob.

Moreover, the description of the documents is also important to be able to accurately identify the consideration. It describes the offer made, therefore, it is used by Alice and Bob during the verification of the documents (T_9 and T_{10}, respectively). It is used by the participants to determine the acceptance of the offer, which in the figure corresponds to the postings of the synchronization tokens, T_{11} and T_{12}, respectively, at which point a contract has been formed.

The handshake document is, in effect, a non-binding memorandum of understanding or letter of interest/intent by the end of Phase I.

16.4.2 *Example of LOI or MOU*

(1) **Items under exchange**: Alice agrees to exchange her X data records of the last six months for a mobile phone app.

(2) **Governing law and jurisdiction**: Alice and Bob agree that if the contract is signed, it will be subject to the applicable laws of a particular jurisdiction and the courts of that jurisdiction will have jurisdiction to hear any claims.

(3) **Start date of the contract**: Alice and Bob agree that the start date of the contract is immediately after the posting of the second sync token, which is to be taken as a signature.

(4) **Completion date of the contract**: It will be made clear that the contract is completed when and only when the exchange has taken place after the posting of both sync tokens.

(5) **Properties of the documents to be exchanged**: Alice and Bob agree that they will locally verify that their respective documents D_A and D_B meet the requirements that the attestable-based FEP expects in order to be able to exchange them.

(6) **The attestable-based FEP, such as FEWD software**: Alice and Bob agree to use, for example, FEWD to conduct the exchange as well as the rules of the protocol.

(a) Each party is independently responsible for downloading the software from the application provider running the implementation and for deploying it on their devices in a manner that:

  (i) The device can be configured with the parameters dictated during off-channel discussions between Alice and Bob for the setup.json document or as predetermined by the application provider.

  (ii) The device responds and passes the remote attestation process initiated by its counterpart.

  (iii) The device is able to execute FEWD, or software for the relevant selected protocol, as dictated by its documentation.

(7) **The public bulletin board (PBB)**: Alice and Bob agree that they will use the PBB identified by a particular unique resource locator (URL) to post their sync tokens.

(a) Each party is responsible for opening an account with the PBB that grants post and retrieval operations.

(8) **Acceptance of offer and contract signature**: Alice and Bob agree that Alice's attestable and Bob's attestable will post their respective sync tokens s_A and s_B to the PBB at an unspecified time in the future to express the acceptance of the documents D_B and D_A, respectively, should they wish to proceed.

(a) The retrievability of s_A from the PBB is to be taken as Alice's acceptance and signature.

(b) The retrievability of s_B from the PBB is to be taken as Bob's acceptance and signature.

(c) The sync tokens s_A and s_B will be taken as valid only if they include a hash of the two documents being exchanged, a hash of the setup document.

(9) **Withdraw from negotiations**: Alice and Bob agree that they are entitled to withdraw from negotiations at any time without any liability or consequences.

(a) To express intention to withdraw from negotiations, Alice and Bob can instruct their respective attestables to post cancel tokens, c_A and c_B, respectively, at any time.

(b) For example, Alice's attestable is free to post c_A to try to withdraw from negotiations at any time after the exchange of documents stage.

(c) A c_A token takes immediate and irrefutable effect if Alice's attestable has not previously posted s_A.

(d) If Alice's attestable has already posted s_A, the withdraw token c_A will take effect only if it is posted before Bob's attestable posts s_B.

(e) Bob is subject to the same withdraw from cancellation policy as Alice.

(10) **The setup document**: Alice and Bob agree that they will use the email channel to establish the setup document.

16.4.3   *Phase II: Contractual formation (T_{11}–T_{12})*

Phase II is primarily concerned with the formation of a contract between Alice and Bob. This is done through the production and posting of tokens by Alice and Bob to the PBB. This phase constitutes an important aspect of the protocol from the standpoint of contractual relations because it may, and it is possible that it could, lead to the creation of binding legal obligations and rights between Alice and Bob. Namely, because at this point binding legal relations may be formed between the parties on the basis of a contract having been formed between them.

(1) **Production of tokens**: As described in Chapter 13, an attestable produces a token only if the outcome from the verification is satisfactory.

(2) **Posting of tokens**: This is also described in Chapter 13. Upon a successful verification of their documents, the attestables proceed to post their tokens to the PBB. To understand the discussion, it might help to regard a token as a signature. Thus, if a participant posts a token to the PBB, she or he signs the contract. Alice's attestable posts its token in T_{11}, which corresponds to Alice's signature on the contract. The figure shows that on his side, Bob's attestable posts its token in T_{12}, which represents Bob's signature on the contract. At this point, the contract has collected two signatures and is therefore formed and in force. Accordingly, Alice and Bob are legally bound after T_{12}.

Note that in the example of the figure, Alice signs the contract first by means of posting her token through her attestable. Therefore, she commits to the contract in T_{11} and waits for Bob's potential signature, post of token in T_{12}. The decision window shown in the figure gives Alice the opportunity to withdraw her commitment by means of invalidating her signature, that is, her posted token. To invalidate her token, Alice is allowed to post a cancellation token to the PBB on the hope that it will arrive at the PBB before Bob's token. A cancellation token is a mechanism that the participants can use to invalidate their signatures after placing them, that is, after posting their tokens. They can also be used by a participant to explicitly utter that she or he is not willing to sign the contract. For example, in T_{11}, Alice could have posted a cancellation token instead of a token that would have cancelled the contract formation immediately. Similarly, Bob could have posted a cancellation token in T_{12}, instead of a token to cancel the contract formation.

A sync tokens includes a cryptographic signature, which is: (a) transmitted and accessible to the other party; (b) signing a hash of the initial setup document that included the memorandum of understanding or letter of interest/intent; in addition to (c) the verification of each party's items that were designated as valid, which occurred in the second part of Phase I.

The posting of the sync tokens appears to also depict the intention of the parties to engage in binding legal relations, included in this particular format given their agreement to the earlier terms and rules of the protocol through the setup document. The posting of the tokens includes their acceptance of the offer having been made, given that they are signing the hash of the setup document as well as the preceding validation of the document which has, at this point, also taken place.

16.4.4 *Phase III: Post-agreement*

This third and final phase refers to two scenarios. Either one of the parties posted their cancellation token and the protocol has been completed cancelled, or both sync tokens were posted and the protocol continues its normal course. If both sync tokens were to have been posted, each attestable would then provide Alice and Bob the ability to access their documents after retrieving the two tokens from the PBB. In the figure, the retrieval of the token is represented by the execution of the synchronization operations in T_{13} and T_{14}, respectively. As described in Chapter 13, once the tokens have been retrieved by each party's attestable, they are used to release the documents from the attestables to the applications. In doing so, both parties would have fulfilled their obligations as part of their agreement and the protocol will have completed successfully.

16.5   Determining the Agreement Between the Parties

This will ultimately be determined on a case-by-case basis and subject to the circumstances at hand. We do not see any reason for why contractual relations could not be formed, or do not occur wholly within the protocol itself, and disputes due to non-performance would be limited to the extent that they do not occur, if the attestables function soundly. Nevertheless, there are instances of great important that may arise and would need to be considered in turn depending on the facts. These may include where any of the requirements for the formation of a contract are absent. Alternatively, where there are any vitiating factors, for example, under English law, that may result in a contract being void or voidable, such as a mistake, misrepresentation, duress, fraud, bribery, among others. Alternatively, the contract may itself be illegal, such as where it is to do something that is prohibited by law.

16.6   Signatures

For the purpose of understanding and identifying one particular stage of FEWD and other attestable-based FEPs, namely, the point at which Alice and Bob post their sync tokens to the PBB and whether the posting of those tokens constitutes a signature, legally speaking. If so, this would entail solidifying each of Alice's and Bob's intention to create legal relations between them by way of having provided their signature. There are and may also be instances where legislation may require a signature.

The posting of the sync tokens by Alice and Bob entails a cryptographic signature, which is to say that it is a signed message using software to authenticate and verify the signature at a particular date and time. At least under English law, it does not appear that it is entirely relevant what a signature looks like (EWHC 772, 2004). Instead, what is important is that both Alice and Bob intended to enter legal relations and sign the document and all of the terms included within it.

Moreover, and as we have described what posting of the sync tokens by Alice and Bob in attestable-based FEPs entails, it is broadly akin to a digital or electronic signature. This is because it is software that is authenticating some information using public-key cryptography, including where the signature is a signed message where some software is used to authenticate the validity of the signature as having happened when it did. On the basis of this form, we do not see any reason for why it would not likely be a form of electronic or digital signature. And because electronic signatures have been broadly accepted as having been capable of meeting the statutory requirement for a signature under English law, so too would posting the sync tokens, as a kind of electronic signature (EWCA Civ 265, 2019).

On the basis of this, the posting of the sync tokens by Alice and Bob appear to lead to the following:

(1) Alice and Bob confirming their agreement and accepting the terms agreed to, which include the attested description of the item and any other terms initially outlined in the setup document;

(2) Alice and Bob transmitting their confirmation to the other party by posting their sync token that is accessible to the other party;

(3) Alice and Bob understanding, from their agreement to the rules of the protocol in the setup document, during the attestation of the setup document, that it is not possible to not proceed with, to end, or to cancel the protocol once both sync tokens have

been posted by each party, but that the protocol would instead complete unsuccessfully;

(4) The posting of the sync tokens are each also a cryptographic signature, denoting securely the time and date of their posting, as well as their acceptance;

(5) Once the posting of the sync tokens by Alice and Bob has taken place, the documents stored in each party's attestable will be released and the exchange will have taken place.

Chapter 17

Operational Concerns

Fair exchange protocols (FEPs) have a variety of risks that are encountered in their regular course of operation. Particularly for protocols that achieve strong fairness guarantees, and therefore make use of independent messaging (IM) environments provided by trusted third parties (TTPs), there is the risk that those parties will not uphold the weight of responsibility that is placed on them, and will either crash or be compromised.

Attestable-based protocols split the monolithic TTP of escrow-based protocols into a public bulletin board (PBB) and a pair of attestables. This provides more places that things can go wrong, but also provides a smaller surface area for wrongness. This design is exploited in this chapter to show techniques for replicating the PBB for crash-tolerance and for compromise-tolerance (which turn out to be the same), and attestables for crash-tolerance — the compromise-tolerance version, which is specific to fair exchange without disputes (FEWD), is covered in Section 17.6). Replication of the dependent environment is also presented, so the participants can join the exchange from multiple different physical devices.

The countermeasures that we suggest are primarily based on redundancy, that is, on replication using design diversity (Avizienis and Kelly, 1994). The idea is that Alice and Bob run instances of software and hardware designed and implemented independently by different programmers and manufactures, respectively, in order to reduce the possibility that all the instances of the protocol fail, for instance, because they all include identical design errors or suffer from identical security weaknesses.

Note that there are many different threats and attack vectors, of which only a handful are covered here. For instance, we do not consider the threat of a participant remotely attacking their counterparty's attestable to prevent them from retrieving sync tokens from the PBB, or denying service to them at the network level (though note that both of those cases are also partially mitigated by replication). While threats like those are possible, the cases we seek to mitigate appear to be the primary risks to fairness in attestable-based FEPs.

We begin with a detailed examination of PBBs.

17.1   The PBB Model

PBB is an immutable, append-only repository of data that can be retrieved by the participants.

Early examples of PBBs can be traced back to the 1970s (Driscoll, 2016) when computer hobbyists started to implement and use them for sharing information by means of posting and retrieving messages and files. The PBB provides synchrony (Peters, 2005) to the asynchronous distributed system comprising the components that make up an attestable-based FEP, which is required for achieving consensus (Fischer *et al.*, 1985), specifically consensus between the participants about the outcome of the synchronize operation.

PBBs have four properties that are required by attestable-based FEPs:

- **Immutability**: Once posted, data on the PBB cannot be altered or removed during the exchange.
- **Availability**: A PBB is an IM environment, and as such it must be reachable by both participants, both for writing data and for reading data, for the duration of the exchange.
- **Linearity**: A PBB must incorporate a strict total ordering into the immutable structure of its posts, such that all correct computer processes will agree on the ordering of any pair of posts.
- **Provenance**: Every PBB must have a unique identity, and all correct computer processes must be capable of determining the provenance of the data returned from a PBB.

Note there is no requirement that a PBB offer any kind of independent computation: it merely collects, orders, and distributes posts. For FEPs that do not provide access to an independent compute (IC) environment, such as gradual release and optimistic front-ends, it is not clear that employing a PBB adds any significant value. It does provide a proof to Alice that Bob can see her message, but without IC, whatever she could do with that proof she can also do without it. Likewise, it provides an ordering to their exchange, but in the absence of IC, Alice could try all the orderings and choose the one that suits her best. If the PBB provided particularly fancy cryptographic artefacts around the postings, it may be possible for a protocol to make use of that, but in this case the PBB is also providing (very limited) independent computation.

The above requirements can be satisfied in several different ways using existing technology. Provenance, for instance, could be satisfied using Secure Sockets Layer (SSL)/transport layer security (TLS) and X.509 certificates (Adams *et al.*, 2001). Note though that such provenance is not transferable, so the attestables must manage the TLS connection themselves. If the PBB digitally signs individual posts, or its aggregate responses, then the network connection can be handled by the participant's application directly, which reduces the complexity of the code running in the attestable. The remainder of this section considers this communication issue in depth.

The messages that the attestables receive from the PBB need to be cryptographically protected to prevent the device's untrusted environment and other parties from altering it. A well-known solution is the deployment of end-to-end secure communication channels between the attestable and the remote device. A secure communication channel is a cryptographic mechanism that enables two communicating parties to pass data under the observance of selected properties such as integrity, confidentiality, and authenticity (Needham, 1993).

In its simplest form, a secure channel can be implemented by means of encryption conducted with a secret key shared between the attestable and the remote platform. More sophisticated channels can be implemented as communication sessions that are opened by the two communicating parties, used as tunnels that provide abstractions for sending and receiving several encrypted messages on behalf to the parties, and closed when no longer needed. As shown in Figure 17.1,

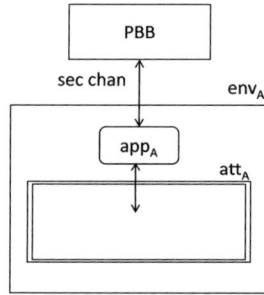

Fig. 17.1.   A secure channel between an attestable and the PBB.

the attestables rely on end-to-end secure channels for communication with each other and with the PBB. Note that the end-point is located within the attestable.

The secure channel shown in Figure 17.1 between the attestable and the PBB can be created on the basis of the TLS protocol, which is known as the SSL protocol. We recall that we make no assumptions about the availability of trusted hardware in the PBB, therefore, we do not assume that the PBB is in possession of an Attestation Identity Key. In this situation, the designer can use the public key associated with the TLS certificate that currently follows the X.509 specification standard.

(1) The attestable is loaded with the URL address and the CA certificate of the PBB, which includes the public key of the PBB. In this manner, the attestable can verify the authenticity of the PBB before contacting it. The validity of the certificate will depend on how frequently the attestable refreshes it.

(2) The attestable contacts the PBB to execute the conventional TLS handshake protocol. The attestable immediately accepts the authenticity of the PBB and continues with the conventional handshake protocol.

(3) During the handshake, the attestable uses the public key of the PBB to encrypt the traffic to protect it against the untrusted environment and other parties.

(4) A successful handshake produces a session key (which represents the end-to-end secure channel) shared only between the PBB and the attestable and is used for encrypting subsequent traffic.

A successful completion of the procedure above would assure the attestable that its operation *posts* stores s in the right PBB and that the operation *retrieves* retrieves *s* from the expected PBB. The implementation of this TLS-based secure channel requires each attestable to run the TLS protocol against the PBB. Following the approach of commercial browsers, the designer can load the certificates of well-known certification authorities to Alice's and Bob's attestables (Foley, 2014). This is a sensible approach provided that the designer is aware of the issues that afflict the versions of the TLS currently in use, such as TLS 1.3, the latest version. There are results that show that the current Internet is plagued with invalid (for instance, self-signed and revoked) certificates (Chung *et al.*, 2016). Several techniques have been suggested to detect revoked certificates such as OCSP (On-line Certificate Status Protocol) Stapling mechanisms and Google's Certificate Transparency service (Google, 2019); however, they do not solve the problem categorically, simply because there is always a time window between revocation and dissemination of revocation (Koschuch and Wagner, 2014; Liu *et al.*, 2015).

Secure channels between attestables can be created on the basis of the TLS protocol if the attestables are in possession of TLS certificates. The possibility of linking remote attestation to the creation of TLS-based secure channels has been explored by several researchers (Goldman *et al.*, 2006). As explained in (Gasmi *et al.*, 2007; Knauth *et al.*, 2019), the approach involves the inclusion of additional information into the X.509 certificate to convey information about the attestable during the TLS handshake.

17.2   PBB Replication

The ability to resolve disputes also usually corresponds to the ability to do bad things, if the trusted party turns out to be untrustworthy. This means having two TTPs in a FEP generally makes things worse, because either of them can invoke their dispute resolution powers to help Bob and hurt Alice, or even just leak D_A to Bob directly.

In attestable-based protocols, the dispute resolution powers have been removed from the PBB, which becomes merely a passive place for tokens to be posted. This provides an opportunity to replicate across PBBs while decreasing the risk of unfair outcomes instead of increasing them.

The failure mode for a PBB that leads to unfairness is simple and universal: it provides one participant with evidence of a successful synchronize operation, and does not provide it to the other participant. This is true for both crash faults and compromise faults: the most a PBB compromised by Alice can do is to provide Alice with s_A and s_B, and to either deny them to Bob or provide him with the cancel token c_A. Conversely, an uncompromised PBB that crashes after Alice retrieves the sync tokens and before Bob retrieves them accomplishes exactly the same result.

The model we provide for replicating the PBB involves changing the sync tokens required by each participant's attestable. att_A needs to see s_A posted on two out of three PBBs, but only needs to see s_B from one of them. As long as only one of the three PBBs fails, Alice can still find the proof she needs to release D_B if Bob releases D_A. Note that cancel tokens make this story more complicated, and are excluded from this model.

Figure 17.2 illustrates the risk interval where the PBB crashing can prevent att_B from retrieving s_A. Bob's attestable is at risk because Alice's has already downloaded s_A and s_B. Note that the vulnerability window also exists in the approach where the two tokens are retrieved through a single operation, rather than one at a time.

A defence mechanism can be built with the assistance of redundancy based on the state machine approach method (Guerraoui and Schiper, 1996; Schneider, 1993; Schneider, 1990). The key idea is that the component to protect the PBB in our scenario is regarded as a state machine; then, to implement a k fault-tolerant state machine,

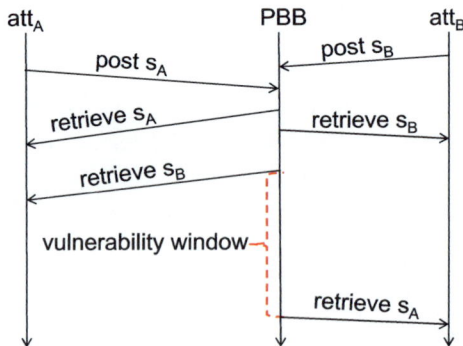

Fig. 17.2.   Vulnerability windows due to potential fail-stop failures of the PBB.

the designer deploys an assembly of $k + 1$ state machine replicas. Since the replicas are assumed to be free from malicious behaviour, any of the replicas that have not been affected by a fail-stop failure are eligible to produce the outcome. A challenge with this approach is that, in general, it requires the support of an underlying protocol to provide replica coordination, that is, a protocol to guarantee that all the replicas keep identical states. Luckily, this requirement can be relaxed in components like the PBB that only serves read requests. The deployment shown in Figure 17.3 can be used for addressing the vulnerability highlighted in Figure 17.2.

In the figure, Alice's attestable and Bob's attestable have access (through their respective apps) to $N = 3$ functionally equivalent but independent PBBs. N can be as large as Alice and Bob decide and agree. Figure 17.4 illustrates the time-line of events. It includes three replicas of the PBB to implement a PBB that can tolerate one fault.

As shown in the figure, att_A posts s_A to all the three PBBs. The requirement that it receive s_A from two out of three PBBs is checked by Alice's attestable, along with the requirement that s_B has been retrieved from one out of three PBBs.

The same conditions apply to Bob's attestable. In the example shown in Figure 17.4, Alice's attestable retrieves s_B from PBB_1, while att_B retrieves s_A from PBB_1. Notice that PBB_2 crashed and therefore does not participate in the retrieval.

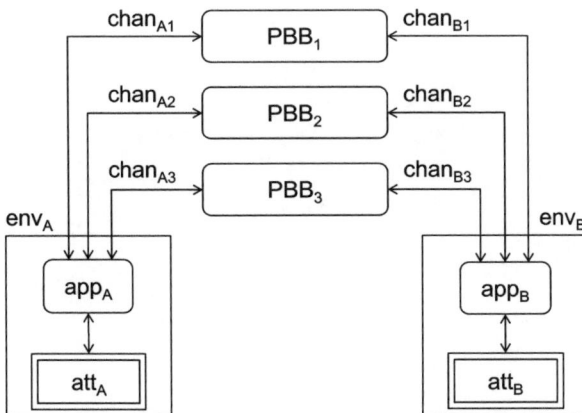

Fig. 17.3.   Replication of the PBB.

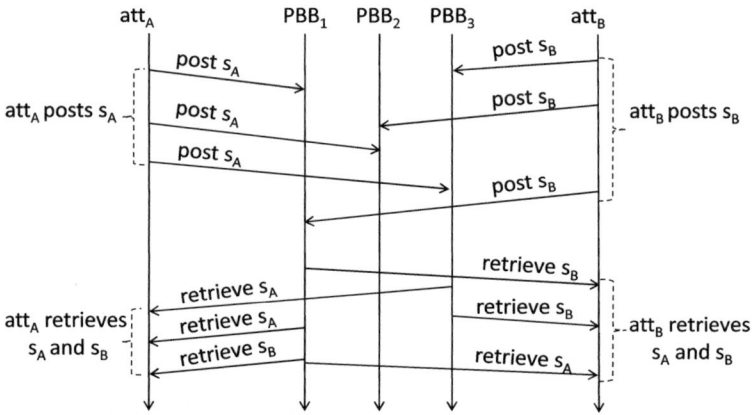

Fig. 17.4.   Fault-tolerant deployment of the PBB.

17.3   Attestable Replication

An attestable failing at the wrong moment can produce an unfair outcome for its owner, as we have already seen. Here we examine an extension to attestable-based protocols, an example of which is seen in Figure 17.5, that allows Alice and Bob to replicate their attestables to mitigate the risk of device failure leading to unfairness.

This kind of deployment can be used to neutralize the impact of fail-stop failures during critical intervals identified in Figures 14.4, 14.5, 14.9, 14.10, and 14.13.

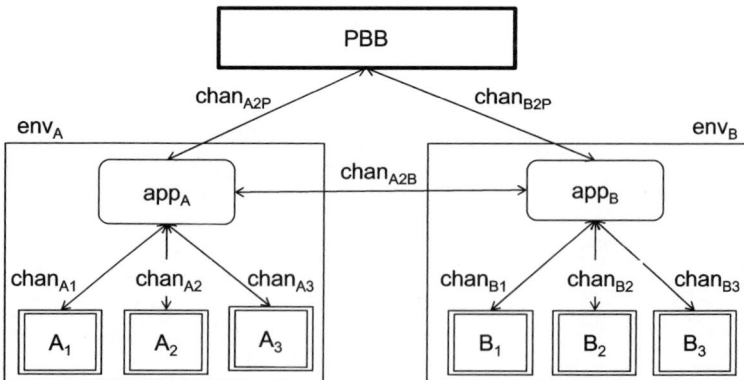

Fig. 17.5.   Replication of the attestables.

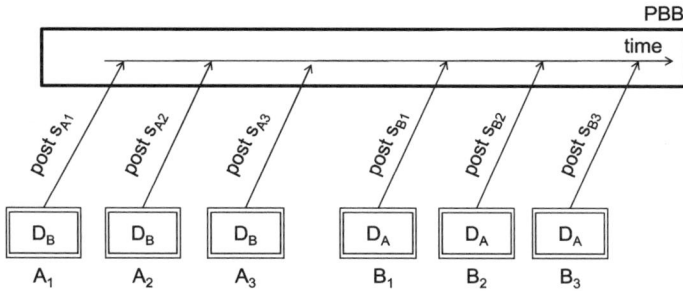

Fig. 17.6. Replication of attestables as a countermeasure to threats of fail-stop failures.

A deployment where Alice and Bob deploy three replicas of their attestable is shown in Figure 17.6. Alice's attestables are in possession of three copies of D_B and Bob's attestables are in possession of three copies of D_A, but the documents have not been released yet to Alice's and Bob's applications, respectively.

To replicate the attestables, we replicate the whole device, which includes the replication of the device's untrusted environment. We emphasize that the untrusted environment of the device does not necessarily host the application. When we replicate the attestables, we use the following notation: A_i is a replica of the attestable operated by Alice and B_i is a replica of the attestable operated by Bob. Thus, $A_1, A_2, \ldots, A_n$ and $B_1, B_2, \ldots, B_n$, represent, respectively, n attestables deployed by Alice and n attestables deployed by Bob to run the protocol to exchange D_A and D_B. A_i and B_i are paired to each other and are responsible for running a replica of the protocol that, at some points, interacts with other replicas. A_i and B_i interact with each other to exchange documents, produce a token, retrieve a token, and release documents. The interaction of A_i and B_i is similar to that of Alice's and Bob's single pair of devices described in Section 13.3.

Simple replication where each pair of attestables A_i and B_i works independently towards the release of their copies of D_B and D_A, respectively, protects against threats of fail-stop failures; for instance, Alice can release a copy of D_B if at least one of her attestables remains operational. The same holds for Bob regarding the release of D_A.

However, this approach opens a door for unfair outcomes. For instance, suppose A_1 crashes after posting s_{A1} and before releasing its copy of D_B. If Bob learns that A_1 has crashed, he can destroy B_2 and B_3 before they post their sync tokens s_{B2} and s_{B3} to the PBB. As a result, B_1 is able to retrieve s_{A1} and s_{B1} from the PBB and release D_A, whereas on Alice's side, none of her attestables are able to retrieve their own matching pair of sync tokens to release their copy of D_B.

Instead, it must be the case that any of Alice's attestables can release D_B to her if any of Bob's attestables release D_A to him. What follows is a mechanism where the attestables release when provided any one of these three pairs of tokens: (s_{A1} and s_{B1}); or (s_{A2} and s_{B2}); or (s_{A3} and s_{B3}).

To help understand the mechanism, it is convenient to regard the execution timeline as consisting of three stages: (i) token dissemination, (ii) token retrieval, and (iii) release of documents. We will describe the protocol only from Alice's attestables' perspective. The protocol is symmetric, so Bob's attestables follow the same procedures. An example of A_1, A_2, and A_3 disseminating their tokens and posting them to the PBB is shown in Figure 17.7.

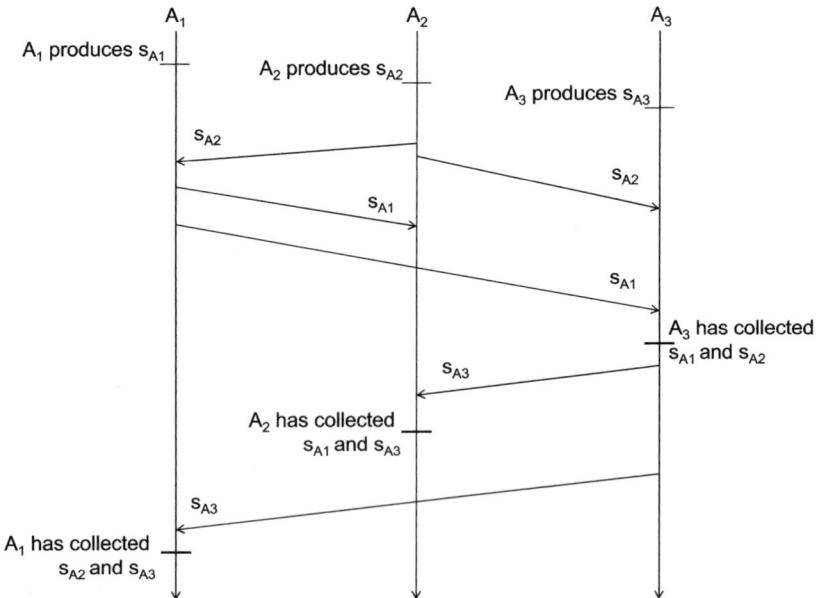

Fig. 17.7.   Example of token dissemination among A_1, A_2, and A_3.

Figure 17.7 shows that Alice's attestables A_1, A_2, and A_3 are programmed to disseminate their tokens, s_{A1}, s_{A2}, and s_{A3}, respectively, to each other. An attestable is able to post its token only after collecting all the tokens from all the replicas. For example, A_2 is able to post s_2 only after collecting s_1 from A_1 and s_3 from A_3.

This means that to have a token available for retrieval from the PBB, at least one of Alice's attestables needs to remain free of fail-stop failures to be able to collect all the tokens from Alice's attestables and post to the PBB, and that the rest of Alice's attestables need to remain free of fail-stop failures at least till they have disseminated their tokens.

On Bob's side, each attestable B_i runs a protocol to send an acknowledgement to all of Alice's attestables to indicate that B_i is in possession of all Alice's tokens, namely, s_{A1}, s_{A2}, and s_{A3}. Figure 17.8 explains the idea with an example; it shows a possible sequence of events of B_1 including its sending of *ack* to A_2, A_3, and A_1 to notify them that it is in possession of the three tokens. There are other sequences that are equally valid. For example, a different order of sending the *ack* would produce a different sequence.

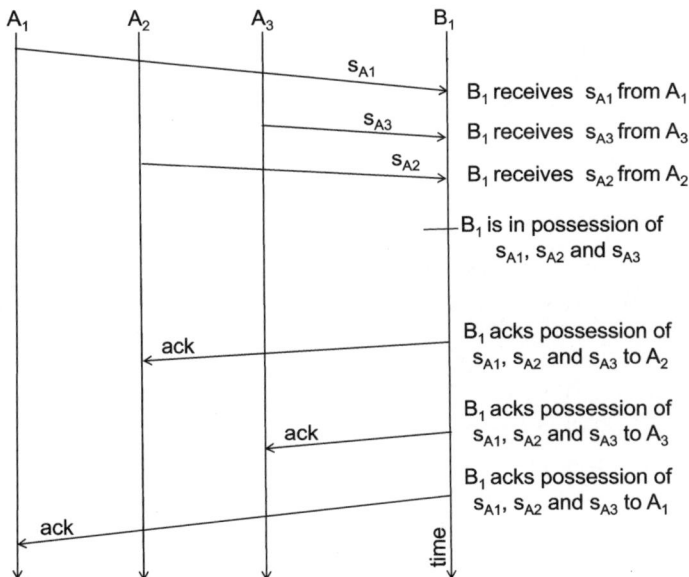

Fig. 17.8. B_1 sends ack of possession of s_{A1}, s_{A2}, and s_{A3} to A_1, A_2, and A_3.

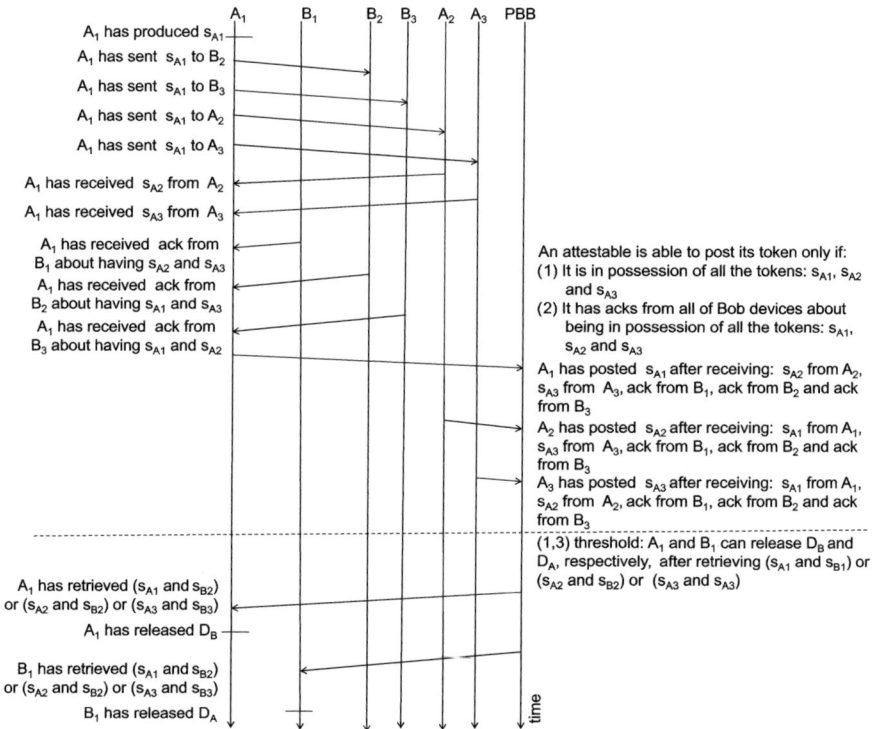

Fig. 17.9.   A (1,3) scheme to defeat fail-stop failures.

The defence mechanism that we suggest against fail-stop failures is shown in Figure 17.9. The figure assumes that token dissemination is conducted on the basis of the protocols described in Figures 17.7 and 17.8. These protocols are embedded in the figure. Note that other event sequences are also possible and valid, yet, the issues and the defence mechanisms remain the same. Events related to A_2 and A_3 are similar.

(1) A_1 follows the protocol of Figure 17.7 to disseminate s_{A1} and to collect tokens s_{A2} and s_{A3}.

   • A_1 sends s_{A1} to A_2, A_3, B_2, and B_3. Next, it collects token s_{A2} from A_2, and s_{A3} from A_3.

(2) A_1 follows the protocol of Figure 17.8 to collect acks from B_1, B_2, and B_3. Each of them acknowledges the possession of s_{A1}, s_{A2}, and s_{A3}.

- All of Alice's and Bob's attestables are now in possession of all the three tokens (s_{A1}, s_{A2}, and s_{A3}) involved in the protocol.

(3) A_1 posts s_{A1} to the PBB.

- A_2 and A_3 execute the same operation as A_1, they post, respectively, s_{A2} and s_{A3}.

(4) A_1 retrieves a pair of tokens, namely, (s_{A1}, s_{B1}) or (s_{A2}, s_{B2}) or (s_{A3}, s_{B3}). FEWD expects that at least one of the pairs will be available from the PBB.

- A $(1,3)$ threshold scheme is in place ($k = 1$ and $n = 3$) to release the documents D_B and D_A.

(5) A_1 uses the retrieved pair of token to release D_B.

(6) If A_1 manages to find and retrieve a pair of tokens, B_1 is able to find and retrieve it, too.

(7) B_1 uses the retrieved pair of tokens to release D_A. The pair of tokens used by B_1 is not necessarily the same used by A_1.

As an example, Figure 17.10 shows that Alice delegates the responsibility of releasing D_B to A_2, whereas Bob uses B_3 to release D_A. The assumption in the figure is that A_1, B_3 and the PBB remain operational and that at least one of the pairs, (s_{A1}, s_{B1}), (s_{A2}, s_{B2}), or (s_{A1}, s_{B1}), is available from the PBB.

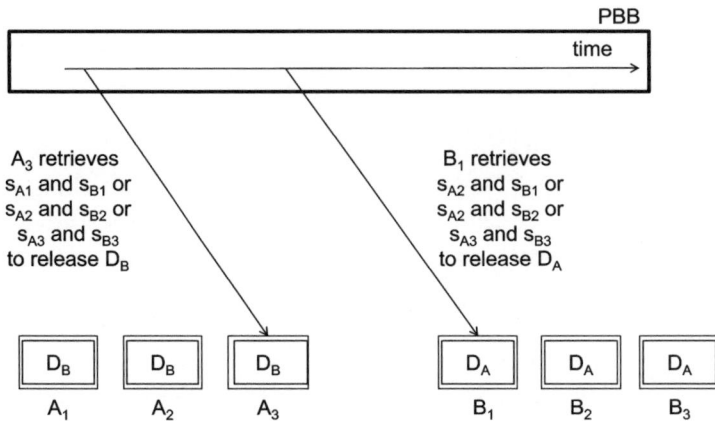

Fig. 17.10. Fail-stop failure defence: Release of documents under $(1,n)$ scheme.

Note that the whole protocol described above is replicated by A_2 and A_3. Therefore, under normal circumstances, the *release* D_B operation is executed by A_1, A_2, and A_3, so Alice will have three equal copies of D_B. She receives a fair outcome as long as one of her attestables is able to release its copy of D_B.

17.4   Attestable Compromise

In addition to crashes, attestables can also be directly attacked in an attempt to compromise their confidentiality.

This can occur in a variety of ways, depending on the mechanisms the attestable uses to provide its guarantees. In this section, we primarily focus on attestables built on embedded trusted hardware, but the concerns raised and general risk profile are applicable to other formulations such as cloud-based attestables, even if the specific tactics differ.

Alice's attestable holds a complete copy of D_B, so if she is able to compromise att_A, she can gain access to D_B during an exchange. She can also compromise att_A after a cancelled exchange: her attestable should destroy itself (including its copy of D_B) once the exchange is cancelled, but Alice can prevent the cancellation message from reaching att_A (among other mechanisms) to force it to maintain a copy of D_B.

If Alice believes her attestable to be compromisable, she may even block the message that sends D_A to att_B, preventing Bob's attestable from ever having access to D_A. This highlights the importance put on securing attestables to prevent Alice and Bob from accessing the plaintext of the documents encrypted inside their attestables.

Unfortunately, it is quite difficult to prove a given piece of hardware is secure. Attacks on trusted hardware are well documented. Examples of attack avenues are presented in Costan and Devadas (2016), and known physical attacks on Intel SGX, for instance, are documented in Adamski (2019), Crowcroft (2019), and Lee *et al.* (2020).

Logical attacks against commercial trusted hardware are also widely documented (Priebe *et al.*, 2019; Tarkhani and Madhavapeddy, 2020). A common pattern of these attacks is that they exploit security holes in the interaction between the application and the hardware, which is often performed through large, informally specified APIs, leaving plentiful surface area for attacks.

17.4.1 *The cost of compromise*

The fact that attacks are possible does not mean that they are cheap however. For instance, the cost of buying the hardware needed to launch a physical attack on the memory bus of an Intel SGX enclave was estimated in 2019 to be roughly $170,000 US dollars (Lee *et al.*, 2020).

Good attestables should be difficult to compromise. This means it should be expensive to successfully attack a given attestable, but it also means that it should take time to perform the attack, or to find new attack vectors when old ones are mitigated.

These two factors work in favour of items that are relatively inexpensive, and also items which lose value over time. Items can be classified, as in Figure 17.11, into three broad buckets depending on how their perceived value changes over time: some tend to go up, some stay constant, and others generally decrease in value over time.

The cost of compromising a hardware attestable can also be modelled as decreasing over time. Depending on the model chosen, this cost may decrease more rapidly than the value of some item D_B stored in att_A, as seen in the red line of Figure 17.12, or it may be mostly comparable to the decrease in value of D_B, like the blue line.

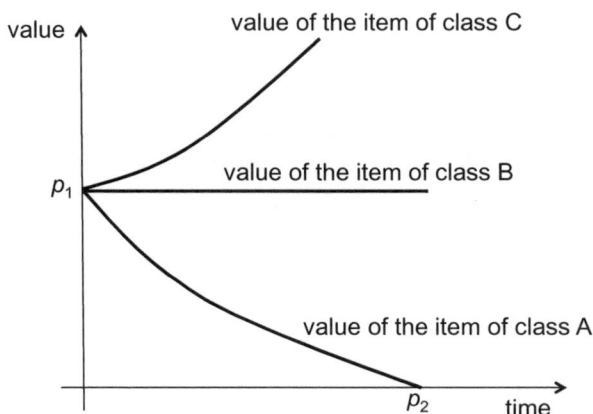

Fig. 17.11. Value of an item of classes A, B, and C.

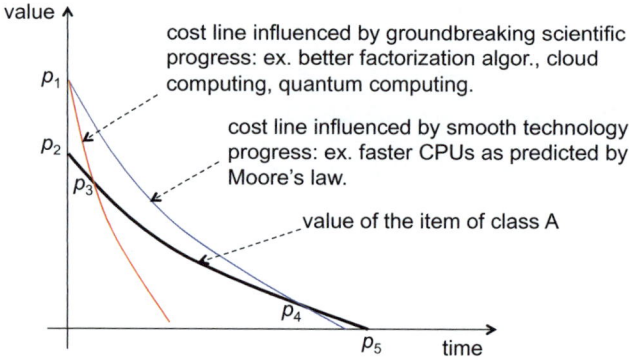

Fig. 17.12.   Value of an item of class A and cost of compromising its attestable.

The inability of an attestable-based protocol to force the deletion of D_B from att_A after Bob cancels the exchange means it is left within the premises of the potential attacker and protected only by the security strength of their attestables.

While in practice we envision a variety of attestable-specific hardware designs that could help mitigate this risk,[1] we provide a protocol-level solution in Section 17.6

17.5   Dependent Environment Replication

The advantage of the modular approach suggested in Figure 17.13 is that it eases the replication of Bob's environment to account for fail-stop failures and malicious threats.

Figure 17.13 shows how the untrusted environment can be replicated as necessary following a $k + 1$ replication state machine to provide the desired level of fault tolerance. Since the functionality of one of the untrusted software is enough to operate FEWD, Alice can deploy $k + 1$ instances of her untrusted software to achieve k fault tolerance. Alice decides to deploy only two replicas of her untrusted environment; on the other side, Bob on his own initiative decides

---

[1]Putting the memory needed by the attestable directly into its chip, for instance, prevents off-chip snooping. Increasing the fragility of that memory, so that it degrades quickly, prevents Alice from retaining a copy of D_B for an extended time, though this needs to be balanced carefully with the crash-tolerance required by attestables.

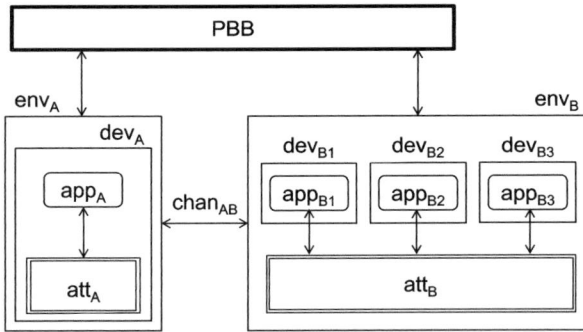

Fig. 17.13.   Replication of Bob's environment.

on three replicas of his untrusted environment; The replication of the untrusted environment is transparent in the sense that Alice and Bob do not need to agree or notify to each other about their number of replicas. Fig. 17.13 shows that the set of untrusted environments communicate (see arrow between untrusted environments) and coordinate among themselves to determine which one is responsible for the task. The complexity of the coordination protocol depends on the logic deployed in the untrusted environments.

17.6   Replicated FEWD

We present a technique at the protocol level for combining the crash-fault attestable replication from Section 17.3 with sharding of items, so that Alice must compromise more than one of her attestables to unfairly release D_B.

This allows Bob to adjust the risk he is exposed to by requiring Alice to use more than one attestable in their exchange, ideally from different sources, so that even if she compromises a minority of them, Bob will still receive a fair outcome.

To start we split the document under Shamir's (k, n) threshold scheme (Shamir, 1979). In this scheme, $1 \leq k \leq n$ is the minimum number of pieces (also called shares) needed to recover a document split into n shares. To use this scheme, D_A and D_B are cryptographically split into n pieces $D_A = D_{A1}, D_{A2}, \ldots, D_{An}$ and $D_B = D_{B1}, D_{B2}, \ldots, D_{Bn}$. Alice's replicas of attestables $A_1, A_3, \ldots, A_n$ collaborate with Bob's replicas $B_1, B_2, \ldots, B_n$ in the following manner: pair A_i and B_i are responsible for exchanging pieces D_{Ai}

and D_{Bi}, for example, pair A_2 and B_2 are responsible for exchanging D_{A2} and D_{B2}.

To focus on preventing Alice and Bob from attacking their attestables, we set $k = n$, thereby requiring all n shares to reconstruct the original document. This is variable: a small k (for example $k = 1$) enhances reliability but weakens the defence against malicious attacks, while a large k like $k = n$ strengthens the defence against the dark arts but weakens reliability — the failure of a single attestable at an inconvenient moment can collapse the whole exchange. With $k = n$, Alice must successfully attack each of her n attestables to reconstruct D_B unfairly.

One issue with this design is that Alice's attestables are no longer able to verify D_B, because each attestable only has access to a share of D_B, not the entire document. To fix this, the verify operation for D_B is done on Bob's side before it is shared, instead of in att_A.

As noted in Section 13.1, D_B can be verified by V_B once extracted from the certified verification module M_B, which is available from the setup document. Bob's attestables can do this work, so that each of his attestables B_1, B_2, and B_3 independently verify D_B before sending it. This independent verification is required to prevent Bob from fooling Alice's attestables via a single compromised attestable of his own.

It is also important to ensure that Bob's compromised attestable cannot feed one or more of Alice's attestables a manipulated shard of D_B, which would prevent her attestables from reconstructing D_B on a successful completion. Therefore, each of Bob's attestables not only independently verifies D_B, but also sends that verification report and the correct corresponding shard to each of Alice's attestables.

17.6.1 *Verification, splitting, and sending of Alice's document*

Figures 17.14 and 17.15 illustrate a countermeasure that defeats attacks on the attestables to extract the documents illegally and to manipulate the verifier. They explain the protocol from Alice's and Bob's side, respectively. We will discuss the former first, which shows how Alice's D_A document is split into n shares and disseminated to Bob's replicas of his attestable.

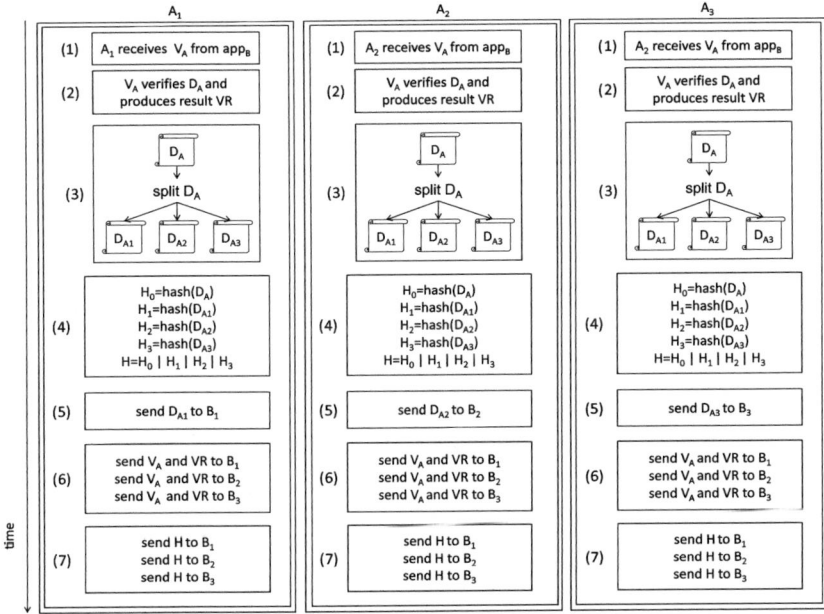

Fig. 17.14. Split document and broadcast.

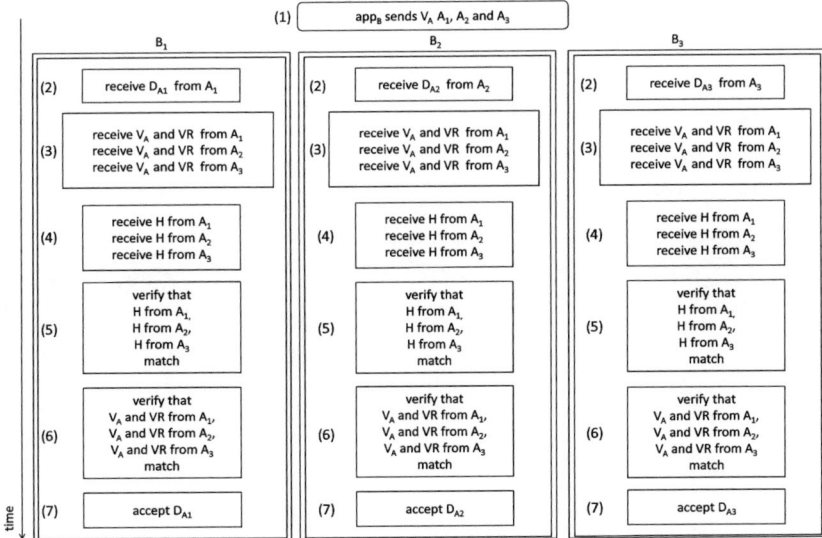

Fig. 17.15. Verification and acceptance of pieces of D_A.

Note that for simplicity, Figure 17.14 shows only the activities that Alice's attestables execute during the interval between the receiving of the V_A verifier from Bob's application and the sending of hashes to Bob's attestables. In the example of the figure $n = 3$, thus, A_1, A_2, and A_3 are three replicas of attestables that Alice deploys to execute the protocol against Bob's replicas, namely, B_1, B_2, and B_3, which are not shown in this figure. We will describe the procedure that the pair A_1 and B_1 executes. The other pairs, A_2 and B_2, and A_3 and B_3, execute the same exchange. We assume that before the exchange starts, A_1, A_2, and A_3 are in possession of copies of D_A. Also, we assume that Bob's replicas of his attestables B_1, B_2, and B_3 as well as Alice's replicas of her attestables can be attested. A particularity of this deployment is that the verify operation takes place at the sender's side. For example, Alice's D_A document is verified with a verifier V_A running in Alice's attestables. Consequently, Bob's attestables need also to verify that the results of the verify operation are actually produced by the verifier V_A running in Alice's attestables.

Alice's attestables perform the following actions:

(1) A_1 receives the V_A verifier from Bob's app.
(2) A_1 runs the verifier against D_A to verify that D_A is accepted. In the figure, VR represents the result, which is boolean: accepted or rejected.

   • A_1 cancels the exchange if the verifier rejects D_A. Let us assume that the verifier accepts D_A, therefore, the execution of the exchange continues.

(3) A_1 splits D_A into D_{A1}, D_{A2}, D_{A3}.
(4) A_1 computes three hashes and H, where | represents a concatenation operation:

   $H_0 = hash(D_A),$
   $H_1 = hash(D_{A1}),$
   $H_2 = hash(D_{A2}),$
   $H_3 = hash(D_{A3}),$
   $H = H_0|H_1|H_2|H_3.$

(5) A_1 sends D_{A1} to B_1, that is, to its counterpart.

(6) A_1 sends
V_A and VR to B_1,
V_A and VR to B_2,
V_A and VR to B_3.

(7) A_1 disseminates H to all Bob's replicas
A_1 sends H to B_1,
A_1 sends H to B_2,
A_1 sends H to B_3.

(8) A_1 continues with the execution of the protocol as explained in what follows.

17.6.2 Verification of hashes and reconstruction of Alice's document

We will describe the protocol executed on Bob's side to verify the correctness of D_A, with the assistance of Figure 17.15. The figure complements Figure 17.14 and for clarity covers only the activities of the interval between the sending of the verifier V_A and the acceptance of the pieces of Alice's document. The figure shows Bob's attestables (B_1, B_2, and B_3) that interact with Alice's that are shown in Figure 17.14. We will explain only the protocol executed by B_1 to verify and accept D_{A1}. B_2 and B_3 execute a similar protocol.

(1) Bob's app sends the verifier V_A to A_1, A_2, and A_3.

(2) B_1 waits to receive D_{A1} from A_1.

(3) B_1 waits to receive V_A and VR (the result of running V_A against D_A) from all of Alice's attestables:
B_1 receives V_A and VR from A_1,
B_1 receives V_A and VR from A_2,
B_1 receives V_A and VR from A_3.

(4) B_1 verifies that the three V_A received from A_1, A_2, and A_3 match and that the three VR received from A_1, A_2, and A_3 also match.

  • B_1 cancels the exchange if it detects a mismatch.

(5) B_1 waits to receive H from all of Alice's attestables:
B_1 receives H from A_1, that is, A_1 version of $H_0|H_1|H_2|H_3$,
B_1 receives H from A_2, that is, A_2 version of $H_0|H_1|H_2|H_3$,
B_1 receives H from A_3, that is, A_3 version of $H_0|H_1|H_2|H_3$.

(6) B_1 compares the content of all three hashes (n out of n), for example, B_1 compares H_0 from A_1 against H_0 from A_2 and H_0 from A_3 to be certain that A_1, A_2, and A_3 are dealing with the same D_A document.

- If B_1 is satisfied, it can be certain that none of Alice's attestables A_1, A_2, or A_3 has been compromised by Alice and continues with the execution of the protocol.
- B_1 cancels the exchange otherwise.

(7) The continuation of the protocol involves the production of the tokens and release of the documents as explained in what follows.

Once a collaborative pair, for example, A_1 and B_1, has accepted their documents (A_1 has verified the hashes and accepted D_{B1}, and B_1 has verified the hashes and accepted D_{A1}), the pair proceeds to produce their tokens s_{A1} and s_{B1}. Similarly, the pair A_2 and B_2 produces the tokens s_{A2} and s_{B2}. And finally, the pair A_3 and B_3 produces the tokens s_{A3} and s_{B3}.

17.6.3   *Token retrieval and release of pieces and reconstruction of documents*

Figure 17.16 shows the last events that take place at Bob's side to reconstruct D_A. To defeat potential attacks perpetrated by Bob, Alice, or both on their attestables, the protocol requires $(3,3)$, that is n out of n pieces of the document to reconstruct it. We assume that

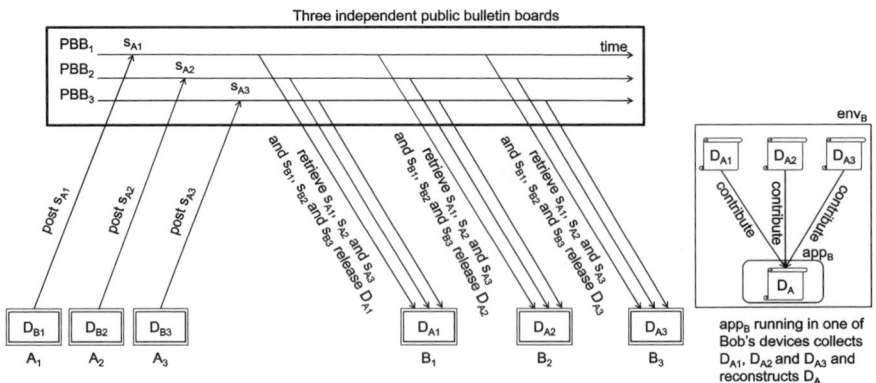

Fig. 17.16.   Reconstruction of D_A under a (3,3) threshold scheme.

Alice's attestables (A_1, A_2, and A_3) and Bob's attestables (B_1, B_2, and B_3) have already validated and accepted their pieces of documents and produced their tokens. Thus, Alice's attestables are in possession of tokens s_{A1}, s_{A2}, s_{A3}, and Bob's attestables are in possession of tokens s_{B1}, s_{B2}, s_{B3}. When the attestables are ready to post their tokens, the protocol proceeds as follows:

(1) A_1, A_2, and A_3 post s_{A1}, s_{A2}, and s_{A3} on PBB_1, PBB_2, and PBB_3, respectively. Though not shown in the figure, Bob's attestables perform a similar operation.

(2) Bob's attestables retrieve the tokens to be able to release their pieces of documents.

- B_1 retrieves Alice's tokens (s_{A1}, s_{A2}, and s_{A3}) and Bob's tokens (s_{B1}, s_{B2}, and s_{B3}). If all the tokens are retrieved successfully, B_1 releases D_{A1}.
- B_2 retrieves Alice's tokens and Bob's tokens. If all the tokens are retrieved successfully, B_1 releases D_{A2}.
- B_3 retrieves Alice's tokens and Bob's tokens. If all the tokens are retrieved successfully, B_1 releases D_{A3}.

(3) The app running in one of Bob's devices collects D_{A1}, D_{A2}, and D_{A3} and reconstructs D_A.

(4) The reconstruction of D_A completes the protocol on Bob's side.

Alice follows the same procedure for reconstructing D_B on her side.

Chapter 18

Commercial Analysis and Use Cases

There are a wide variety of use cases for fair exchange. Here we examine a number of them and provide a commercial analysis of the benefits of using various fair exchange protocols (FEPs). Classic use cases include the exchange of signatures on legal contracts, exchange of an electronic message against a non-repudiable proof of receipt like in certified email, exchange of electronic items against payment in online shopping, and exchange of secret strings.

18.1 Exchange of Signatures on Legal Contracts

One of the most straightforward commercial applications of FEPs is in the exchange of signatures on legal contracts, also referred to in the literature as exchange of digital signatures and as contract signing protocols.

The idea is to model the signing of traditional business contracts where both signatory parties place their hand-written signatures simultaneously on the same piece of paper. The same effect can be achieved online if Alice and Bob first agree on the text to be signed, then individually and separately sign two separate copies of the document (D_A and D_B, respectively), and then finally fairly exchange D_A and D_B.

Note that D_A and D_B are easily verifiable, and fit within the class of copyable items. Any FEP that can exchange copyable items can handle this process, and once exchanged, these signed documents bind Alice and Bob to reciprocal commitments and create legal rights and obligations, as seen in Chapter 16.

Which FEP is appropriate for this situation depends on the sensitivity of the document being signed, the relationship between the two parties, and in general the cost and risk profile of the exchange. If it is important that the document remain confidential, for instance, in the case of mergers and acquisitions (M&A) paperwork, then a protocol like fair exchange without disputes (FEWD) that guarantees strong fairness and verifiability without revealing sensitive information to an escrow service may be most appropriate. In other cases, a weaker protocol like gradual release could be sufficient.

18.2   Exchange of Delivery and Receipt

A general use case includes all those that fall within the category of exchange of delivery and receipt. It covers a whole swath of different types of use cases in different industries and sectors that has to do with being able to exchange and verify information in the form of digital items where information is shared and a receipt is returned confirming some authorization, permission, or confirmation or lack thereof being shared in return.

One such example is medical data being sent to a research group for aggregate inclusion. In such a case, the research group is interested in knowing the data are valid, and Alice, who's data are being transmitted to the research group, wants to know that the research group has received Alice's data and that Alice's data have not been leaked (and potentially will not be).

Their attestables:

(1) verify the data Alice sends;
(2) compress or aggregate Alice's data to ensure the data's integrity; and
(3) guarantee that Alice's data never leaves the attestable and have therefore not been leaked.

Once Alice's data have been verified securely, the research group can send something of value to Alice that notifies Alice of receipt and provides proof that Alice's data have not been leaked.

A further example has to do with payments and proof that a payment has been made, processed, or is being processed, otherwise referred to as the receipt of a payment. For example, normally where Alice makes a transfer to Bob using some electronic method of payment transfer, Alice will be provided with some confirmation number or code that is a reference to Alice having made and authorized the transfer of monies. In addition, what can be sent in return is confirmation of receipt of that thing of value for the payment being made, such as a confirmation pursuant to an invoice of the funds having been paid and being satisfied.

This category of use cases is broadly simple, it is a form of notification that the transfer of value, of a digital item, has taken place, for example, by being initiated. It may also be applied in cases where it has been received. In each case, it may be to Alice, sending the digital item, but also to other parties where and as needed. It is especially useful where such proof of receipt is information that may be needed for something else, for example, accounting records. It is also a way to receive, in return, certain confirmations, such as in the healthcare records example of Alice's data not having been leaked.

18.3   Health Certificates

A practical application of FEPs is the exchange of health certificates that provide a good evidence about the fitness of a person to engage in an activity. For example, Alice can agree to meet Bob for coffee only if they exchange health certificates with evidence that both are free from contagious deceases like COVID.

This exchange can be handled by FEWD, executed from Alice's and Bob's mobile phones. Alice and Bob will only need to have their health certificates on their mobile phones and find a public bulletin board (PBB) to help their devices to execute the synchronize operation. Such a PBB can be offered by the shopping mall where Bob and Alice are planning to meet. Furthermore, there are no technical difficulties in extending FEWD to more than two participants. For example, FEWD can be used by a group of friends to exchange health certificates about heart and other medical conditions before heading off skiing.

There are other similar examples of practical interest. The general idea is that attestable-based protocols can be used by individuals to share health information that is relevant in particular situations without revealing it to third parties. An application on Alice's mobile phone can take into account her health conditions (for example, allergies and immunodeficiencies) and alert her of the risks of joining a group of people at a concert, conference, party, and other gatherings or particular locations.

Alice wants to ensure that if she provides her health certificates to the other participants that she receives their information in turn, in a privacy preserving way. FEPs allow Alice to efficiently share her certificate with everyone else with the guarantee that they will not be able to see her certificate unless Alice also sees theirs.

Alice's device could provide her with an alert when she is entering high risk scenarios, depending on her risk criteria: allergies, for instance, or high sensitivity to certain transmissible diseases. This is also applicable in a range of other instances, for example, where age is a requirement for entry.

A specialized sync token may be devised that provides additional benefits when used on a PBB. For instance, by embedding a small amount of information in the sync token that can provide a rough probabilistic count of conditions in a certain area, researchers may be able to more quickly understand the spread of various conditions across a geographic region. This could also be restricted further to only allow analysis of the sync token in conjunction with the certificate data, in cases where probabilistic embeddings would not provide enough privacy.

18.4   Completing Missing Information

FEPs can also be used to exchange partial information. This is what humans have done for millennia when they meet at a crossroads: exchange information about what to expect on the journey to come. FEPs allow us to do the same thing digitally, with guarantees around the exchange that are difficult to achieve otherwise.

A wide range of examples fit this use case: road conditions, animal tracking, market conditions, social factors, network routing conditions, and all kinds of cases where people want to expand the coverage of their incomplete information. FEPs allow those who share more to be guaranteed they will receive more, reinforcing healthy dynamics and shifting us away from relying on large data brokers who constantly take but rarely give.

Another example is supporting federated and decentralized machine learning (ML), where Alice and Bob can offer each other improvements to their ML models in a fair exchange process. When we can train locally and spread those local improvements to others in our communities, then we have the opportunity to make highly efficient local models that are specialized for our particular concerns.

18.5 Online Shopping Without Non-performance Disputes

Many e-commerce platforms operate dispute resolution mechanisms to counteract the various forms of disputes that may arise, such as non-delivery of the items and delivery of the incorrect items (or incorrect description).

Sometimes this involves the platform acting directly as a mediator when a dispute arises, but this has serious drawbacks, such as the burden of contacting the platform and the time it takes them to solve the dispute. For example, if Alice receives an item that has been accidentally damaged by the delivery service, she must raise the issue with the platform and return the item to the seller before she is able to receive a replacement or refund — which might take weeks. It also opens up Alice to the potential for arbitrariness on the part of the platform or the centralized arbitrator to decide whether Alice is right or not.

To take another example, many online sellers operate as pay before delivery of services. Sometimes these sellers charge for items that are out of stock and unable to be delivered. When this happens, it may take several days for the seller to notify the buyer about the mistake, and additional days to refund the money.

A different approach that many large e-commerce platforms take is to provide escrow services either directly or through third-party escrow services. In doing so, the platform functions as a trusted third party (TTP) in an escrow exchange between Alice and Bob.

This works in many situations, but has the standard cost and risk drawbacks of escrow-based FEPs.

An alternative to each of these standard approaches is to use attestable-based FEPs, which requires Alice and Bob to have access to attestables, but reduces the cost of the exchange by putting the work on Alice and Bob and allowing them to choose their own PBB. Attestable-based FEPs can also reduce the risks presented by an all-seeing escrow TTP, as described in Chapter 12. By doing this, the typical disputes relating to non-delivery or delivery of the incorrect item can be eliminated.

Chapter 19

Additional Uses and Future Work

There are a wide variety of use cases where attestable-based FEPs like FEWD can be applied. However, it is worth mentioning that attestables can serve as a low-cost and low-risk point of mutual trust in many applications beyond fair exchange. We examine some of those here, and additionally consider the intersection of various computational and cryptographic systems with fair exchange, beginning with smart contracts.

19.1 Smart Contracts

Generically, a smart contract is just a computer program that manages assets or information according to its rules, though this definition is broad enough to encompass almost any computer program. The term is commonly used to refer to computer programs on blockchains that manage the assets that have been created in that blockchain system, but we will extend this idea slightly to consider any system, centralized or distributed, that exposes its functionality as a programming language and allows programs in that language to be run on that system.

Smart contracts on blockchains are used for creating assets, exchanging assets that have been created within that specific system, establishing lotteries and games using those assets, coordinating voting and governance over the use of those assets, and various kinds of workflows involving assets or information.[1]

Smart contracts are a natural device for fairly exchanging items that reside entirely in a single system. If D_A and D_B are both within the same system, and that system has the capacity for smart contracts, then a smart contract can be used to act as a escrow service in the exchange. Since both items are already within the escrow system, and presumably Alice and Bob already trust the safety and liveness of that system, it is relatively straightforward to achieve strong fairness in this context.[2]

If one or both items are outside of the smart contract's system, then it becomes more difficult to exchange them within a FEP. A deposit of an external asset could be made using verifiable encryption, in theory, but it would introduce additional cost (perhaps considerable cost) and risk compared to making that deposit as isolated storage directly within Alice's dependent environment. If the system is private, it may offer independent compute (IC), but in an open distributed system like a public blockchain the only way to perform computation without leaking the deposited values is to use verifiable encryption.

It is possible to use a smart contract system for the deposit, verify, and release/restore operations for an asset expressed within that system. This can be done as part of an asymmetric protocol like the one discussed in Chapter 14, where the digital money's ledger acts as a trusted third party (TTP) that executes the synchronize operation in the FEP.

Any system that maintains unique assets and expresses the required interfaces can provide this, but a system that supports smart contracts allows those APIs to be created by end users, rather

---

[1]These same applications can of course be performed on any centralized system that exposes its functionality in a programming language like Daimio, but we focus on smart contracts on blockchains in this section as they are currently a more popular host.

[2]Whether there are other significant risks depends on the specifics of the system: some systems allow smart contracts to be updated after they are deployed, for instance, which could easily cause an unfair outcome for one or both parties. Formal verification may be another important consideration, as a bug in the smart contract could also produce unfair outcomes.

than requiring the system operators to provide them. Additionally, expressing the asset as a TODA file allows the exchange program to be written anywhere, instead of needing to reside within the issuer's own system.

Public systems can provide an independent messaging (IM) environment, so a smart contract on a public system can be a public bulletin board (PBB) in an attestable-based protocol. This allows them to perform the synchronize operation in an IM environment, providing the possibility of strong fairness in protocols such as ZKCP and ZKCPlus (Li *et al.*, 2021).

It is also possible to use public systems more directly by combining their PBB and asset escrow capabilities. However, it should be noted that they cannot serve as trusted entities for secret verification without fully homomorphic encryption or similar methods. Currently, smart contracts can only provide a fair exchange guarantee over a small class of items: unique assets created within that specific blockchain.

Attestable-based protocols can perform certain kinds of smart contracts and are ideal for one-shot, short-term processes with a single output. The handshake document in FEWD describes two different assets and how to validate them programmatically. Therefore, it is in fact a smart contract. Protocol extensions can handle multiparty exchanges and private computation over private data, such as credit scores or health research.

It is interesting to note that while blockchains provide fair exchange for their own unique items, cryptographic protocols can exchange copyable items: they play opposite roles with respect to these item classes. Systems responsible for creating assets and managing their state over time can generally support the trust burden of providing the API access to their own items that is required for fair exchange, but today it is rare to find such systems that can also be trusted to provide exfiltration-resistant computing.

One use case for which smart contracts on a public blockchain excel is lotteries. This is a difficult case in a distributed system, because all of the participants except the winner have an incentive to break the lottery process, if they can. Running the lottery on a public blockchain generally means many actors that are not part of that particular lottery have an incentive to continue the process, so it is likely to finish.

We can adapt FEWD to provide a "lottery guarantee": either one party will receive both things, or nothing will happen. This is effectively an "anti-fair exchange guarantee", which picks up the two outcomes that a fair exchange rejects (Alice receives both, or Bob receives both), rejects the one fair exchange accepts (Alice receives Bob's and Bob receives Alice's), and retains restore.

The lottery exchange proceeds as usual for FEWD until the final operation of release/restore. If the exchange is cancelled by a cancel token posted on the PBB, the restore operation is invoked as usual, so that no unique items are lost. However, if both parties post their sync tokens on the PBB before either of their cancel tokens are posted, then both items are released to a single party by their attestable. This could be based on, for instance, the parity of the PBB's signature over the sync tokens.

Because the PBB is trusted to not collude with either party, neither party can know until the second sync token is posted by the PBB which one is going to win, so there is no advantage gained by Bob cancelling after seeing Alice's sync token. Because the attestables are trusted to provide IC, both parties can be confident that if they win, they will receive both items, and the other party will receive neither.

Another possibility in a smart contract system is taking a deposit, which is paid out if certain conditions are met and restored to the depositor otherwise.

If those conditions are the verify operation in a FEP, then this smart contract resembles a FEP over a generative instrument, where the generation of the other party's item has been replaced by claiming their deposit. Given a deposit of sufficient risk-adjusted value, trust in the smart contract that provides the fair exchange process (including verifying the item and releasing the deposit), and explicit trust in the safety and liveness of the smart contract's underlying system, this can provide a strong back-end to an optimistic FEP.

Several FEPs have been proposed that do something similar, and using this method allows the exchange of items that are not naturally generatable or revocable, by covering the risk of loss with a sufficient deposit (Bentov and Kumaresan, 2014; Eckey *et al.*, 2020; GauthierDickey and Ritzdorf, 2012). Note, however, that it requires up-front interaction with the TTP to make the deposit, so it is not truly optimistic — though as we saw earlier, a one-time deposit might be made in an amount large enough to cover several exchanges, provided there is a mechanism to prevent overuse (this requires solving double spend, but might be much lighter weight than the deposited assets themselves, which also require IM).

It is also possible to go the other direction, and have, for instance, the sender of a secret item pay a deposit that is granted to the recipient should the sender cheat. This effectively turns the secret into a revocable instrument. Alice and Bob might do this if D_A is a secret that neither party wants to make public. They cannot pass it into a smart contract on a public blockchain for verification, because that would expose D_A to everyone. Instead, Bob releases his payment to Alice first, and then she delivers D_A to him. If she fails to do so, he can put a claim on the deposit contract by depositing a small amount himself. If she produces the secret for all to see, then she is paid, otherwise Bob takes the deposit. Counterfactual games of this sort can be played to produce fairness, but often at some expense to the players, which may not be distributed fairly: an analysis under marginal fairness may yield interesting results.

Attestable-based FEPs are capable of exchanging unique items, so they are naturally amenable to these techniques as well. The simpler generative case is especially promising, as attestables can exchange secrets without resorting to revocation instruments. Conversely, attestables are efficient enough that it may generally be preferable to simply skip the optimistic step and exchange exclusively through the attestables.

Finally, we consider an area where smart contracts on a long-lived system have a distinct advantage over attestable solutions. Processes that are long-term, multi-step, or iterative, such as governance or workflows, require state management that is maintained across the lifespan of the process, which may be measured in years or decades.

In a system that expresses its functionality as a programming language, users can build their own workflow processes. If that system is trusted to provide long-lived service with costs and risks that fit within a user's thresholds, then they can use it for their long-lived process.

A FEP, in contrast has a single outcome: the items are either released, or they are restored. FEPs generally also have a limited lifetime, either through a wall clock timer for protocols with weak timeliness or through party cancellation for protocols with strong timeliness. Being able to cancel an exchange is important for timeliness (which in turn is an important consideration in the overall fairness of the outcomes), but smart contracts by default do not allow cancellation, so there are different use cases for which one or the other is more well suited.

It is not entirely clear how to extend an attestable-based protocol to manage long-lived processes where the participants might not always be incentive aligned with the process continuing. In the lottery example mentioned earlier, this was avoided by having the outcome be determined by the actions of the PBB, which arrives late enough in the exchange that neither party can negatively impact the other by loss of liveness.

In an iterative process, the participants have to return after discovering the outcome, and continue the process together. If the attestables the participants used were in the control of a third party, for instance, a cloud service, who made promises of their own about the continued liveness of those attestables, then they have the same effect as any other smart contract system. Whether such an IM environment is necessary for iterative processes is an area of future work.

19.2   Secure Multiparty Computation

Secure multiparty computation (SMC)[3] is a broad class of techniques that enable two or more parties to provide inputs to a function, compute the results, and retrieve the results without disclosing their inputs to each other. Yao's Millionaires' problem is an example of SMC that allows two parties to each compute a function $f(x_A, x_B)$, where x_A and x_B are provided by Alice and Bob, respectively, without disclosing them to each other (Yao, 1982).

Many examples of SMC protocols do not provide fairness guarantees to the participants. For instance, in the previous example Alice may not be guaranteed to learn $f(x_A, x_B)$ if and only if Bob does, depending on the solution used.

---

[3]Also known as secure multiparty computation (SMPC), multiparty computation (MPC), and privacy-preserving computation (PPC).

This is a natural evolution of the field after Cleve's work (Cleve, 1986) in 1986 showed the impossibility of fairly distributing the results of a coin flip without a TTP. Many interesting computations turned out to be impossible to produce with fairness guarantees in the two-party version.

An interesting counterpoint is a protocol (Gordon *et al.*, 2011) for achieving fairness over certain kinds of binary computations, including Yao's Millionarie's problem, that can be expressed as a lower-triangular matrix. If Alice stops early with the result, then Bob has enough information to generate the result accurately. Note though that Bob can't be certain that the result is accurate, as the stopping player may have stopped without the result. This leaves Alice knowing she has an accurate result, while Bob is uncertain.

A solution based on gradual release protocols is proposed in Pinkas (2003). This solution does not require the participation of a TTP, and therefore, can only provide weak fairness guarantees, as we saw in Chapter 11.

Optimistic fair exchange is used as the basis of another solution proposed in Cachin and Camenisch (2000). It uses verifiable encryption, and involves a TTP only when one of the parties misbehaves or messages of the SMC process are lost.

Verifying input is a challenge in SMC. It is often ignored entirely, as in Yao's Millionaires' problem, where Alice does not know if Bob used his actual bank account balance. When it is available, it is limited to verifiable encryption, because there is no independent computation.

In some protocols involving a large number of participants, a non-collusion assumption is made to provide a TTP through a consensus protocol. Conversely, if Alice is unsure whether the other participants are colluding, then from her perspective this reduces to a two-party exchange. Alice must explicitly trust the consensus over the other participants to not collude, and introduce them as a TTP into her trust stack, or risk unfairness.

Multiparty FEPs, considered in the next section, can generalize protocols like FEWD, and combined with techniques like those seen in Section 19.4, they may be able to supplement or replace SMC for some use cases, particularly when strong fairness and programmatic item verification are important.

19.3   Multiparty Fair Exchange

FEPs can be extended from exchanges between two parties to support an arbitrary number of parties.[4]

Both SMC protocols and FEPs allow multiple parties to interact while retaining strong guarantees on the outcomes. SMC focuses primarily on privacy guarantees, while multiparty FEPs focus on fairness guarantees.

Designing a multiparty escrow-based FEP is relatively trivial. The handshake document provides a map of each party's expected input and output, as well as a unique identifier for this particular exchange. Each party deposits its items for that handshake document with the escrow service, which verifies them. If all the inputs for a handshake document arrive at the TTP before any party cancels, then it releases those inputs accordingly. Otherwise, it restores the inputs to their original parties.

In contrast, designing multiparty FEPs that do not rely on a TTP to provide all of the operations is quite tricky. The cancellation problem in optimistic protocols, already complicated for two parties, is compounded considerably in the multiparty case, leading to subtle attack vectors that yield unfair outcomes (Mukhamedov and Ryan, 2008). Gradual release (GR) has been used as the basis of fair SMC protocols (Garay *et al.*, 2011), though as we have seen, the definition of fairness in SMC is substantially different from its meaning in fair exchange, and adding more parties to gradual release can considerably increase the number of messages required. It is not entirely clear that even the weak (and marginally unfair) fairness that is available in two-party GR can be achieved in a multiparty gradual release FEP.

Escrow-based and optimistic multiparty protocols that rely on the assistance of a TTP have been suggested (Asokan *et al.*, 1996; Franklin and Tsudik, 1998; Khill *et al.*, 2001; Liu and Hu, 2011; Mukhamedov *et al.*, 2005a), though several attack vectors and flaws have been revealed that highlight the difficulties of multiparty

---

[4]Though note that this extension is not always trivial: many definitions of fairness fail in the presence of multiple malicious parties, who may exchange their items regardless of the result of the synchronize operation (Garbinato and Rickebusch, 2010).

protocols outside the escrow model (Chadha *et al.*, 2006; Mukhamedov *et al.*, 2005b; Mukhamedov and Ryan, 2008).

Another source of complexity in multiparty protocols is the topology of interaction among the participants. A ring of participants exchanging with each other — for instance, A -> B -> C -> D -> A — can have different properties at the protocol level than if everyone is exchanging with everyone else in a complete graph (Chadha *et al.*, 2006). The nature of the items exchanged, which may not be homogeneous, can also add complexity (Asokan *et al.*, 1996).

Attestable-based protocols, which use an explicitly trusted IM environment for sync, have the same advantage as escrow-based exchanges when it comes to their multiparty extension. A variety of other services that a TTP can perform, like matchmaking and auctions, can be ported to an attestable context while maintaining the original protocol dynamics and complexity but reducing the cost and risk to the participants.

19.4 Zero-knowledge Information Exchange

One of the problems with computers is also one of their greatest strengths: they very rarely forget things.

If you show someone your driver's license, they are very likely to forget all the important details later. Show your driver's license to a computer, however, and it can remember it in perfect detail for an arbitrarily long time. We rely on computers to provide long-term immutable memory, just as our ancestors relied on paper, but computer systems can be quite rapacious, and unethical datamongers abound. We need to be able to provide proof of our claims — that we are allowed to drive, for instance, or are old enough to enter — without revealing any unnecessary information.

Zero-knowledge proofs (ZKPs) can provide exactly this. Interactive ZKPs are built in protocols executed between two parties, typically referred to as the prover and the verifier. They enable the prover to convince the verifier that the former knows a secret without revealing it. They were formally described in 1991 (Goldreich *et al.*, 1991) and since then they have been used in several applications in computer security (Almuhammadi and Neuman, 2005). For example, a ZKP protocol can be used by Bob to prove to Alice that he has enough money in his bank account to perform a purchase, without revealing anything else about the amount.

Protocols for ZKPs and FEPs have a richly interconnected history. In a classic interactive ZKP example like Yao's Millionaires' problem, where Alice and Bob would like to know who is wealthier without revealing their wealth to each other, there is a need to fairly exchange the outcome, as both Alice and Bob would like to know the result. Depending on the specific protocol used to solve the problem, this may be a purely implicit protocol, for instance, by assuming Bob is a trustworthy party who will send Alice the result, or it may explicitly involve a gradual release style synchronize operation, where Alice and Bob are both interactively querying the other.[5]

We saw examples earlier of going the other direction, with various FEPs built from non-interactive ZKPs coupled to a blockchain-based synchronization system. This can be seen as extending the domain of verifiable encryption for the deposit and verify operations by using ZKP, and pushing the synchronize operation into an IM environment to get strong fairness. This requires explicitly adding the safety and liveness of the blockchain system to the trust assumptions of the protocol, and introduces the corresponding costs and risks.

There are two primary issues with ZKPs. The first is that they can be computationally expensive when compared to the equivalent computation without zero-knowledge. The second is that they are often quite specific to the information being exchanged, so new protocols must be devised for each new type of item. These same problems also affect other verifiable encryption systems, and the two problems are correlated: typically, the more general a solution is, the more computationally expensive it is.

In situations amenable to using an independent computation environment provided by a TTP, both of those concerns are alleviated, by allowing general purpose programs to be written in regular programming languages. Evaluating those programs inside an

---

[5]Typically, this occurs with an assumption that both parties will continue providing answers until the other party is satisfied, rather than a proper gradual release "work for result" backchannel (Yao, 1982).

attestable provides the same exfiltration resistance as ZKPs, without the computation and complexity overhead. The trade-offs between adding an attestable to the stack of trust assumptions and employing ZKPs often results in a clear winner once both options are considered for a given use case.

Note that the program in the attestable can perform whatever verification computations are desired, and can produce whatever result is desired — a binary result, a specific number, or a more complex data structure, all without exposing the underlying input. This result can be structured as a transferable proof, where anyone who sees it in the future will also be convinced by it, or as a non-transferable proof, where an arms-length third party in the future will not be convinced by the proof.

Fair exchange problems often arise in zero-knowledge use cases, such as receiving access upon showing authorization credentials. Attestables can be used in the verify operation instead of ZKPs within scenarios like these. The attestable performs a post-processing step on the item just prior to release.[6] Running both the verify and the release/restore operation in IC enables zero-knowledge information exchange.

This motivates introducing two new properties for FEPs. The first is the ability for one party to gain information about the other party's item — for instance, whether it passes the verification check or not. Learning that D_B did not pass the verify operation might provide Alice with valuable information, which may yield a marginally unfair outcome to Bob. Contrarily, if she learned that the exchange was cancelled, but did not know whether it was because the verify check failed or because Bob cancelled it, then she learns nothing definitive about D_B. Conflating these signals requires them to both enter the same environment, which generally means doing the verify operation within the IM environment used for the synchronize operation.

The second is the ability to limit the information one participant can gain about the other's item. In particular, in FEWD Bob can always gain one bit of information about Alice's item, which is that Alice's item is either valid or invalid. This can be useful in

---

[6]We examined some related risks, and possible mitigation through post-processing, in Chapter 15.

Table 19.1.   Information leakage in the exchange of copyable items.

Protocol Family	Leakage to TTP	Leakage When Exchange is Cancelled	Zero-knowledge Information Exchange
Escrow-based	**Total:** TTP directly verifies information	**None:** if TTP sends only "cancelled" on cancel	**Supported:** can facilitate any zero-knowledge information exchange
Optimistic	**Significant:** total leakage whenever a dispute occurs, possible leakage on deposit	**Significant:** originator sends information directly to receiver	**Not supported:** contains no information protection mechanisms
Attestable	**None:** sync and cancel tokens contain no sensitive information	**Insignificant:** participants learn whether verification succeeds	**Supported:** can facilitate any programmable zero-knowledge information exchange

cases where Alice wants to prove her item is valid, and receive a proof of the validity of Bob's item, without revealing anything else. The post-processing phase of the release/restore operation can be used to release only the boolean validity of the original document, instead of the whole thing.

When comparing these features across different families of FEPs, one advantage that arises from escrow-based exchanges is the use of human intervention during the verify operation. This is a natural thing for an escrow service to provide, and allows them to extend the range of items they can exchange to include digitally accessible items.

FEWD can also be extended to allow humans to intervene during the verify operation, but this comes at the cost of information leakage to a TTP.[7] In Table 19.1, we do not consider this extension

---

[7]Recall that Alice is in control of the messaging from her attestable, hence, even if it is compromised, she can still prevent it from leaking information to another party. This is quite unlike an escrow service, where the information is already in

for attestable-based protocols: because it is an opt-in extension, participants can choose to take on those risks if the benefits of having trusted humans in the loop outweigh the drawbacks.

The first column of the table lists the main categories of FEPs: escrow-based, optimistic, and attestable-based FEPs.

The second column of Table 19.1 shows what information is leaked to TTPs involved in the protocol.

- **Escrow-based FEPs**: In these protocols, all the messages and the items that Alice and Bob exchange go through the escrow service, which operates as a TTP, so information leakage to the TTP is total and unavoidable. Accordingly, these protocols are suitable only when the information that Alice and Bob disclose to the escrow service is not particularly sensitive.
- **Optimistic FEPs**: In these protocols, no information is leaked to the TTP when there are no disputes, because the TTP is not involved. However, when a dispute is triggered by a party that has not received its item, the TTP gets involved and operates as an escrow service (see Figure 10.1). Consequently, the amount of information leaked to the TTP is significant. The reason is that the messages and the items that the participants exchange during dispute resolution must go through the TTP.
- **Attestable-based FEPs**: In these protocols, the TPP gathers only sync and cancel tokens. Since no sensitive information is included in the tokens, no information is leaked to the TTP.

When the protocol completes in success, the parties receive their expected item, thus, there is no question about information leakage. Information leakage to counterparties is an issue only when the exchange is cancelled. This is examined in the third column.

- **Escrow-based FEPs**: In these protocols, the TTP can be programmed to prevent the flow of sensitive information from Alice to Bob and vice versa (see Figure 9.1). If the exchange is cancelled, the escrow service can simply send a *cancel* notification to Alice and Bob without revealing sensitive information. Therefore, an escrow-based protocol can be designed

---

the hands of that other party. It is interesting to consider a design in which Alice has similar veto power over messages escaping from Bob's attestable.

where there is no information leakage to counterparties when the exchange is cancelled.

- **Optimistic FEPs**: In these protocols, information leakage is significant because a participant sends all the information about their item directly to their counterparty. This issue becomes relevant in the exchange of contract signatures, which ideally should be abuse-free (Garay *et al.*, 1999) so that Alice is not able to gather information about Bob's intentions to sign the contract and abandon the protocol (Garay *et al.*, 1999).

- **Attestable-based FEPs**: In these protocols, information leakage is insignificant because information about the items is sent to the attestables rather than to the applications. Sensitive information is never exposed outside the attestables when the exchange is cancelled.

  However, information leakage between the participants is difficult to completely prevent, because the attestables report the verification status to their owners. Consequently, if the exchange is cancelled after the verify operation, a participant always learns that their counterparty has an item that does or does not satisfy the verifier.

  In FEWD, for example, there is nothing to prevent Bob from cancelling the exchange after learning that Alice has a valid document. Thus, due to the peer-to-peer validation process, FEWD always leaks one bit of information (document accepted or rejected by the verifier).

Let us analyse that final point further with the help of Figure 13.1, which shows that the attestables do not post or retrieve tokens to and from the PBB directly; that task is delegated to the application.

In state 1, Alice's attestable att_A runs the verifier V_B to verify D_B. If the verification fails, the Finite State Machine (FSM) progresses from state 1 to the final state 4. Note that in this case FEWD completes fairly, but leaks a little information: Alice learns that Bob did not send a document that satisfies the verifier.

If D_B is accepted by V_B, then Alice's attestable provides Alice's application with sync and cancel tokens s_a and c_A, which the application is free to post to the PBB. Alice now knows that Bob possesses a document that satisfies V_B, but to retain strong timeliness she still has the ability to cancel the exchange. If she posts c_A at this point, then she has learned something about D_B, potentially without Bob having learned the same thing about D_A.

For most use cases this particular leakage is irrelevant, but it can be prevented when needed by adding an additional confirmation step to the interaction between att_A and att_B, for instance, by using the PBB to do a pre-validation synchronization. Other use cases may actively benefit from this ability, or from the more elaborate post-processing version mentioned earlier.

19.5 Exchange of TODA Files

So far we have primarily discussed unique items whose state is managed by the issuer, whether a centralized service or a blockchain, but this isn't the only way of expressing a unique digital item. Mobile objects (Chapter 2), such as TODA files (Coward and Toliver, 2022), allow the state of the item to be managed locally by the owner instead of remotely by the issuer.

When ACME Corporation creates a digital anvil and sells it to Alice, this might be done by creating the anvil as a row in their database, and associating that row with Alice's account (itself another row in their database). Alice interacts with the anvil by asking ACME Corporation to modify that row, which they may do if she properly authenticates herself as the owner of her account and authorizes the transaction. For instance, she might ask ACME to associate her anvil with Bob's account instead, in exchange for receiving Bob's ACME digital tornado kit.

If ACME creates the anvil as a TODA file, this process looks rather different. Instead of a row in a database, the anvil is expressed as a file on disk. Instead of associating it with Alice's account, ACME associates the anvil with a hash provided by Alice, updating the TODA file in the process. Once Alice has the TODA file, she can update it as desired, and can prove that her updates are unique.[8]

This structure splits the ownership of unique items across three distinct properties: integrity, possession, and control. The integrity of a unique item is its uniqueness, which is maintained by the issuer:

---

[8]Specifically, they are as unique as if they were made in ACME's database itself, instead of being made in Alice's untrusted environment.

ACME Corporation is highly motivated to not allow its products to be duplicated or counterfeited. Control determines who has the ability to make a legitimate update: typically in a database this is anyone, because there are no asset-level invariants, but many systems today use cryptographic signatures as a control mechanism. And possession answers the question of where the update must take place. If Alice's anvil is a row in a database or blockchain, then that is the only place it can be updated; if it is a TODA file, then she can move it to a custodian of her choice, including a device she owns.[9]

When exchanging TODA files, all three of these dimensions need to be accounted for. In particular, att_A not only needs to change the control of D_A by modifying its keys to ensure that Alice cannot update it, it also needs to change the possession of D_A to ensure that it is somewhere reachable by both Bob and Alice, to support both release and restore. If possession stayed local to Alice's system, this could lead to unfairness for Bob. Conversely, if possession transferred to Bob, then it might not be possible for att_A to restore D_A back to Alice, leading to unfairness for her.

An analogy to a lockbox is helpful: the steel of the lockbox provides its integrity; its location determines possession; and a lock can be attached which determines control. Alice's attestable att_A can swap out the lock so that only it has the key, but if the lockbox is still in Alice's house, then its release to Bob cannot be guaranteed. Conversely, if it was in Bob's house, restoring it to Alice if the exchange fails is not guaranteed.

What is needed is some kind of neutral ground, where either side is guaranteed access to the box — in other words, an IM environment. Such environments function for TODA files much like PBBs function in FEWD: in general, they cannot steal an item or discriminate against a particular actor. By placing a TODA file within such an environment, fairness can be guaranteed within an attestable protocol like FEWD.

An alternate way of exchanging TODA files involves adding a mechanism for conditional exchange into the semantics of the files

---

[9]This device can be explicitly untrusted by everyone else in the system, because the proof structure of the TODA file provides a proof of integrity that transcends its location.

themselves. This can ensure that D_A is transferred to Bob if and only if D_B is transferred to Alice, by incorporating the proof of such transfers directly into the TODA file proof structure. This proof information must be transferred between the participants to ensure fairness, though, because without it D_A is in an indeterminate state. Because the new proof information is required whether the exchange succeeds or fails, this technique does not reduce to an exchange of copyable items, and in general, it seems better to exchange TODA files as opaque unique items rather than trying to push the exchange mechanism into the proof structure.[10]

19.6 Future Work

Widespread use of FEPs can change our world. Today, our experience of digital commerce is hamstrung by expensive risk-mitigation mechanisms like credit cards, which add a significant tax to every purchase. We pay this credit card tax primarily because it offers us a weak FEP: if we do not receive our goods, the credit card company might refund our money.[11]

Worse still, our purchases are concentrated into just a few trusted merchants. For the last quarter century, we have been trained to never buy things online from an unknown merchant. This is radically different from the real world, where one can walk into any unknown shop and confidently make a purchase. Fair exchange can provide that same experience digitally, and help to break the monopoly hold a few large companies have on our digital experience.

This book was written to help us take the first few steps towards a world of ubiquitous fair exchange. It presents a framework for understanding the limitations of different FEPs, and for crafting new protocols that are a good fit for their intended purpose. It introduces attestables, a minimal interface for independent computation, and PBBs, a minimal interface for IM, and shows how we can use them to create strong FEPs with minimal costs and risks.

---

[10]This realization lead directly to the development of FEWD.

[11]Note that this fairness is not only weak, but often one sided: merchants have little recourse when they receive inappropriate chargebacks.

There is much left to do. If this book is anything, let it be a rallying cry: fair exchange is important. We need it in our world. It is a pillar that can help support an efficient and prosperous digital ecosystem. But to get there, we need more research, more implementations, and more real-world uses of fair exchange, at scale and in the wild.

Some of this work has already been started. The Centre for ReDe-Centralisation, whose history is deeply entwined with the work that lead to this book, is running a multiyear project to bring attestables to the cloud.[12] Implementation of a version of FEWD is part of that project, and work continues on extending both the framework and the formalization of FEWD.

Also deeply entwined with the work on this book are TODA files, which recast computational objects as distributed data structures that carry their own proof of uniqueness, as mentioned earlier. Fair exchange becomes increasingly important as our digital assets become more flexible and ubiquitous. We designed FEWD carefully to ensure it is forward compatible with changes to the way unique items are managed in the future, but work remains to modularize the implementation details of such assets.

It is also important to continue to improve our understanding of the nature of mobile items, to be able to build specialized FEPs that minimize the costs and risks of exchanging mobile objects, like the specialized FEPs seen in Chapter 14. In particular, to reach areas of the use case space like micropayments, a FEP is needed that can perform efficient exchanges of very low value. Attestable-based protocols provide a good basis for building out specialized systems like this, and the operational model of fair exchange provides abstractions and restrictions for guiding the work.

Extending FEWD to multiparty exchange is a natural next step. A taste of the model is provided in the replication section: adding more parties to the exchange is not entirely dissimilar from replicating the trusted agents. Indeed, it may be the case that an extended model of device replication could overlap significantly with multiparty exchange, and explain both of them in a single consistent model. Applying verification tools to FEWD's specification and

---

[12]Cloud Attestables on Morello Boards (CAMB).

implementation enables a better understanding of its properties and requirements, for instance, with respect to safety and liveness.

Another line of work involves applying the framework presented here to more existing protocols, both to better understand those protocols and also in the hope that these additional examples would allow the framework itself to be tightened, evolved, and more precisely formalized. This applies as well to the individual components in the framework: for instance, examining the interaction of the PBB and attestables in attestable-based protocols within the context of the extensive literature on consensus, or identifying applications that can be supported with variations on PBBs, ranging from pure IM environments to those that are aware of their role within the system and are able to perform specific computations.

More generally, there is much work remaining to understand how to extend fair exchange in various ways, for instance, to handle ongoing operations and incremental workflows rather than individual one-shot transactions, and to create new practical FEPs that are risk-and-cost-efficient and are well suited to their use cases.

Fair exchange is important. This is increasingly true as the digital world becomes a larger part of our daily lives, and as digital assets begin to take on new forms and fulfill many of the roles that physical assets like paper have held in the past.

We encourage you to look for opportunities to apply fair exchange to your work, and to your life. Let's build the digital world we want to live in.

Chapter 20

Glossary

att_A: An attestable (Alice's in this case).

app_A: Alice's application. Bob's is app_B.

D_A: An item: probably copyable, definitely Alice's.

I_A: A unique item, used when necessary to distinguish copyable from unique.

s_A: Alice's sync token.

c_A: Alice's cancel token.

K_A: A key. This one is used by Alice.

env_A: Alice's environment.

$chan_{AB}$: A channel between A and B.

$\{D_A\}_K$: Item D_A encrypted under key K.

Abusable: A FEP where some participant can prove that they can unilaterally decide how the protocol completes.

Abuse-free: A FEP where no participant can prove to an independent observer that they can unilaterally decide whether the protocol completes in success or cancellation.

Account item: A unique item that can only be directly accessed.

Asset item: A unique item that can be moved between accounts.

Asymmetric: A FEP where different actions are available to the participants depending on their roles.

Attestable-based: A FEP that splits the TTP apart.

Attestables: A minimal interface for independent computation.

Clockful: A FEP in which the participants rely on wall clock time to coordinate their actions.

Clockless: A FEP that does not rely on globally synchronized clocks.

Collusion-free: A FEP which bears no risk that its TTP can abscond with both items, even if colluding with a participant.

Collusion-risky: A FEP where an untrustworthy TTP could steal the items, either directly or by colluding with a participant.

Confidentiality: A FEP that guarantees that only the intended parties have knowledge of the items sent during the exchange.

Copyable item: An item that maintains no invariants.

Dependent environment (D): A participant completely controls this environment.

Deposit operation: The second FEP operation, where items are secured outside their owners control.

Escrow-based: A FEP that embraces the TTP entirely.

Exfiltration resistance: A computational process that can keep its secrets.

Fair exchange protocol (FEP): A procedure the participants can follow to try to ensure they receive a fair outcome.

FEWD: An attestable-based FEP described in this book.

Generatable: An instrument that can be generated by a TTP.

Gradual release: A FEP that eschews the TTP altogether.

Handshake document: Result of the handshake operation, aligns the participants' expectations and provides a unique identifier for the exchange.

Handshake operation: First step in a fair exchange, resulting in a handshake document.

Homomorphic encryption: A variety of techniques for performing computation directly on encrypted items.

Inaccessible item: An item that is not digital.

Independent compute (IC) environment: A participant cannot change the rules of this environment.

Independent messaging (IM) environment: A participant cannot block messages from this environment.

Independent storage (IS) environment: A participant cannot see inside this environment.

Instrument: A copyable item that can be generated or revoked by a TTP.

Invasive: A FEP that requires changes to the items being exchanged.

Invisible: A FEP where there is no observable difference between an item that was exchanged optimistically and the same item exchanged through the TTP back-end.

Leaky protocol: A FEP where there is a risk that unintended parties gain knowledge of the items exchanged.

Monolithic: A FEP where the TTP is required to be the single environment in which all protocol operations occur.

Non-invasive: A FEP that can be used without making any changes to the items that are being exchanged.

Non-replicable: Replication of TTP is significantly detrimental or even impossible.

Non-repudiation: A FEP guarantee that the exchange will produce evidence conclusively linking the participants to the sending of their items.

Opaque: A FEP where items exchanged through the TTP back-end are observably different from items exchanged optimistically.

Optimistic: A FEP that minimizes TTP interactions on the happy path.

Polylithic: The TTP environment for each operation can be specified independently.

Public bulletin board (PBB): A publicly accessible append-only data store.

Public key: The publicly viewable half of an asymmetric cryptographic key pair.

Redecentralization: The process of providing entities the power to solve their own problems.

Release/restore operation: The fifth operation in a FEP, where the items are either released to their new owners or restored to their previous owners.

Replicable: The FEP where the TTP can be replicated to mitigate the risk of behaviour unbecoming to a TTP.

Repudiation: A FEP that does not guarantee evidence connecting the participants and their sent items.

Secret item: A basic copyable item.

Secret key: The private half of an asymmetric cryptographic key pair.

Secure multiparty computation: A way to compute a function and share the output while keeping the inputs private.

Smart contracts: A computer program run by a trusted third party.

Stateful: A FEP whose TTP is aware of the exchange and responsible for keeping some of its state, and modifying its behaviour based on that state.

Stateless: A FEP whose TTP's behaviour does not change, regardless of how it is used in an exchange.

Strong fairness: A FEP guarantee that non-performance disputes can't occur.

Strong timeliness: A FEP guarantee that either party can drive the exchange to completion at any time.

Symmetric: A FEP where the actions available to each party are independent of their role in the exchange.

Symmetric key: A cryptographic key used for symmetric cryptography.

Synchronize operation: The fourth step in a FEP, where the decision to succeed or cancel is made.

TODA file: A digital item that carries its own proof of integrity.

Trusted third party (TTP): A party that both participants explicitly trust.

Unique item: An item that maintains invariants with integrity.

Vercrypt item: An item that can be verified under encryption.

Verify operation: The third step in a FEP, where the deposited item is checked against the handshake document.

Weak fairness: A FEP that relies on external adjudication for resolving disputes.

Weak timeliness: A FEP guarantee that it will end before some particular time.

Zero-knowledge proof (ZKP): A proof that reveals no additional information.

References

Adams, C., Cain, P., Pinkas, D., and Zuccherato, R. (2001). Internet x.509 public key infrastructure time-stamp protocol (TSP), Standards Track 3161, ietf.

Adamski, A. (2019). Overview of intel SGX — Part 2, SGX externals, https:// blog.quarkslab.com/overview-of-intel-sgx-part-2-sgx-externals.html.

Akkoyunlu, E. A., Ekanadham, K., and Huber, R. V. (1975). Some constraints and tradeoffs in the design of network communications, in *Proceedings Fifth ACM Symposium on Operating Systems Principles SOSP'75*.

AliPay (2020). Alipayservices agreement (updated as of 28 February 2020), https://render.alipay.com/p/f/agreementpages/alipayserviceagreement. html, Section 3: Alipay Services for Online Transactions.

Almuhammadi, S. and Neuman, C. (2005). Security and privacy using one-round zero-knowledge proofs, in *Proceedings Seventh IEEE Int'l Conf. on E-Commerce Technology (CEC'05)*.

Amazon Pay (2019). Transaction disputes, https://pay.amazon.com/uk/help/ 201754740, accessed on 9 February 2019.

Asokan, N. (1998). Fairness in electronic commerce, Ph.D. thesis, Computer Science, University of Waterloo, http://https://asokan.org/asokan/research/ Asokan98.pdf.

Asokan, N., Schunter, M., and Waidner, M. (1996). Optimistic protocols for multi-party fair exchange, Tech. Rep. RZ 2892 29/11/96, IBM, https:// www.researchgate.net/publication/228550422_ Optimistic_Protocols_for_ Multi-Party_Fair_Exchange.

Asokan, N., Schunter, M., and Waidner, M. (1997a). Optimistic protocols for fair exchange, in *Proceedings 4th ACM Conf. on Computer and Communications Security (CCS'97)*.

Asokan, N., Shoup, V., and Waidner, M. (1998). Asynchronous protocols for optimistic fair exchange, in *Proceedings IEEE Symposium on Security and Privacy*.

Asokan, N., Janson, P., Steiner, M., and Waidner, M. (1997b). State of the art in electronic payment systems, *Advances in Computers* **53**, pp. 425–449.

Ateniese, G. (2004). Verifiable encryption of digital signatures and applications, *ACM Transactions on Information and System Security* **7**.

Avizienis, A. and Kelly, J. P. J. (1994). Fault tolerance by design diversity: Concepts and experiments, *IEEE Computer* **17**, 8.

Avoine, G. and Vaudenay, S. (2004). Fair exchange with guardian angels, in *Information Security Applications: 4th International Workshop, WISA 2003 Jeju Island, Korea, August 25–27, 2003 Revised Papers 4* (Springer), pp. 188–202.

Ben-Or, M., Goldreich, O., Micali, S., and Rivest, R. L. (1990). A fair protocol for signing contracts, *IEEE Transactions on Information Theory* **36**, 1.

Bentov, I. and Kumaresan, R. (2014). How to use bitcoin to design fair protocols, in *Advances in Cryptology–CRYPTO 2014: 34th Annual Cryptology Conference, Santa Barbara, CA, USA, August 17–21, 2014, Proceedings, Part II 34* (Springer), pp. 421–439.

Bilge, L. and Dumitras, T. (2013). Investigating zero-day attacks, *Login* **38**, 4.

Blum, M. (1983). How to exchange (secret) keys, *ACM Transactions on Computer Systems* **1**, 2.

Cachin, C. and Camenisch, J. (2000). Optimistic fair secure computation (extended abstract), in *Proceedings CRYPTO'2000*.

Chadha, R., Kremer, S., and Scedrov, A. (2006). Formal analysis of multiparty contract signing, *Journal of Automated Reasoning* **36**(1–2), 39–83.

Choudhuri, A. R., Green, M., Jain, A., Kaptchuk, G., and Miers, I. (2017). Fairness in an unfair world: Fair multiparty computation from public bulletin boards, in *Proceedings ACM SIGSAC Conference on Computer and Communications (CCS'17) Security*.

Chun, B.-G., Maniatis, P., Shenker, S., and Kubiatowicz, J. (2007). Attested append-only memory: Making adversaries stick to their word, in *Proceedings 21st ACM Symposium on Operating Systems Principles (SOSP'07)*.

Chung, T., Liu, Y., Choffnes, D., Levin, D., Maggs, B. M., Mislove, A., and Wilson, C. (2016). Measuring and applying invalid SSL certificates: The silent majority, in *Proceedings Internet Measurement Conf. (IMC'16)*.

Cleve, R. (1986). Limits on the security of coin flips when half the processors are faulty, in *Proceedings of the Eighteenth Annual ACM Symposium on Theory of Computing*, pp. 364–369.

Costan, V. and Devadas, S. (2016). Intel SGX explained, https://eprint.iacr.org/2016/086.pdf.

Coward, K. and Toliver, D. R. (2022). Simple rigs hold fast, https://arxiv.org/abs/2208.13617, doi:10.48550/ARXIV.2208.13617.

Coward, K., Toliver, D. R., *et al.* (2022). Rigging specifications, Tech. rep., T.R.I.E.

Crowcroft, J. (2019). Threats to SGX, Tech. Rep. UCAM-CL-TR—, University of Cambridge, Computer Laboratory.

Driscoll, K. (2016). Social media's dial-up ancestor: The bulletin board system, *IEEE Spectrum*.

Eckey, L., Faust, S., and Schlosser, B. (2020). Optiswap: Fast optimistic fair exchange, in *Proceedings of the 15th ACM Asia Conference on Computer and Communications Security*, pp. 543–557.

Even, S. and Yacobi, Y. (1980). Relations among public key signature systems, Tech. Rep. Technical Report CS0175, Technion: Israel Institute of Technology: Computer Science Department, http://www.cs.technion.ac.il/users/wwwb/cgi-bin/tr-get.cgi/1980/CS/CS0175.pdf.

Even, S., Goldreich, O., and Lempel, A. (1985). A randomized protocol for signing contracts, Tech. Rep. Volume 28, Communications of the ACM.

EWCA Civ 265 (2019). Golden ocean group limited v salgaocar mining industries pvt ltd & or 2011 ewca civ 265; uk jurisdiction taskforce, the lawtech delivery panel, legal statement on cryptoassets and smart contracts, at 2.2.4, https://uk.practicallaw.thomsonreuters.com/D-008-7640?transitionType=Default&contextData=(sc.Default)&firstPage=true, accessed on 27 February 2023.

EWHC 772 (2004). Newell v tarrant, https://sas-space.sas.ac.uk/6518/1/ElectronicSignaturesStephenMason.pdf, accessed on 27 February 2023.

Fischer, M., Lynch, N. A., and Paterson, M. S. (1985). Impossibility of distributed consensus with one faulty process, *Journal of the Association for Computing Machinery* **32**, 2.

Foley, J. (2014). Provisioning x.509 certificates using rfc 7030, *Linux Journal* **2014**, 245.

Franklin, M. and Tsudik, G. (1998). Secure group barter: Multi–party fair exchange with semi-trusted neutral parties, in *Proceedings Financial Cryptography (FC'98), LNCS vol. 1465*.

Garay, J. A., Jakobsson, M., and MacKenzie, P. (1999). Abuse-free optimistic contract signing, in *Proceedings Annual International Cryptology Conf.: Advances in Cryptology (CRYPTO'99), LNCS vol. 1666*, pp. 449–466.

Garay, J. A., MacKenzie, P., Prabhakaran, M., and Yang, K. (2011). Resource fairness and composability of cryptographic protocols, *Journal of cryptology* **24**, 615–658.

Garbinato, B. and Rickebusch, I. (2010). Impossibility results on fair exchange, *10th International Conference on Innovative Internet Community Systems (I2CS)–Jubilee Edition 2010*.

Gasmi, Y., Sadeghi, A.-R., Stewin, P., Unger, M., and Asokan, N. (2007). Beyond secure channels, in *Proceedings ACM workshop on Scalable Trusted Computing (STC)'07*.

GauthierDickey, C. and Ritzdorf, C. (2012). Secure peer-to-peer trading for multiplayer games, in *2012 11th Annual Workshop on Network and Systems Support for Games (NetGames)* (IEEE), pp. 1–6.

Goldman, K., Perez, R., and Sailer, R. (2006). Linking remote attestation to secure tunnel endpoints, in *Proceedings First ACM workshop on Scalable Trusted Computing (STC'06)*.

Goldreich, O., Micali, S., and Widderson, A. (1991). Proofs that yield nothing but their validity or all languages in NP have zero-knowledge proof systems, *Journal of the Association for Computing Machinery* **38**, 1.

Google (2019). Certificate transparency, https://www.certificate-transparency.org/what-is-ct, accessed on 11 August 2019.

Gordon, S. D., Hazay, C., Katz, J., and Lindell, Y. (2011). Complete fairness in secure two-party computation, *Journal of the ACM (JACM)* **58**, 6, 1–37.

Gray, J. N. (1978). Notes on data base operating systems, in R. Bayer, R. Graham, and G. Seegmuler (eds.), *Operating Systems: An Advanced Course*, chap. 3.F, Lectures notes in Computer Science, Vol. 60 (Springer–Verlag), pp. 394–481.

Guerraoui, R. and Schiper, A. (1996). Fault-tolerance by replication in distributed systems, in *Proceedings Ada-Europe Int'l Conf. on Reliable Software Technologies, LNCS Vol. 1088.*

Khill, I., Kim, J., Han, I., and Ryou, J. (2001). Multi-party fair exchange protocol using ring architecture model, *Computer and Security* **20**, 5.

Knauth, T., Steiner, M., Chakrabarti, S., Lei, L., Xing, C., and Vij, M. (2019). Integrating intel SGX remote attestation with transport layer security, https://arxiv.org/abs/1801.05863.

Koschuch, M. and Wagner, R. (2014). Papers, please... x.509 certificate revocation in practice, in *Proceedings 5th Int'l Conf. on Data Communication Networking (DCNET).*

Lee, D., Jung, D., Fang, I. T., Tsai, C.-C., and Popa, R. A. (2020). An off-chip attack on hardware enclaves via the memory bus, https://arxiv.org/pdf/1912.01701.pdf, arXiv:1912.01701 [cs.CR].

Levin, D., Lorch, J. R., and Moscibroda, T. (2009). Trinc: Small trusted hardware for large distributed systems, in *Proceedings 6th USENIX Symposium on Networked Systems Design and Implementation (NSDI).*

Li, Y., Ye, C., Hu, Y., Morpheus, I., Guo, Y., Zhang, C., Zhang, Y., Sun, Z., Lu, Y., and Wang, H. (2021). Zkcplus: Optimized fair-exchange protocol supporting practical and flexible data exchange, in *Proceedings of the 2021 ACM SIGSAC Conference on Computer and Communications Security,* pp. 3002–3021.

Liu, Y. and Hu, H. (2011). An improved protocol for optimistic multi–party fair exchange, in *Proceedings Int'l Conf. on Electronic and Mechanical Engineering and Information Technology.*

Liu, Y., Tome, W., Zhang, L., Choffnes, D., Levin, D., Maggs, B., Mislove, A., Schulman, A., and Wilson, C. (2015). An end-to-end measurement of certificate revocation in the web's pki, in *Proceedings Internet Measurement Conf. (IMC' 15).*

Micali, S. (1997). Fair electronic exchange with virtual trusted parties, https://ecir.mit.edu/publications/research-papers, accessed on 18 March 2020.

Mukhamedov, A. and Ryan, M. D. (2008). Fair multi-party contract signing using private contract signatures, *Information and Computation* **206**, 2–4, 272–290.

Mukhamedov, A., Kremer, S., and Ritter, E. (2005a). Analysis of a multi–party fair exchange protocol and formal proof of correctness in the strand space model, in *Proceedings Financial Cryptography and Data Security (FC'05), LNCS vol. 3570.*

Mukhamedov, A., Kremer, S., and Ritter, E. (2005b). Analysis of a multi-party fair exchange protocol and formal proof of correctness in the strand space model, in *Financial Cryptography and Data Security: 9th International Conference, FC 2005, Roseau, The Commonwealth of Dominica, February 28–March 3, 2005. Revised Papers 9* (Springer), pp. 255–269.

Needham, R. M. (1993). Cryptography and secure channels, in S. Mullender (ed.), *Distributed Systems*, 2nd edn., chap. 20 (Addison–Wesley, acm PRESS), pp. 531–541.

Onieva, J. A., Zhou, J., and Lopez, J. (2004). Enhancing certified email service for timeliness and multicasting, in *Proceedings of 4th International Network Conference (INC'04)*, pp. 327–336.

Orzan, S. and Dashti, M. T. (2008). Fair exchange is incomparable to consensus, in *Proceedings 5th Int'l Colloquium on Theoretical Aspects of Computing*, pp. 349–363.

Pagnia, H. and Gärtner, F. C. (1999). On the impossibility of fair exchange without a trusted third party, Tech. Rep. TUD–BS–1999–02, Darmstadt University of Technology, https://www.cs.utexas.edu/~shmat/courses/cs395t_fall04/pagnia.pdf, accessed on 10 July 2019.

Pagnia, H., Vogt, H., and Gärtner, F. C. (1999). Modular fair exchange protocols for electronic commerce, in *Proceedings 15th Annual Computer Security Applications Conference (ACSAC'99)*.

Pagnia, H., Vogt, H., and Gärtner, F. C. (2003). Fair exchange, *The Computer Journal* **46**, 1.

Pass, R., Shi, E., and Tramièr, F. (2017). Formal abstractions for attested execution secure processors, in *Proceedings EUROCRYPT*.

PayPal (2019). Resolving a dispute with your seller guide to handling a dispute, https://www.paypal.com/uk/webapps/mpp/first-dispute, accessed on 9 February 2019.

Peters, R. (2005). *A Secure Bulletin Board: Master's Thesis*, Master's thesis, Technische Universiteit Eindhoven. Department of Mathematics and Computing Science.

Pinkas, B. (2003). Secure two-party computation (extended abstract), in *Proceedings Int'l Conf. on the Theory and Applications of Cryptographic Techniques (EUROCRYPT'03)*.

Piva, F. R., Monteiro, J. R. M., and Dahab, R. (2009). Regarding timeliness in the context of fair exchange, in *Proceedings IFIP Int'l Conf. on Network and Service Security (N2S'09)*.

Priebe, C., Muthukumaran, D., Lind, J., Zhu, H., Cui, S., Sartakov, V. A., and Pietzuch, P. (2019). Sgx-lkl: Securing the host os interface for trusted execution, https://arxiv.org/pdf/1908.11143.pdf, arXiv:1908.11143 [cs.OS].

Rabin, M. O. (1981). How to exchange secrets with oblivious transfer, Tech. Rep. Report 81, ePrint Archive: Report 2005/187, Harvard University, accessed on 9 November 2019.

Ray, I. and Ray, I. (2002). Fair exchange in e-commerce, *ACM SIGecom Exchange* **3**, 2.

Schneider, F. B. (1990). Implementing fault-tolerant services using the state machine approach, *ACM Computing Surveys, Vol. 2* **22**, 4.

Schneider, F. B. (1993). Replication management using the state–machine approach, in S. Mullender (ed.), *Distributed Systems*, 2nd edn., Chap. 7 (Addison–Wesley, acm PRESS), pp. 169–197.

Shamir, A. (1979). How to share a secret, *Communications of the ACM* **22**, 11.

Shmatikov, V. and Mitchell, J. C. (2002). Finite–state analysis of two contract signing protocols, *Theoretical Computer Science* **283**, 2, 419–450.

Sinha, R., Gaddam, S., and Kumaresan, R. (2019). Luciditee: Policy-compliant fair computing at scale, https://eprint.iacr.org/2019/178.

Tarkhani, Z. and Madhavapeddy, A. (2020). Sirius: Enabling system-wide isolation for trusted execution environments, https://arxiv.org/pdf/2009.01869.pdf, arXiv:2009.01869 [cs.CR].

Tygar, J. D. (1996). Atomicity in electronic commerce, in *Proceedings Fifteenth Annual ACM Symposium on Principles of Distributed Computing, Keynote paper*.

Vogt, H., Gärtner, F. C., and Pagnia, H. (2001a). Supporting fair exchange in mobile environments, *Mobile Networks and Applications* **8**, 2.

Vogt, H., Pagnia, H., and Gärtner, F. C. (2001b). Using smart cards for fair exchange, in *Proceedings Electronic Commerce. Second Int'l Workshop, (WELCOM 2001), LNCS Vol. 2232*.

Werker, M. (2017). *The role of Alipay in commerce in China FACILITATOR OF TRUST OR ABUSER OF BIG DATA?* Master's thesis, Leiden University, MA Asian Studies: Chinese Studies.

Yao, A. C. (1982). Protocols for secure computations (extended abstract), in *Proceedings 23rd Annual Symposium on Foundations of Computer Science, (SFCS'08)*.

Zhou, J. and Gollmann, D. (1997). An efficient non-repudiation protocol, in *Proceedings 10th Computer Security Foundations Workshop*.

Index